T0330106

RESOURCE NATIONALISM IN INDONESIA

RESOURCE NATIONALISM IN INDONESIA

Booms, Big Business, and the State

Eve Warburton

SOUTHEAST ASIA PROGRAM PUBLICATIONS

AN IMPRINT OF CORNELL UNIVERSITY PRESS   ITHACA AND LONDON

First published 2023 by Cornell University Press

Library of Congress Cataloging-in-Publication Data

Names: Warburton, Eve, author.
Title: Resource nationalism in Indonesia : booms, big business, and the state / Eve Warburton.
Description: Ithaca [New York] : Southeast Asia Program Publications, an imprint of Cornell University Press, 2023. | Includes bibliographical references and index.
Identifiers: LCCN 2023004244 (print) | LCCN 2023004245 (ebook) | ISBN 9781501771965 (hardcover) | ISBN 9781501771972 (paperback) | ISBN 9781501771989 (epub) | ISBN 9781501771996 (pdf)
Subjects: LCSH: Natural resources—Government policy—Indonesia. | Government ownership—Indonesia.
Classification: LCC HC447.5 .W369 2023 (print) | LCC HC447.5 (ebook) | DDC 333.709598—dc23/eng/20230511
LC record available at https://lccn.loc.gov/2023004244
LC ebook record available at https://lccn.loc.gov/2023004245

For Dad, my dearest friend

Contents

Figures

Tables

Acknowledgments

This book was made possible with the support of a wonderful cast of colleagues and friends over the course of several years. My interest in resource nationalism began during my time as a doctoral student at the Australian National University's (ANU's) Department of Political Social Change at the Coral Bell School of Asia Pacific Affairs. Many of the questions and ideas that shape this book emerged through stimulating discussions with the staff and students at ANU, in particular John McCarthy, Nick Cheesman, Marcus Mietzner, Greg Fealy, Liam Gammon, Dom Berger, Colum Graham, Danang Widoyoko, Ahmad Muhajir, and Tom Power.

The most special thanks go to Edward Aspinall, my former supervisor. During the early years, Ed patiently read through my embryonic ideas about nationalism and natural resources, providing me with invaluable feedback and pushing me to think in more critical and original ways about my data. After finishing the dissertation, Ed continued to be a generous mentor and colleague. We collaborated on a range of research projects about Indonesia's economic elite and the country's broader democratic political economy, and those projects have gone on to inform many aspects of this book. The ANU introduced me to two other outstanding academics with whom I have had the good fortune to collaborate—Burhanudidn Muhtadi and Diego Fossati. I am indebted to both Burhan and Diego for expanding my understanding of surveys and many aspects of Indonesia's political economy as well.

Parts of this manuscript have benefited from the feedback of scholars beyond the ANU. Natasha Hamilton-Hart, Dan Slater, and Tom Pepinsky have offered critical comments at various stages of this project's development. I also wish to thank participants at the 2018 SEAREG workshop at Yale-NUS, where I presented one part of this book, and special thanks must go to Allen Hicken, Amy Liu, Cesi Cruz, and Eddy Malesky whose feedback prompted me to rethink my conceptual framework. Generous input from two anonymous reviewers also helped me transform the theoretical and conceptual parts of this book for which I am immensely grateful.

There is a long list of people in Indonesia whose kindness and knowledge I depended on while conducting my research. Special mention must be made of those people with whom I met regularly to discuss Indonesia's resource politics: Gusti Budiartie, Hendra Sinadia, Rangga Fadillah, Tim Scott, Raras Cahyafitri,

Sita Dewi, Douglas Ramage, Sidney Jones, Sukhyar, Linda Siahaan, Annelise Young, Kiki Andi Pati, Cillian Nolan, Yasril Rhilone, Wijayono Sarosa, Matt Busch, and all of the staff at Publish What You Pay, especially Agung Budiono. Universitas Gadjah Mada provided institutional support that made parts of my fieldwork possible, and I wish to thank Prof. Purwo Santoso, Amalinda Savirani, and Dian from ASPAC who provided a warm and stimulating intellectual space to discuss and present my early findings. Chitra Retna and Ermy Prasetio of Article 33 also helped enormously during my field research. In more recent years, conversations with La Ode Syarif, an inspiring intellectual and activist, also shaped my thinking on state-business relations in the resource sectors. Many people from Indonesia's business community gave me their time as well but wished to remain anonymous.

The first draft of this book was completed in Singapore at the Asia Research Institute (ARI), NUS, where I held a postdoctoral fellowship from 2019 to 2021. ARI is a rare and supportive home for early career researchers working on Asia. While there, I benefited from incisive feedback and encouragement from a range of colleagues, including Sana Jaffrey and Amit Julka, as well as Jamie Davidson, Michelle Miller, Ted Hopf, and in particular from ARI's director, Tim Bunnell.

Thank you to my wonderful partner, Matt, whose love and patience helped me bring my first book project to life.

Finally, I wish to thank my parents, Greg and Alicia, for their unwavering support, and for tolerating the distance my work put between us for all those years. My dear father fell ill and passed away as I was completing the manuscript. I dedicate this book to him.

Abbreviations

APINDO	Asosiasi Pengusaha Indonesia, Indonesian Employers Association
APKASINDO	Asosiasi Petani Kelapa Sawit, Palm Oil Farmers Association
BP MIGAS	Badan Pelaksana Kegiatan Usaha Hulu Minyak dan Gas, Regulatory Body for Upstream Oil and Gas Activities
CCoW	coal contract of work
CoW	contract of work
CPO	crude palm oil
DMO	domestic market obligation
DPR	Dewan Perwakilan Rakyat, People's Representative Council
FDI	foreign direct investment
GAPKI	Gabungan Pengusaha Kekapa Sawit, Association of Palm Oil Companies
GDP	gross domestic product
Gerindra	Gerakan Indonesia Raya, Great Indonesia Movement Party
Golkar	Golongon Karya
IBRA	Indonesian Bank Restructuring Agency
ICMA	Indonesian Coal Mining Association
ICW	Indonesia Corruption Watch
IMA	Indonesian Mining Association
IMF	International Monetary Fund
IPA	Indonesian Petroleum Association
IPOP	Indonesian Palm Oil Pledge
IRESS	Indonesia Resource Studies
IUP	Izin Usaha Pertambangan, Mining Use License
IUPK	Izin Usaha Pertambangan Khusus, Special Mining Use License
JOB	joint operating bodies
KADIN	Kamar Dagang dan Industri Indonesia, Indonesian Chamber of Commerce and Industry
KPK	Komisi Pemberantasan Korupsi, Corruption Eradication Commission
KSP	Kantor Staf Presiden, Presidential Staff Office
Nasdem	National Democratic Party
NGO	nongovernmental organization

NIL	Negative Investment List
OEP	open economy politics
PAN	Partai Amanat Nasional, National Mandate Party
PDIP	Partai Demokrasi Indonesia-Perjuangan, Indonesian Democratic Party-Struggle
PKS	Partai Keadilan Sejahtera, Prosperous Justice Party
PLN	Perusahaan Listrik Negara, National Electricity Company
PSC	production-sharing contract
SKK MIGAS	Satuan Kerja Khusus Pelaksana Kegiatan Usaha Hulu Minyak dan Gas Bumi, Special Task Force for Upstream Oil and Gas Activities
SOE	state-owned enterprise
TAC	technical assistance contract

RESOURCE NATIONALISM IN INDONESIA

NATIONALISM AND NATURAL RESOURCES

In June 2016, American mining giant Newmont Mining decided to close its Indonesian business. After two decades exploring and operating the Batu Hijau gold and copper mine on Sumbawa Island, Newmont sold its majority stake to a domestic firm. Arifin Panigoro, an Indonesian businessperson and ally of the incumbent president, Joko Widodo (known as Jokowi), acquired the mine. The government enthusiastically promoted the deal, with one minister telling the press months earlier that "it has always been thought that Indonesians don't have the ability [to run large mines]," but this deal, he said, would prove otherwise (Syahrul 2015). To finance the US$2.6 billion acquisition, Panigoro's company, Medco, borrowed from three state-owned banks—Bank Mandiri, Bank Negara Indonesia (BNI), and Bank Rakyat Indonesia (BRI). Rumors circulated that President Widodo had to intervene to bring these banks on board and push the deal through. The company chairperson cast the deal as a major achievement, not just for the firm but for the entire nation: "[This deal] proves that with the collaboration of Indonesian companies, state-owned banks, the government and the public at large, we can solve every challenge the country faces. . . . [Newmont] deserves praise for setting a new precedent for international investors in the natural resource sector, and for being cooperative and supportive towards realising the Indonesian people's aspiration" (Medco Energi, June 30, 2016).

Indonesia's land and resource industries were historically the domain of foreign firms. From the seventeenth century, Dutch private, state, and later Anglo-American companies, dominated the extraction and trade of the archipelago's commodities. The Netherlands East Indies government gave Dutch agrifirms and trading companies, as well as mining firms like Royal Dutch Shell, Billiton, and Caltex, privileged access to Indonesian resources under the most favorable terms for the companies, with few benefits channeled to indigenous communities. On declaring independence in 1945, Indonesia's nationalist leaders drew up a constitution explicitly outlining that the land and the subsoil resources beneath it were the property of the new republic and must be used for the benefit of its citizens.[1] Yet, for another half century, foreign multinationals dominated many of the country's primary export sectors and especially precious minerals. Medco's acquisition of the Newmont mine was, therefore, a moment of political significance and nationalist pride.

The Newmont acquisition took place against the backdrop of a wider nationalist turn that accompanied the worldwide resources boom, which took place from roughly 2004 to 2013. Prices of commodities such as coal, oil, nickel, gold, and palm oil climbed to historic highs. During this time, Indonesian lawmakers introduced a range of new restrictions on foreign ownership, investment, and labor in mining and other sectors (Patunru and Rahardja 2015; Warburton 2017b). Indonesia was not alone in this regard. Anti-foreign agitation had surged throughout resource-rich countries around the world during the global commodity boom, and the governments of countries as diverse as Mongolia, Tanzania, Bolivia, Argentina, Australia, the Philippines, and Papua New Guinea tightened foreign ownership rules in response to rising demands from a range of state and nonstate actors (Wilson 2015). This phenomenon is often described as *resource nationalism*.

Resource nationalism is at once both a discursive tool and a set of substantive policy prescriptions. As a discourse, resource nationalism links land and subsoil resources to a community of national citizens and makes a set of normative claims about who has rightful ownership over and who should benefit economically from those resources (Childs 2016; Koch and Perreault 2018). State and nonstate actors deploy nationalist narratives to oppose foreign exploitation of their land and resource industries and to promote a vision of national sovereignty and local control over natural wealth (Koch and Perreault 2018).

To realize such visions, nationalist protagonists advocate concrete *policy* outcomes that can transform how resources are owned and exploited. This study is concerned with understanding the conditions under which such policy transformations take place. I use the term *resource nationalism* to describe a range of policy efforts that seek to restrict foreign access to land and resources and to create opportunities for different types of national actors to own, exploit, and benefit from a country's natural wealth. Further, while nationalization is usually understood as the (often hostile) takeover of private assets by the state, this book widens the conceptual parameters of nationalization in order to investigate the different ways local ownership can be engineered for the benefit of either domestic private actors *or* for state-owned enterprises. Indeed, a question that drives this study is why different forms of nationalization occur—sometimes expanding state ownership and at other times giving private domestic business actors control over land and natural resource projects.

During the boom years, demands for resource nationalism intensified around the world. By the mid-2000s, industry experts and corporate risk analysts had come to view resource nationalism as one of the most serious threats to foreign investors in the commodities sectors and began dedicating regular reports to measuring, indexing, and assessing expressions of resource nationalism and attendant restrictions on foreign firms.[2] Indonesia featured heavily in such global industry analyses. For example, one prominent corporate consultancy, the Fraser Institute, conducted a survey in 2013 of 742 mining companies from around the world and found that Indonesia was perceived to be the worst place to do business out of 96 global jurisdictions (Wilson, McMahon, and Cervantes 2013, 26). During the first two decades of the twenty-first century, an increasing number of multinational firms like Freeport, Churchill Mining, BHP, and Chevron sold down or out of their investments in Indonesia.

Indonesia is one of the largest economies in Asia and a major global supplier of strategically important commodities like coal, nickel, bauxite, and palm oil. These primary sectors have long attracted much of the foreign direct investment (FDI) that enters the country and are critical to the export economy and a major source of foreign exchange. There was much consternation from foreign trading partners, risk consultancies, and foreign journalists about the impact that nationalist policies would have on international trade and the domestic economy.

Yet, at the same time, few economists and industry observers expected the nationalist trend to last beyond the boom. Market-cycle theories maintain that resource nationalism is epiphenomenal: when prices are high, government coffers are awash with resource rents, which puts state actors in a better bargaining position with foreign investors and they can afford to shift regulations and increase taxes, royalties, and divestment requirements; once prices cool and economies slow down, however, state managers will again try to court foreign investors and multinational corporations, as they search for new sources of revenue (Monaldi 2020; Vivoda 2009).

Arguments put forward in historical studies of economic policymaking in Indonesia cohere with this market-cycle theory. Mohammad Sadli, a prominent liberal economist during the New Order government (1966–98), argued famously that in Indonesia, "bad times may produce good economic policies, and good times frequently the reverse" (Hill and Wie 2008, 154). Throughout the New Order, oil booms prompted more assertive nationalist intervention in favor of state-owned enterprises and domestic firms (which Sadli saw as bad), while oil busts and downturns compelled the Suharto government to roll back its nationalist approach and create more incentives for foreign investment (which Sadli viewed as good) (Hill and Basri 2004). "Sadli's law," as it became known, and the notion that booms and busts moved the policy pendulum between nationalist and liberal policy approaches, has enjoyed immense traction among analysts of Indonesia's economy.

Similar ideas were circulating among experts in Indonesia when I arrived in Jakarta in late 2013 to conduct my field research. The Indonesian government was embarking on what would be a long, fraught process of renegotiating foreign mining contracts to bring them in line with new divestment rules. I recall one of my first interviews was with a foreign journalist who had been covering the negotiations. He dismissed the growing pressure on foreign companies as little more than a passing phase: "This nonsense will all blow over soon," he said. "Prices are going down, and those shortsighted guys in government will remember how badly they need foreign investors. These things are always cyclical."[3] Foreign mining managers, political risk consultants, and analysts in foreign embassies similarly believed that resource nationalism would soon reverse.

This position rested on two assumptions: first, that nationalist aspirations among Indonesian policymakers were relatively shallow and were merely a short-term response to the lure of excess rents; second, that outside of boom conditions, Indonesia's government, state-owned enterprises (SOEs), or private business class would be incapable of acquiring and running major extractive projects. Such assumptions turned out to be incorrect. By 2022, at the time of writing, almost all of the country's major oil, coal, and mineral contracts were in the hands of domestic companies. Resource nationalism persisted well beyond the boom, reshaping patterns of ownership and investment in major export industries, and compelling analysts to rethink the causes and consequences of nationalist change.

This book is about the changing landscape of ownership in Indonesia's land and natural resources sectors during the first decades of the twenty-first century. This was a period marked not only by a major resources boom but also by Indonesia's political transition from a centralized authoritarian regime to a decentralized, competitive, and patronage-driven democracy. These twin forces, one economic and the other political, constitute a critical backdrop to the emergence and persistence of resource nationalism in the contemporary period.

The Indonesian Puzzle

During the boom years, the Indonesian government introduced a range of interventions designed to squeeze out the foreign players that had long dominated lucrative export industries: new divestment rules, denial of contract renewals, and new limits on foreign shareholding. Two features of this process are particularly puzzling. A first feature that makes Indonesia's experience of resource nationalism so remarkable is its *persistence*. In many instances, the intensity of nationalist change increased *after* the boom. In Indonesia, resource nationalism generated a series of takeovers and buy-ins by both domestic private firms and SOEs over the course of the boom and in the decade that followed. This shift amounted to a slow nationalization of the country's land-based resource industries.

The second puzzling feature of the Indonesian case is the uneven nature of nationalist intervention. There was variation in both the *intensity* of nationalist policy interventions and in the *beneficiaries*. In some cases, like the Newmont acquisition described above, the government helped domestic capitalists take over foreign contracts; in other cases, like the divestment of Freeport McMoran from the Grasberg gold and copper mine in Papua province, the Jokowi administration excluded domestic tycoons and instead ensured the shares went to a major state-owned mining company. There was important variation across sectors, too. Whereas foreign investors were being squeezed out of the coal and minerals industry well beyond the boom, the government rejected demands from legislators and sections of business to tighten restrictions on foreign investments in commercial plantations. Meanwhile, the legislature started debating new nationalist changes to the foreign investment regime for oil and gas in 2012; at the time of writing in 2022, lawmakers had still not agreed on a new law to govern the terms of investment, leaving this sector in a state of regulatory limbo for over a decade. Nationalist policies were fragmented and uneven both within and among Indonesia's three major commodities sectors, all of which were attracting much FDI and generating massive export revenues at the height of the boom (figure 0.1). In short, despite each sector being the object of nationalist demands, outcomes varied: nationalist regulations prevailed in the mining sector, remained weak in the oil and gas sector, and failed in the plantations sector.

These two puzzles—nationalist persistence and variation—motivate the book and give rise to a series of questions about the causes and consequences of resource nationalism in Indonesia:

a) Against the backdrop of a boom, why do nationalist efforts prevail and persist in some contexts but fail or stagnate in others? Who are the major advocates for and beneficiaries of nationalist transformation, and under what circumstances do their preferences for resource nationalism get channeled into concrete policy change?

b) What do subnational patterns of resource nationalism reveal about the nature of Indonesia's contemporary political economy? What can the

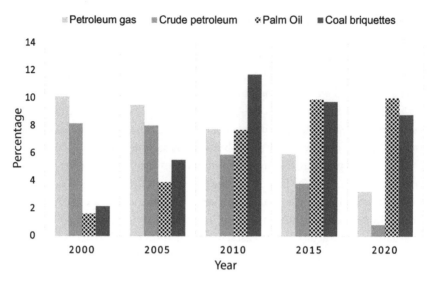

FIGURE 0.1. Percentage contribution of natural resources to exports

Source: Observatory of Economic Complexity, international trade data, 2000–20

form and fate of nationalist demands tell us about the relative power of different policy actors (state, business, and popular forces) in Indonesia's resource sectors during and following the boom?

c) What are the consequences of resource nationalism for the governance of Indonesia's land and natural resources and for developmental outcomes more broadly? Specifically, does the transformation of ownership structures have observable benefits, and if so, where do those benefits ultimately flow?

d) Finally, what do the answers to these three sets of questions mean for the comparative scholarship on resource nationalism and for the frameworks that analysts use to understand variation in nationalist policy outcomes across countries? And can Indonesia's experience help to sharpen the analytical tools we use when studying resource nationalism in other middle-income democracies?

Existing theories of resource nationalism provide limited answers to questions of subnational variation raised by the Indonesian case. Much previous scholarship on resource nationalism is focused on explaining *timing* and subscribes to the market-cycle theory highlighted above (Monaldi 2015; Vernon 1971; Vivoda 2009). Among the studies that are concerned with variation, the trend is to engage in cross-national comparisons and seek the source of distinct nationalist trajectories in country-level variables like weak rule of law, rentier state features, or the leftist developmental ideology of state managers and incumbent governments (Berrios, Marak, and Morgenstern 2011; Wilson 2015). Such research is invaluable for understanding global trends, but subnational variation remains underexplored.

One possible answer is that characteristics of sectors themselves—oil, mining, and cash crops—are what determines their different nationalist trajectories. These industries are, after all, distinct kinds of economic ventures. The nature of capital investments, technology, labor dynamics, and the size of economic rents vary among them. But as this book will show, these sectors share important similarities that make them susceptible to nationalist agitation. Specifically, coal, minerals, oil, and cash crops like palm oil all experienced a global price boom during the first decades of the twenty-first century, they make significant contributions to Indonesia's export income and foreign reserves, and each experienced the entry of new domestic private players in the wake of the Asian financial crisis in 1997–98, but they all attract large amounts of foreign investment, too.

These sectors are also all mired in rent seeking, conflict, and corrupt practices surrounding the allocation of concessions and permits (Casson, Muliastra, and Obidzinski 2015). Studies of resource nationalism often assume that extractives are especially vulnerable to state intervention, rent seeking, and protectionist mobilization because they are nonrenewable, capital intensive, and geographically concentrated—otherwise known as a "point source" resource (Isham et al. 2005). Yet often land resources and in particular cash crops are contested in ways similar to extractive resources. For this reason, studies of natural resource economies and the resource curse regularly place forestry and cash crop industries in the same analytical category as extractives because they all suffer boom-bust vulnerabilities and are subject to similar patterns of rent seeking and protectionist intervention during a boom (Boschini, Pettersson, and Roine 2007; Isham et al. 2005; Ross 2001).[4]

Indeed, all around the world, agricultural industries are among the most protected sectors because land ownership, and in particular ownership of productive farmlands, is politically sensitive and therefore subject to nationalist mobilization and protectionist policy interventions. In Indonesia specifically, the plantation sector has a long history of protectionism and was closed to foreign investors on and off throughout the 1990s. But during the most recent boom, commercial plantations remained open to foreign capital. Figure 0.2 illustrates the puzzling pattern of nationalist intervention in Indonesia when compared to other similar countries.

The Organisation for Economic Co-operation and Development's (OECD) FDI Regulatory Restrictiveness Index assesses a country's FDI rules and allocates scores based on the degree of restriction placed on FDI in four areas: foreign equity restrictions, discriminatory screening or approval mechanisms,

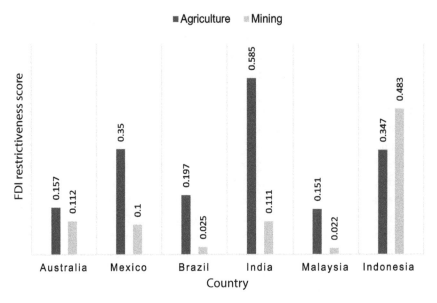

FIGURE 0.2.   FDI restrictiveness (average score, 1997–2020)

Source: OECD FDI Restrictiveness Data Set, 2022

restrictions on key foreign personnel, and operational restrictions. Annual scores are given for all OECD and select non-OECD countries for each of their major sectors, where zero reflects no restrictions and one reflects a sector being closed to FDI. The average scores presented in table 1.2 demonstrate that in countries with major mining (including oil) and agricultural industries, governments on average place far more restrictions on FDI in agriculture. Whether in a high-income economy like Australia or in upper- or lower- middle-income economies (like Malaysia or India, respectively), the agricultural sector tends to be the target of more protectionism than the mining sector—except in Indonesia. So why are subnational patterns of resource nationalism different in Indonesia? Given that during the boom years, minerals, coal, oil and gas, and commercial plantations all experienced similar demands to restrict foreign ownership and investment, why is it that nationalist policy outcomes varied to such a degree across sectors?

The Arguments

This book makes the following arguments about nationalist variation in Indonesia, each of which responds to the sets of questions outlined previously.

The Rise of Domestic Business

The main contention of this book is that *business power* determined both the persistent and varied nature of resource nationalism in contemporary Indonesia. For much of Indonesia's modern history, local private capital played a minor role in the country's commercial plantation and resource industries, and instead, foreign capital and SOEs controlled the exploitation and export of the country's raw commodities. But domestic business expanded rapidly into these industries over the course of the late twentieth and early twenty-first century. After the Asian financial crisis (1997), local business elites began rebuilding their fortunes by accessing cheap land and mining concessions. The fortuitously timed boom in coal and crude palm oil prices that took off during the early to mid-2000s dramatically increased the profits of domestic businesses in these sectors, in turn enhancing their capacity to buy into or take over foreign resource contracts and expanding their influence at the policymaking table. This book traces and demonstrates the distinct forms and uses of private sector power in Indonesia's land and resource sectors and the consequences of such power for nationalist policy trajectories.

For example, in the mining sector, laws and regulations came to reflect the protectionist demands of domestic mining magnates, some of whom are oligarchs with direct links to the centers of political power. In classic political economy parlance, these corporate actors enjoy superior *instrumental power*— direct political lobbying skills and influence and often deep personal connections to politicians and lawmakers (Fairfield 2015; Lindblom 1977)—which they use to seek access to lucrative contracts and to push for a regulatory framework that privileges the interests of domestic capital.

In the plantations sector, major domestic business actors favored a more liberal investment regime with few restrictions on foreign flows. When the government opened plantations to allow almost full foreign ownership following the Asian financial crisis, investors from Malaysia and Singapore poured in at a pace, targeting the palm oil sector. The flow of foreign capital led to a rapid expansion in the production and export of crude palm oil. Unlike in the mining sector, however, major domestic companies operating in this sector came to support, rather than oppose, the open investment regime. I trace this variation back to the contemporary evolution of the sector, its integration into networks of regional capital, and critically, to important differences in the character and behavior of local businesses—differences that have deep historical roots. Specifically, Chinese Indonesian businesses that dominate palm oil production are less likely to lobby against FDI or to seek stringent foreign divestment rules. For a range of historical reasons, these businesses are more ambivalent in their dealings with the contemporary democratic state, maintain more political distance from it, and seek a more international footprint for their companies. Such businesses have invested massively up and down the value chains of the country's vast food and agricultural industries, which endows them with immense *structural power* and gives their preferences and business decisions weight within economic policy-making circles. As this book will show, histories of capital accumulation and state predation toward ethnically Chinese Indonesian businesses (Chua 2008; Robison 1986) underpin the ownership structures of today's resource industries and, in turn, help to explain distinct nationalist policy trajectories, too.

This study of resource nationalism also provides insight into the *limits* of business power in contemporary Indonesia. As theorists of state-business relations have long emphasized, state policy is never purely a "passive register . . . of dominant sectoral pressures" (Schneider 1998, 117). Business capacity to influence outcomes is contingent not just on structural power and material resources but also on other variables that lie beyond businesses' control. Even materially powerful capitalists can fail to get what they want during policy negotiations because state actors must consider a range of other intervening problems, including the "climate of public opinion" (Vogel 1987, 63).

There were key moments when a *statist* form of resource nationalism prevailed over the demands of powerful business interests because government leaders deemed SOEs as either more capable or politically preferrable to private actors. More specifically, this book argues that state-led nationalizations prevailed in cases where private business faced structural economic constraints (capital and technology) or where the political stakes were high such that state actors preferred to keep profitable natural assets out of the hands of oligarchic forces. For example, as the historical chapters demonstrate, the state-owned oil giant Pertamina has greater capabilities in the oil and gas sector compared to much of the local private sector, despite the latter's remarkable expansion into the upstream sector. Competition between powerful statist advocates and a small group of politically connected domestic investors in oil and gas generated extended regulatory stasis, but the push to squeeze out foreign multinationals in upstream oil and gas ultimately advantaged Pertamina, which enjoyed both economic and political advantages over its domestic competitors.

In the mining sector, meanwhile, Freeport's major gold and copper mine was one of the few foreign-operated mines taken over by a state-owned enterprise, rather than by domestic private businesses, because President Jokowi deemed this particular mine too economically and politically strategic to be controlled by one or a group of tycoons. There was a strong sense among the president's advisers that public opinion would favor a state takeover of the Freeport mine, which in turn would help Jokowi's reelection bid. The *political salience* of particular extractive projects, therefore, can lead to nationalist transformation in favor of the state over private capital.

Beyond these important moments of statist nationalism, however, this study argues that the most remarkable feature of contemporary resource nationalism in Indonesia is the role of private capitalist actors in driving or containing nationalist proposals. Even in the oil and gas sector, where Pertamina ultimately came to dominate the country's upstream production, the instrumental power of local private enterprise reached new heights and complicated efforts to seek legislative change in favor of SOEs' privileges. Historically, in Indonesia's land-based and natural resource sectors, the state partnered with foreign capital to exploit, extract, and export; today, these industries are dominated by local tycoons and domestic business elites with growing economic and political influence. Robison's (1986) influential study of capital during the New Order characterized the state as the incubator of an emergent domestic capitalist class. In the historical chapter of this book, I demonstrate that process of incubation and the degree to which major private interests in these sectors depended on the state for capital, protection, and opportunity. Today, however, business has achieved a new level of autonomy and influence over the state's policymaking apparatus.

The observations I make about the variability of resource nationalism in Indonesia can be summarized as such: where dominant domestic businesses interests were locally oriented with low levels of internationalization and high levels of instrumental power, nationalist efforts prevailed (the mining sector); where the dominant business actors were conglomerates with a more international orientation and high levels of structural power, nationalist efforts failed (the palm oil sector); and where private investors faced economic constraints or where projects were especially politically salient, state capital prevailed (specific oil, gas, and minerals projects).

Indonesia's Contemporary Political Economy

The argument outlined above makes two interventions into existing scholarship on Indonesia. The first intervention pertains to what the dynamics of resource nationalism reveal about the nature of Indonesia's political economy in the democratic era. When Indonesia began its democratic transition at the end of the 1990s, the structure of the economy was also in the midst of change. Over the course of the 1980s and 1990s, Indonesia had become less dependent on oil rents; but at the turn of the century, as the country recovered from the devastating economic crisis of 1997, Indonesia became much *more* dependent on coal and crude palm oil as sources of export income and foreign exchange.

As Indonesia's young democracy evolved, patronage came to play an increasingly central role in electoral politics and democratic governance more generally. Election campaigns became more costly with each cycle (Aspinall and Berenschot 2019; Muhtadi 2019), and laws are often designed and decided through expensive deals brokered by political parties and senior bureaucrats (Mietzner 2013a). Political parties seek out candidates from the private sector to help underwrite their activities, and from party leaders down to the regional legislatures, politicians with a business background have become commonplace (Mietzner 2015; Poczter and Pepinsky 2016; Warburton et al. 2021). So, as the commodities boom took off in the mid-2000s, the land and resource industries, and especially the coal sector, became an attractive source of rents that could be used for political purposes at both the local and national levels. Political parties and ministries became populated by people with direct interests in either extractives or plantations, and sometimes both.

Throughout this book, I show how these two trends—the increasing centrality of patronage to Indonesia's young democracy and the increasing centrality of mining and palm oil to the economy—expanded both the instrumental and structural power of domestic agribusiness and mining companies. In turn, land and resource policy, including the trajectory of resource nationalism, came to reflect the preferences of domestic capital during and after the boom.

In other parts of the world, and especially in Latin American countries like Bolivia and Ecuador, popular forces and social movement activists play a pivotal role in anti-foreign mobilization and in defining the terms of resource nationalism (Kohl and Farthing 2012; Riofrancos 2020). In Indonesia, however, such actors have played a minor part in nationalist campaigns. Indeed, land rights movements, environmental activists, and indigenous groups that oppose foreign and corporate control of Indonesia's natural resources found themselves increasingly excluded from negotiations over land and environmental regulations during the decade following the boom (2014–). Indonesia's democracy took an illiberal turn during Jokowi's presidency, and civic activism of all kinds came under pressure from a more repressive and assertive state (Power and Warburton 2020; Warburton and Aspinall 2019). But the transformation of ownership in the land and resource industries from foreign to domestic private hands has been especially critical to the exclusion of popular forces from the terms of debate over resource management. Resource nationalism in Indonesia is, thus, a top-down, corporate project that has been largely determined by a rising class of domestic business elites.

This book's arguments build on well-established critical political economy portrayals of Indonesia's political landscape. Scholars from this tradition have long maintained that oligarchs and predatory politicobusiness elites captured

Indonesia's democracy after the fall of the autocrat, President Suharto, in 1998, and since that point, the direction of political and economic policy has been driven by the efforts of oligarchs to expand and defend their personal wealth (Robison and Hadiz 2004; Winters 2011). Oligarchy theorists thus emphasize continuity between the political economy of Suharto's authoritarian regime and Indonesia's contemporary democratic context, while at the same time pointing to an increase in the relative power of wealthy business elites vis-à-vis politicobureaucrats (Fukuoka 2012).

My study of corporate control over resource nationalism confirms oligarchy theorists' main contention that wealthy holdovers from the Suharto era continue to exercise immense economic and political influence. The book extends and complicates such observations. I argue that oligarchic characterizations of Indonesia's political economy should be a starting point for an alternative set of analytically important questions about variation and change that are rarely broached by oligarchy theorists themselves, such as when and why do big business interests express conflicting or changing preferences? And do economic elites exercise power in different ways? By specifying those preferences and attending to competition and conflict between the state and private sector actors, this book sets out to provide a sharper picture of how business power varies within and between sectors.

This study of resource nationalism demonstrates not only how and why domestic corporate influence has intensified in these sectors but also delineates the *limits* to business power. The case study of oil and gas provides a powerful illustration of how, in some contexts, state capital continues to enjoy superior structural power. Public opinion mattered, too. In the mining sector, the political salience and public spectacle of specific resource projects drove politicians and state managers down a more statist-nationalist path, which meant excluding tycoons and oligarchs from lucrative upstream extractive projects. In democratic countries, these moments of "loud" politics (Culpepper 2011) often act as a constraint on the policy power of capitalist actors.

The arguments outlined here make a second intervention into the narrower literature on natural resource governance in Indonesia. Although there are many empirically rich studies of Indonesia's resource industries, most research to date has focused on the travails of decentralized management of forests and plantations, and the environmental and social costs of poorly regulated extractive spaces (see, e.g., Erb 2016; Erman 2007; Hamilton-Hart 2015; McCarthy 2010, 2012; Resosudarmo et al. 2012; Spiegel 2012). Most scholars have also homed in on only one sector, and few have attended to the policy consequences of shifting ownership landscapes across land and resource industries. Studies of Indonesia's experience of resource nationalism, of which there are very few, have focused on conflict and competition between the state and global capital (Kaup and Gellert 2017), and especially on the rent-seeking activities of the state (Buehler 2012). To date, we have no cross-sectoral political economy studies that compare and contrast the role capital plays in designing regulation. This book thus adds to the rich body of work on this topic by providing a historically grounded study of nationalism, business power, and sector-level policymaking in three of Indonesia's strategic economic industries.

The Developmental Consequences of Resource Nationalism

Moving beyond the causes of nationalist variation in Indonesia, this book also grapples with the *consequences* of Indonesia's changing ownership landscape for the governance of the country's precious natural wealth. Advocates of nationalist policies often claim that land and resource projects will be better managed when under the stewardship of local rather than foreign actors and that more of the wealth such projects generate will stay within the country's borders rather than taken offshore. It is common to hear nationalist actors in Indonesia argue that state or domestic private enterprise will pay more tax and invest more in local labor, skills, and downstream industrialization than their foreign counterparts. From this perspective, a locally owned resource industry will bring greater developmental and distributional benefits to the domestic economy and to the population more broadly.

The Indonesian case presents a complex picture of the developmental consequences of nationalist change. For example, I find evidence that local mining firms were more willing than foreign miners to renegotiate their contracts at the height of the boom and to commit to downstream industrialization by investing in technology that foreign businesses spent years eschewing. But it is also the case that as their companies have become more profitable and as their investments have expanded, domestic resource giants have used their superior instrumental power to reshape the regulatory architecture in ways that help them to avoid paying higher taxes and royalties, to sustain and expand their land concessions, and to reduce their environmental responsibilities.

Indeed, this book argues that the slow nationalization of Indonesia's extractive projects and the fusion of business-state interests in major export sectors more generally has contributed to a marked deterioration in the country's environmental protections and to the shrinking of civic space for activists and communities with alternative visions for resource ownership and management. As the following chapters will show, unlike in other parts of the world, popular forces and other sorts of nonstate actors have featured only in the margins of

Indonesia's experience of resource nationalism. Instead, social movement activists, environmental economists, and the communities living near sites of exploitation found themselves increasingly isolated from policymaking processes affecting resource ownership and governance. As a result, resource nationalism and the attendant transition to local ownership in Indonesia has, in many ways, failed to improve on or remedy the problems of land and resource exploitation that emerged during earlier periods of foreign control.

Comparative Contribution

The book's final argument concerns the comparative literature on resource nationalism. Much of the political economy work on this subject portrays resource nationalism as a zero-sum contest pitching states against foreign firms. A common conclusion is that in weak states with poor property rights protections and high levels of corruption, bureaucrats and politicians will be especially likely to pursue the nationalist path during a boom, altering contracts, demanding concessions, and extorting foreign firms while there are excess rents to grab (Mahdavi 2020; Stevens 2008; Vivoda 2009; Wilson 2015). This prevailing focus on institutional weakness and corrupt state actors has meant that studies of resource nationalism rarely attend to how the structure, preferences, and identities of domestic corporate actors might drive—or sometimes derail—nationalist trajectories or how local capitalists might help to sustain the nationalist turn long after a boom has ended.

When it comes to middle-income and patronage democracies such as Indonesia, I argue, accounts of resource nationalism would benefit from a sharper focus on the specific role of domestic business. General theories of business power have long demonstrated the political influence that corporate actors enjoy in capitalist economies, especially when it comes to policies that govern trade and flows of foreign capital (Doner 1991; Kim and Osgood 2019; Puente and Schneider 2020). We should expect such influence to be even more pronounced in patronage democracies, where the line between business interests and public office is especially thin and where businesspeople increasingly enter politics directly (Szakonyi 2020). Current theories of resource nationalism tend only to treat local capital as a rent-seeking partner of corrupt bureaucrats. Even though such arrangements are a feature of resource nationalism in many countries, and especially patronage democracies like Indonesia, I suggest that domestic business can also exact a more independent influence on nationalist outcomes and should therefore be brought into the analytical foreground.

An objective of this study is to bring the growing body of research on resource nationalism into dialogue with scholarship on state-business relations and foreign investment flows. Within the open economy politics (OEP) tradition, for example, one stream of scholarship emphasizes the importance of studying the interests and capabilities of business actors, arguing that even *within sectors*, different sorts of businesses will seek different sorts of foreign investment and trade regulations (Kim and Osgood 2019; Osgood et al. 2017). Characteristics such as firm size, whether a company exports or imports, and its ownership structure have all been theorized to play a role in determining the policies a business wants and the actions it will take in pursuit of those policies (Puente and Schneider 2020). This book delves into ownership structures in particular and argues that the Indonesian case compels an exploration of the role that owner identity plays in explaining economic interests and the political behavior of businesses. Departing from much of the scholarship in the OEP tradition, in this study I suggest a more historically grounded and context-sensitive approach to explaining how and why different kinds of corporate actors hold such a range of nationalist preferences. This is especially important in postcolonial countries like Indonesia, with politically fraught historical processes of capital accumulation. A comparative contribution of this book is, therefore, to demonstrate the value of studying business identity for tracing the form and fate of resource nationalist mobilization and transformation.

Design, Method, and Data

Most comparative work on resource nationalism makes states the primary unit of analysis, asking how different state-level institutions might produce different kinds of nationalist outcomes. This book, however, provides a *within*-country study of resource nationalism, homing in on subnational variation at the sector level. Why conduct a single-country study of Indonesia? The Indonesian case warrants particular attention because of the country's role as a key natural resource exporter. It is the world's leading producer of palm oil, the second largest for thermal coal, and among the world's top producers of nickel, tin, gold, copper, and bauxite. It is important, therefore, to understand the causes and consequences of nationalist change in the leading export sectors of Southeast Asia's largest economy. Indonesia is also home to one of the world's largest tracts of tropical forest, second only to Brazil and the Democratic Republic of the Congo, spread out across its outer islands. Changes in the ownership and use of Indonesian land and the levels of deforestation that can accompany those changes are of major significance given international efforts to protect primary forests, reduce global carbon emissions, and meet climate targets (Jong 2021). In short, the ownership and exploitation of Indonesia's land-based resource sectors matters beyond the country's borders, and its political and economic status make it a "crucial case" deserving an in-depth single country study (Goertz and Mahoney 2012).

This study is designed around a structured comparison of Indonesia's three leading primary commodity sectors. As the chapters in this book will demonstrate, all three sectors have long histories of anti-foreign mobilization and protectionist state interventions. Yet, in the contemporary era, nationalist regulations prevailed in the mining sector, failed in the plantations sector, and remained ambiguous and unresolved in the oil and gas sector. The chapters that follow document the process behind several nationalist policy proposals. Each sectoral case study homes in on nationalist demands associated with a piece of legislation and the debates and conflicts that such demands generated. When it comes to the mining sector, nationalist agitation was focused on the development of Law 4/2009 on Mineral and Coal Mining, which outlined a new divestment regime for foreign mining companies and a disruptive ban on the export of raw minerals. In the plantations sector, I examine a failed proposal to cap foreign ownership as low as 30 percent and to compel divestment of foreign-owned plantation companies as part of the new Law 39/2014 on Plantations. In the oil and gas sector, I focus on nationalist mobilization that was directed at revisions to Law 22/2001 on Oil and Gas, and the fate of a proposal to provide state-owned Pertamina with a formal first right to accept or refuse expiring foreign contracts.

To conduct the comparative analysis, I draw on several types of data that together paint a picture of business power in Indonesia's resource sectors. To describe the case studies and the variation in nationalist policy trajectories, I bring together a range of sources, including parliamentary records, court hearings, media reports, and interviews. These data were collected mostly during fieldwork visits to Indonesia between 2014 and 2019, including to Jakarta and to islands that produce the bulk of Indonesia's mining and agrocommodities, like Sumatra, Kalimantan, and Sulawesi. Over that period, I was either living in Indonesia or traveling regularly between Australia, Singapore, and Indonesia.

I conducted over 160 interviews with businesspeople, politicians, legislators, members of the relevant state ministries and departments, academics, journalists, and other industry folk in Indonesia. Some respondents met with me numerous times. We spoke at length and at regular intervals about the nature of nationalist change, the seemingly endless revisions to the laws and regulations that set the terms for foreign ownership and investment. These conversations helped me to understand the preferences of different actors with a stake in the resource industries and to perceive how business power shapes nationalist outcomes in Indonesia.

I specify business preferences via two means. I use qualitative methods to capture actors' response to nationalist demands. For example, I analyzed the public statements of industry associations and major firms and conducted interviews with key stakeholders from each industry: representatives of peak bodies, company representatives, industry consultants, and the bureaucrats and legislators who regularly engaged with private sector actors during the policymaking process. I also identify the major businesses in each sector and profile their ownership structures, assets, and where possible, document their political connections. My observations of how the structure of business ownership has changed in each sector rely on several sources. Information on corporate ownership is notoriously difficult to access in Indonesia, and the task required collecting company information taken from the Orbis database, together with listed firms' annual reports and media coverage of ownership changes.[5] The data illustrate the incremental takeover of foreign resource projects by Indonesian firms and also suggest differences in the ownership structures of major agribusiness, mining, and oil companies in Indonesia: compared to extractive businesses, agrifirms tend to be larger, more often owned by ethnically Chinese Indonesians, and more of their business interests are domiciled abroad.

Second, I supplement these qualitative data with an original and representative survey of business elites from across Indonesia's major economic sectors. This is one of only a few representative surveys ever done of Indonesia's business class. Implemented in 2019, the survey was part of a larger project funded by Australia's Department of Foreign Affairs and Trade on "Southeast Asia's Rules Based Order" (SEARBO) and was designed by a team of scholars at the Australian National University's Department of Political and Social Change in partnership with the Indonesian Survey Institute.[6] One goal of the survey was to investigate corporate preferences more systematically when it comes to FDI. Such data are unique, not just in the context of the Indonesia-focused literature but also in terms of scholarship on FDI more broadly. Most research in this field infers what businesses want based on (often limited) data on firm-level characteristics. I combine this kind of data with the representative survey that asked 670 business elites, of which over 180 come from the extractive and agricultural sectors, directly about their policy preferences on foreign involvement in the Indonesian economy. The results confirm not only that firms have a wide range of preferences within each sector but that firms' size and their owners' identity are significant predictors of nationalist preferences. The survey also probed corporate managers about their company's lobbying activities and their relations with the state, which help to build a picture of how state-business relations can vary between sectors and firms and how those relations correlate with identity and with preferences for protection.

A Brief Note on Key Concepts
Business

Business in treated throughout this study as having heterogeneous policy preferences and behaviors. As Schneider (1997, 213) argues, it is reasonable to assume that businesses' principal preference is profit, but it is far more difficult to know their strategies and, in turn, their policy preferences. For example, in developing and middle-income countries like Brazil and Mexico, and indeed Indonesia, diversified conglomerates dominate several industries which can make their preferences and strategies more "flexible, contingent and complex" (214). Upstream businesses have distinct preferences to those operating in the downstream of a sector, and smaller companies will seek regulatory regimes different to those wanted by large and diversified companies. Business preferences, therefore, require empirical attention and explanation.

Throughout this book, I use several related terms to describe different sorts of business actors. I use "business" and "private capital" interchangeably to refer in the broadest sense to private sector interests and actors. Descriptors such as "firm," "company," or "enterprise," are used to indicate the corporate entities that a specific business actor owns. When I refer to the "major" business interests in each sector, I am speaking of those business actors who are responsible for a large volume of the sector's production and exports. Throughout this book, terms like *tycoons* and *big business* are used interchangeably as a way to refer to the most prominent businesspeople in a given sector. Finally, I use the term *oligarch* to mean those major business actors who inhabit a space "near the centre of the [political] regime" (Winters 2011, 15) but who still retain an "economic base outside the state" (Hutchcroft 1991, 424). In other words, such business actors enjoy immense political influence without depending solely or primarily on the state for generating their private wealth.

The State

I also refer routinely to "the state" and "state actors" throughout this book. In institutional terms, the state consists of the bureaucracy, executive, judiciary, and legislature. These are the state's policymaking, implementing, and accountability apparatus, which are conceptually distinct from the interest groups and political parties that "transmit societal demands" (Hall 1997, 276).

The reality, however, is that in most countries, the state apparatus is often not clearly distinguished or separate from societal forces. Indeed, when it comes to Indonesia, the executive and bureaucracy are heavily politicized, the worlds of business and politics overlap, and the judiciary remains a site of collusion and corruption. Indonesia's state institutions are fragmented by cross-cutting patron-client relations (Aspinall 2013), with senior bureaucrats tied to individual politicians or parties, and ministers who not only hold senior positions in political parties but also have significant business investments in the sectors that they regulate.

This study adopts Migdal's (1994, 9) disaggregated view of the state in which he sees "officials at different levels of the state ... interacting—at times conflicting—with an entire constellation of social forces in disparate arenas." In other words, across different sectoral arenas, state actors engage with societal forces and participate in policy conflicts without necessarily pursuing the same goals or acting as a coherent or unified whole. Therefore, in the chapters that follow and in each sectoral case study, I endeavor to be as specific and as detailed as possible when explaining state actors involved in nationalist campaigns and policy conflicts and when delineating the source of nationalist support within particular ministries, parts of the executive, or within the legislative branch.

The Rest of the Book

The rest of book is organized as follows. Chapter 1 locates the study within existing international research on resource nationalism, reflects critically on extant approaches to explaining the phenomenon, and elaborates in more detail the book's conceptual and theoretical framework. Chapter 2 provides a history of foreign control and nationalist mobilization in Indonesia's resource industries. Starting from the colonial era, moving through the early years of independence, up to the end of the New Order period (1998), this chapter traces and describes shifts in patterns of ownership in each sector and demonstrates the conditions under which domestic business was able to make incremental but only limited inroads into Indonesia's lucrative export industries.

Chapter 3 outlines varied patterns of resource nationalist policies that emerged in response to the commodities boom and against the backdrop of Indonesia's democratic transformation. This chapter is largely descriptive. Its purpose is to set up the empirical puzzles that motivate the book, illustrating the persistent but also uneven nature of nationalist change across my case study sectors. The book's main analytical contentions are laid out in chapters 4, 5, and 6. Chapter 4 compares the fate of nationalist proposals in the mining and palm oil sectors and demonstrates how local corporate actors have evolved, grown, and become critical policy actors—but their preferences for protection varied. Chapter 5 looks at the constraints on private business: the structural power of SOEs in the oil and gas sector and the conditions under "political salience" guides state managers' approach to resource nationalism. Chapter 6 explores the basis of businesses' distinct nationalist preferences, drawing on insights from OEP theory and leveraging new survey data to specify more systematically how firm-level characteristics can be linked to nationalist preferences and policy outcomes. The concluding chapter confronts the consequences of corporate control of resource nationalism in Indonesia. I argue that resource nationalist policies and changes to the ownership of major resource projects have had discernible developmental impacts, but overall long-term distributional outcomes remain uncertain. At the same time, the transformation of ownership in these sectors has had clear and negative consequences for environmental protection and for the rights of communities at sites of land and resource exploitation.

The concluding chapter also reflects on what the Indonesian case tells us about patterns of resource nationalism more broadly. By providing a detailed window into Indonesia's experience, this book's objective is to move political economy studies of resource nationalism beyond the prevailing state-centric approach, which gives most analytical weight to factors like boom-bust cycles and bureaucratic myopia. The Indonesian case demonstrates the political impact that domestic corporate actors have in middle-income patronage-driven democracies. In such contexts, commodity booms do not just enhance the power of the state vis-à-vis foreign firms. Instead, booms can enhance the instrumental and structural power of major domestic business actors, giving them an especially influential seat at the policymaking table and, in turn, transforming ownership structures and reshaping developmental trajectories.

RESOURCE NATIONALISM IN PATRONAGE DEMOCRACIES
A Framework

This chapter sets out an analytical framework for studying resource nationalism in competitive patronage democracies like Indonesia. In these sorts of settings, domestic capital enjoys outsized influence on political decision makers, and local business interests can drive or derail nationalist agendas in the sectors they dominate. Much of the industry analysis and political economy research on resource nationalism is preoccupied with the nature of the state, the incentives that drive bureaucrats to pursue the nationalist path, and the state-level institutions that might constrain bureaucrats' nationalist ambitions. Although invaluable for explaining cross-national trends, I argue that such an approach overlooks important within country differences and subnational variation and understates the role played by societal actors, including business, in the production of nationalist policies. When holding state-level institutions constant, we can see that bureaucrats and elected politicians face a range of constraints and pressures at the subnational and sector levels that shape distinct policy paths (Evans 1995). Such constraints include the preferences and political influence of business.

By adopting this analytical approach, I bring studies of resource nationalism into dialogue with a rich political economy literature on economic policymaking and business power. The framework I propose renders domestic business a major force in determining the trajectory of land and resource policy in competitive patronage democracies and makes the case for tracing nationalist variation back to the major corporate interests in each sector.

Theories of Resource Nationalism: Bargains, Booms, and State Institutions

Conceptualizations of resource nationalism vary, often reflecting analysts' distinct professional or disciplinary concerns. Corporate risk consultancies, which produce a large volume of analysis on resource nationalism, aim to assess the damage that nationalist interventions might do to foreign investments. From their perspective, resource nationalism constitutes a set of risky, flawed, and inefficient economic interventions (Ernst & Young 2014; Maplecroft 2019; Stratfor 2018). Media outlets often take a similar position and characterize resource nationalist policies as shortsighted, thinly veiled asset grabs by the state (Buehler 2012; Castle 2014; *The Economist* 2012a, 2012b; Kurtz and Van Zorge 2013; McBeth 2014a).

At the opposite end of the conceptual spectrum, sociologists and political geographers view resource nationalism as primarily a discursive tool. Scholars working in this field are concerned with the way nationalist demands are formulated and deployed by both state actors and social movements to express sovereignty over land and resources and to articulate more inclusive extractive models and developmental outcomes for the state as well as for communities living close to sites of extraction (Bebbington and Humphreys-Bebbington 2011; Koch and Perreault 2018; Kohl and Farthing 2012; Perreault and Valdivia 2010; Riofrancos 2020; Veltmeyer 2013; Yates and Bakker 2013).[1]

Sitting between these two starkly different approaches is a large body of political economy scholarship to which this book speaks most directly. In the broadest sense, political economists cast resource nationalism as an attempt by governments to rectify a perceived imbalance between the state and foreign multinational firms when it comes to the benefits that accrue from commercial resource exploitation. This perception motivates state managers to introduce a range of policy prescriptions that enable greater state control over foreign investors and more domestic ownership of major resource projects, so as to ensure a larger share of resource profits flow into state coffers (Mahdavi 2020; Stevens 2008; Vivoda 2009). Most political economists adopt a realist approach and characterize resource nationalism as a zero-sum game between states and foreign companies, each vying with the other to maximize their own gains when it comes to lucrative resource projects.

To explain why resource nationalism emerges at a particular moment in time, political economists emphasize shifts in host states' bargaining position. Raymond Vernon's (1971) pioneering "obsolescing bargain thesis," for example, argues that resource nationalism surfaces when the government gains the "upper hand" at a certain point during the life of an oil contract. Even though a state must initially entice investors into its oil industry (with tax holidays or subsidies and few obligations to engage local firms, investors, or labor), once a foreign firm has sunk its capital into a resource project, that capital cannot be easily moved, and the bargaining power shifts back to the host. More recently, scholars of resource nationalism have pointed to exogenous changes in commodity prices—booms and busts—as the major reason for a shift in state-firm bargaining power. This "market-cycle" explanation argues that resource nationalism is a function of high commodity prices (Wilson 2015). The logic is twofold: first, boom times provide governments of resource-rich countries with windfall profits, which in turn gives them greater leverage in their negotiations with foreign investors and more influence over international commodity markets (Herberg 2011; Humphreys 2013); second, there is more money to be made during a boom, which motivates state officials to seek greater access to resource rents via enhanced state intervention (Click and Weiner 2010; Kurtz and Van Zorge 2013; Solomon 2012; Stevens 2008).

This market-cycle explanation first emerged in response to programs of nationalization in the oil industries of Middle Eastern and Latin American countries from the 1950s through to the booms of the 1970s and 1980s. Vlado Vivoda's (2009, 518) more recent analysis of international oil companies' bargaining power similarly characterizes resource nationalism as "a by-product of high prices." Resource nationalism is thus rendered epiphenomenal, rising in tandem with commodity prices and producing similar state responses across resource-rich countries.

The concept of rent seeking is often at the heart of these bargaining theories because from this perspective, price booms in minerals, hydrocarbon, and cash crop sectors are thought to motivate short-term rent-seeking behavior among state actors. There are synergies with the expansive resource curse literature. One stream of resource curse scholarship argues that booms produce myopia among policymakers and politicians, in turn increasing the likelihood of nationalist, protectionist, and rent-seeking behavior, leading eventually to slower economic growth and institutional decline (Deacon and Rode 2012; Karl 1997; Ross 2015). Michael Ross's (2001) seminal study of the timber industry in Southeast Asia found that resource windfalls from the timber boom triggered a frenzy of rent seeking and corrupt behavior among state managers. The result was the large-scale retreat of foreign capital and multinational companies from this industry and institutional decline across Asia's leading timber-exporting economies. There is, therefore, much consensus that booms trigger an increase in state interventionism, which analysts have often tied explicitly or implicitly to rent seeking. The market-cycle theory of resource nationalism, however, assumes that booms will produce similar sorts of myopic state responses across resource-rich countries, which means variation goes unexplained.

To address the question of variation, scholars have focused primarily on the role that state institutions play in conditioning how countries respond to booms, in turn leading to different degrees and types of resource nationalism (Domjan and Stone 2010; Gardner 2013; Haslam and Heidrich 2016b; Wilson 2011). Again, these studies intersect with parts of the resource curse literature that emphasizes resource-rich countries do not all suffer the same cursed fate. Instead, the quality and strength of state institutions act as the mechanism via which a boom will either have a net positive or negative impact on a country's developmental trajectory (Busse and Gröning 2013; Luong and Weinthal 2010; Mehlum, Moene, and Torvik 2006). Comparative studies of resource nationalism similarly trace cross-country variation back to institutional weakness: where rule of law is patchy or arbitrary and where corruption is common, foreign resource firms are more likely to find themselves the target of nationalist attacks (Arbatli 2013; Click and Weiner 2010; Wilson 2015).

Frameworks that divide states up into nationalist countries (rentier states and those with weak rule of law) and liberal countries (those with strong rule of law and property rights protections) cannot explain why a single state might behave differently in different sectors. For example, Jeffrey Wilson's (2015) typology of states and resource nationalisms places Indonesia in a "developmental state" category because of the government's drive to industrialize parts of the country's mineral mining sector; however, other cases of resource nationalism in Indonesia also reflect the characteristics of Wilson's "rentier"-type state in which the government directly takes over foreign-run resource projects as a means of capturing rents. Both during and after the boom, the Indonesian government ended the contracts of multinational companies in the mineral and oil sector and handed state-owned firms control of several strategic resource concessions, like the Mahakam oil and gas block, once operated by France's Total, and Freeport McMoran's gold and copper mine in Papua province. How can we explain a state's tendency to pursue this mix of rentier, developmental, and in some cases, even economically liberal interventions across different parts of its resource-based economy?

This study builds on the previous work reviewed here by developing a conceptual framework that deals with two limitations in the extant literature. First, much political economy work is focused almost exclusively on the state as the source of nationalist change, and thus, there is a tendency to overlook and undertheorize the role of nonstate actors in determining nationalist outcomes. Second, the zero-sum picture painted by many political economy studies suggests resource nationalism constitutes a victory of the state over capital and free markets.

Such a picture glosses over complex relationships between the state and domestic capital and obscures the ways in which sections of the state do the bidding of domestic business elites. To be sure, state actors are always central to any story of resource nationalism; however, as Ignacio Puente and Ben Schneider (2020) put it, there is much to be gained by occasionally pushing the state into the "analytic background" in order to reveal the policy power of societal forces, including business. I set out, therefore, to develop a conceptual framework that can provide analytical space for domestic business actors and establish a more detailed picture of the conditions under which nationalist demands prevail, and why they sometimes fail, in a democracy such as Indonesia.

Conceptualizing Resource Nationalism

It is first important to recognize the normative and ideological content of resource nationalism. In the broadest sense, all forms of nationalism are an expression of loyalty and belonging to one's own nation above other nations. Such sentiments are necessarily articulated in relation to an "other" that falls outside a national boundary, whether defined in political, territorial, or sometimes ethnic terms (Gellner 2008, 1–3). Looking back to some of the classic work on economic nationalism can help to bring clarity to the concept of resource nationalism. Nationalism in the economic realm is the belief that membership of a national community, however defined, confers special material privileges and benefits that should not extend to those rendered foreign (Clift and Woll 2012). Harry Johnson's (1965, 179) seminal study describes economic nationalism as a policy effort to "extend the property owned by nationals" or members of the "national group," because domestic ownership and domestic industrial achievement satisfies both an emotional and material desire to strengthen the economic position of nationals and the nation.

Advocates for resource nationalism similarly perceive land and natural resources to be the economic domain of nationals over foreigners and as the inherent property of the national group. Advocates oppose a free-market approach to economic policy because they perceive that markets alone cannot fairly allocate land and natural resources to groups who *should* own, exploit, and benefit from them. I thus define resource nationalism as a *policy effort to expand local ownership over land and resource industries (localization) and to advance the economic position of the national group vis-à-vis foreign groups by leveraging land and natural resources for industrial achievement (industrialization).*

What specific sorts of policy efforts are associated with resource nationalism? Many studies offer remarkably broad, all-encompassing descriptions of what constitutes a resource nationalist policy, including everything from the introduction of higher taxes and royalties for private companies to the unilateral modification of private companies' contracts, limitations on the import or export of particular commodities, local content requirements, compulsory corporate social responsibility contributions, forced divestment of foreign assets to the state or domestic companies, and in the most extreme cases, nationalization of entire industries (Dargin 2010; Marston 2016; Wilson 2015).

There is a need for greater conceptual clarity when it comes to delineating, and in turn explaining, the policies associated with resource nationalism. For instance, taxation and royalties are often cast as manifestations of resource nationalism. But there are important differences in terms of how taxation impacts local versus foreign firms. Taxes that aim to increase state profits and redistribute rent from private companies are qualitatively different to the interventions that target foreign companies in particular. In the Democratic Republic of the Congo (DRC), for example, the government introduced a new tax in 2018 specifically for multinational miners but not state-owned or local companies involved in the booming cobalt industry (Mahdavi 2020, 8). In Indonesia, on the other hand, proposed royalty hikes in the 2009 Mining Law negotiations were tabled to draw in more income from all mining firms. This is a substantively different policy to the tax introduced in the DRC and should be distinguished conceptually and analytically.

Again, it is instructive to look back at how economic nationalism has been defined in policy terms. Economic nationalists advocate for more local ownership of valuable economic assets and industries and seek privileges for state-owned companies or domestic private firms through restricting FDI and mandating foreign ownership limitations (Girvan 1975). Economic nationalism is also associated with protectionist trade policies, domestic market obligations, and the use of tariffs, quotas, subsidies, and other interventionist forms of industrial policy (Auty 1994).[2] The goal of such interventions is to develop and protect domestic industry, increase local manufacturing capacity and the production of high-value products, and reduce a country's reliance on imports and markets as a means to economic "self-sufficiency" (Colantone and Stanig 2019). Economically nationalist policies can also extend to state support for domestic firms abroad and the leveraging of domestic resources for the sake of supporting national champions and helping them to compete with foreign firms on global markets (D'Costa 2009).

Resource nationalist policies can similarly be divided into those that seek to *localize* ownership and those that seek to advance the economic position of national groups by pursuing domestic *industrial* achievement in the land and natural resource industries. When it comes to the latter, policies for resource-based industrialization aim to shift a country's resource sectors higher up in global value chains by investing in downstream industrial activity through subsidies, trade restrictions, and beneficiation regulations (Auty 1994; Neilson et al. 2020; Wilson 2015). Domestic market obligations (DMOs) are used for similar industrial purposes, forcing companies to supply their raw commodities to downstream industries. DMOs are also used to supply the public with low-priced commodities such as petroleum, gas, or coal for electricity or crude palm oil for cooking. In such instances, demands for public access to these commodities is often framed in nationalist terms—these resources belong first and foremost to the nation and its people, not foreign trading partners and communities abroad.

This book is primarily concerned with *localizing* forms of resource nationalism, asking how and under what conditions the ambition to localize land and resource industries gets transformed into concrete policies and, in turn, changes to ownership landscapes. Such policies include forced divestment regulations, caps on foreign investment, and in extreme cases, nationalization of projects and industries (Berrios, Marak, and Morgenstern 2011; Guriev, Kolotilin, and Sonin 2011; Mahdavi 2020). I propose that these localizing forms of resource nationalism can be further differentiated into policy efforts that seek ownership or privileges for the state, domestic business, or communities at sites of extraction and exploitation (figure 1.1). Nationalization is, thus, not only a statist effort whereby private assets are transferred to the state; rather, this concept of resource nationalism allows for a form of localization and nationalization that is driven by private domestic interests.

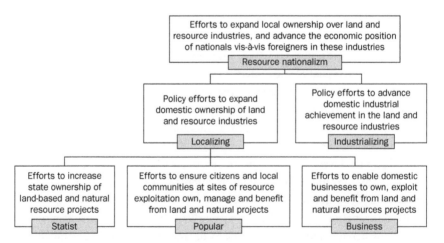

FIGURE 1.1. Conceptualizing resource nationalism

1. *Statist resource nationalism*: Proponents of a statist nationalism view the state as the legitimate owner, manager, and beneficiary of a country's natural riches and as such, seek to increase state ownership of land-based and natural resource projects while opposing private ownership and exploitation. Statist advocates promote the role of state-owned enterprises in primary production and resource extraction, either through direct ownership of major strategic projects, shares in foreign-operated projects, or through forced partnership between foreign and state-owned firms. Government expropriations of foreign oil assets in Libya in the 1970s or in Venezuela in the early 2000s are examples of extreme forms of statist resource nationalism, whereby foreign firms' assets are seized by the state and handed to state-owned firms (Karl 1997; Mahdavi 2020; Monaldi 2020). There are many less dramatic examples, too. For example, in 2018, the DRC doubled the state's equity interest in foreign-operated mines to 10 percent, and that share increases by 5 percent with each license renewal (Matthews-Green 2018). In Indonesia, proponents of a statist resource nationalism in the oil and gas sector demand state-owned giant Pertamina be given special privileges to all expiring foreign oil and gas concessions before such concessions get opened to tender for either foreign or local private enterprises. These sorts of initiatives enable governments to extend state ownership over the resource sector at the expense of private investors.

2. *Popular resource nationalism*: Proponents of a popular resource nationalism advocate for the rights of citizens and local communities at sites of resource exploitation to own, manage, and benefit from natural resources. This type describes the more "bottom-up" nature of resource nationalism that observers have identified in countries such as Bolivia and Ecuador, where demands for local control of natural resources have come from social movement organizations and leaders seeking greater economic distribution of extractive profits to local and indigenous communities (Kohl and Farthing 2012; Perreault and Valdivia 2010; see also Bebbington and Humphreys-Bebbington 2011; Yates and Bakker 2013). Demands for "local" control are especially narrow in this case, premised on the notion that a specific community's physical and cultural attachment to a piece of territory or point of extraction imbues members with a right to its riches, over and above other communities who live within the wider borders of the state. For example, the movement to have indigenous native title recognized within Australia's legal system gives Aboriginal Australians an opportunity to claim special ownership rights to lands where they can prove a historical and

precolonial connection (Sutton 2003).³ In Indonesia, meanwhile, separatist movements in Aceh and Papua made control of natural resources a critical component in their demands for independence from Indonesia (Aspinall 2007). Although neither movement has achieved political independence, as part of different special autonomy deals, the central government gave local administrations in these provinces greater resource tax and royalty benefits and special equity interest in major resource projects in order to recognize the rights that Acehnese and Papuans have over the resources within their territories (Resosudarmo et al. 2014, 454).

3. *Business-centered resource nationalism*: Finally, proponents of a business-centered nationalism oppose ownership of the resource sectors by foreign actors and argue against state monopolies, too. Instead, this brand of resource nationalism demands domestic private actors should have special and privileged opportunities to own, exploit, and benefit from a country's natural resources. From this perspective, local entrepreneurs are uniquely positioned to transform natural riches into national wealth, ensuring that the profits of land and extractive industries are not channeled into foreign corporate hands. Private sector nationalists may also seek state support to help expand their interests abroad. This type of resource nationalism is achieved through interventions that force foreign companies to divest part or a majority of their shares to domestic firms or that compel foreign investors to partner with local companies. Local content requirements fit within this category, too, because such rules force foreign companies to purchase more products from local firms than they otherwise would. The overarching goal of this form of resource nationalism is to build a domestic business class in the resource sectors, to help develop domestic champions and to reduce foreign and multinational involvement in land and resource industries.

There are many cases from around the world where domestic firms in these sectors lobby the state to do their bidding and attempt to limit or squeeze out foreign competition. For example, the global soybean boom in the mid-2000s triggered an influx of foreign investment—much of it from China—into Brazilian farmlands. In response, the country's "Soy Kings," giant family-owned soybean exporters, demanded the Brazilian government stop what became termed the "foreignization" of Brazilian farmlands (Oliveira 2018). In Australia, too, a campaign developed in the late 2010s to better monitor and then limit foreign investment into farmlands out of fears that foreign entities were crowding out private family-owned farms (Sippel and Weldon 2020). Back in Indonesia, meanwhile, the government has long maintained a negative investment list that limits or excludes foreign investment and ownership in a broad range of sectors and subsectors in order to meet the demands of local businesses. During the boom, as we shall see throughout this book, the mineral mining sector and its subsectors were sites of nationalist campaigns by domestic mining firms that sought privileged access to foreign-operated extractive projects.

Other scholars have similarly delineated various types of resource nationalism, usually suggesting that specific state-level institutional arrangements predict particular nationalist policy approaches (Wilson 2015). I depart from such studies and argue instead that resource nationalist efforts can seek different sorts of ownership structures, and such variation is not anchored to a particular regime or state type; instead, statist, popular, and business-centered claims coexist and compete at the subnational level. Resource nationalism is constituted by competing sets of claims, and advocates for each will lobby incumbent governments to recognize and protect their claims to own and extract natural resources at the expense of both foreign and other national groups. Such competing claims often lead to protracted policy conflicts. For example, Indonesia's oil sector was the site of a years-long conflict between statist advocates and proponents of a business-centered resource nationalism. Statists wished to allocate the state-owned oil firm Pertamina a first right to take up or refuse all expiring foreign-operated oil contracts; business advocates, on the other hand, although agreeing that overseas firms should be excluded from the first round of such tenders, argued domestic firms must be given equal opportunity to compete with Pertamina. This conflict proved so intractable that a new law regulating the country's strategic oil and gas sector languished in parliament for over a decade, leaving the sector in a perpetual state of legal ambiguity.

So, although ultimately it is the state that regulates land and resource policy, resource nationalism should not be viewed as simply work done by and for the state. Instead, governments manage and act on a range of nationalist demands emanating from different parts of the bureaucracy and society, too; some of those demands are statist, others seek more popular ownership of and participation in resource projects, and some nationalist demands reflect the interests of powerful business actors. Attending to these competing claims and, most importantly, explaining why one type of nationalist claim prevails over another can provide insight into the forces behind subnational variation in nationalist policy trajectories and can offer a window into the relationship between state, business, and popular forces. In Indonesia, I argue, popular forms of resource nationalism were relatively weak and became weaker over the course of the boom and the years that followed. Instead, nationalist debate and policymaking in all three sectors was dominated by statist and business claims, with domestic business often playing a decisive role in the form and fate of nationalist intervention.

Building Business In

Why has business been a major determinant of how resource nationalism has taken shape in Indonesia, and how can a focus on business help to explain subnational variation? In this section, I draw on business-centered theories of economic policymaking to lay out a framework for explaining: first, why we should expect capital to play an outsized role in determining the regulation of foreign flows in a middle-income competitive patronage democracy such as Indonesia; second, why different kinds of domestic businesses want different kinds of nationalist outcomes; and third, the conditions under business sometimes fails to get what it wants, such that statist demands for resource nationalism can prevail.

Business Power in Competitive Patronage Democracies

One limitation of the growing literature on resource nationalism is that domestic business actors have so far been given little independent analytical attention. Debate about resource nationalism has taken place largely without reference to an expansive scholarly literature on the role that domestic capital plays in economic policymaking. Why should we expect business to shape economic policy outcomes?

Political economists have long recognized that private sector actors can exercise immense political muscle (Lindblom 1977). However, in recent years, there has been a new wave of scholarly interest in business power, particularly in the context of emerging economies. This wave marks an "important theoretical shift away from a statist literature" that explained economic, regulatory, and developmental outcomes with almost exclusive reference to state capacity and institutions (Puente and Schneider 2020, 1354). Scholars' renewed focus on business is in part a response to the neoliberal turn that many emerging economies experienced throughout Latin America, Eastern Europe, and parts of developing Asia since the 1990s, which carved out more space for market-led, pro–private sector growth strategies, in turn supporting the expansion of domestic private sectors and giving rise to sprawling conglomerates in these parts of the world (Fairfield 2015; Fuller 2016; Lim, Gomez, and Wong 2021). As the business class has grown and become more complex in emerging and middle-income countries, analysts have increasingly sought to understand how the specific characteristics of business might be tied to patterns of growth, industrial policy, corruption, taxation, investment, trade policy, and welfare outcomes (Bauerle Danzman 2020; Doner 1991; Doner and Schneider 2016; Fairfield 2015; Jaffrelot, Kohli, and Murali 2019; Schneider 2014; Szakonyi 2020; Yadav and Mukherjee 2016).

In a similar vein, I argue that understanding the regulation of land and re-source investments in emerging economies requires a shift in analytical focus away from the state and toward the structure, ownership, and preferences of do-mestic businesses. Such a focus is especially critical when explaining national-ist economic outcomes in Indonesia. At the end of the 1990s, the collapse of Suharto's centralized authoritarian state and the introduction of new and more market-oriented investment rules under the guidance of the World Bank and the International Monetary Fund (IMF) created conditions for a rebalancing of the relationship between state and capital, whereby capital came to enjoy far greater autonomy from, and influence over, the state apparatus (Aspinall 2013; Chua 2008; Rosser 2001). In the two decades since democratic reform and eco-nomic liberalization and propped up by a global commodities boom, Indonesia has seen the rise of mining magnates, agribusiness giants, and domestic oil and gas companies. The transformation of ownership in these sectors and the power and preferences of local business elites are critical for understanding patterns of nationalist policymaking in the contemporary period.

At the same time, the source of corporate actors' policy power varies and is neither homogenous nor unconstrained (Culpepper 2011; Fairfield 2015; Hacker and Pierson 2002). Equally, that major business interests hold power should not lead us to assume that they wield influence in the same way or to the same de-gree. Tasha Fairfield's (2015) reworking of Charles Lindblom's (1977) classic dis-tinction between structural and instrumental power is particularly instructive. Structural power stems from the economic weight of corporate actors' invest-ments. More specifically, concerns about "reduced investment, capital flight, or declining production" in a given sector make policymakers sensitive and respon-sive to the interests of major business actors. The threat, or perceived threat, that corporate actors may "exit" (that is, remove their investments) or "withhold" future investment in economically strategic sectors constrains politicians' and bureaucrats' capacity to enact legislation that challenges private interests (Fair-field 2015, 43). Structural power varies over time and across sectors within a sin-gle country. Investments in fixed assets like mines and plantations makes the threat of "exit" less proximate than in sectors where capital is more mobile; yet, underinvestment, slowed productivity, and reduced employment in commod-ity export industries can constitute major concerns for a government. And booms can, of course, make commodity-exporting industries more critical to an econ-omy at particular junctures. So, to the extent that a country such as Indonesia depends on agro- and extractive commodities for revenue, foreign exchange, growth, employment, and the like, the major business actors in these sectors will enjoy structural power and inherent influence over regulations governing their investments.

On the other hand, some businesses enjoy superior instrumental power, which refers to "deliberate political actions," including "lobbying, direct participation in policymaking, financing electoral campaigns, editorializing in the press, or engaging in various types of collective action" (Fairfield 2015, 28; see also Lindblom 1977). Fairfield further identifies forms of instrumental power as consisting of deep political relationships (for example, partisan linkages, recruitment into government, election to office, informal ties like familial or friendship connections) and necessary material resources (money, expertise, media access, etc.). We can expect instrumental power, and in particular the importance of deep relationships, to be especially significant for business influence in electoral systems where party discipline is weak and politics are highly personalized and clientelist because individual politicians and bureaucrats will be more responsive to the deliberate, targeted, and sometimes personalized political activities of business actors (Eaton 2002; Fairfield 2015, 37). Still, even withing such contexts, business actors' instrumental power can vary across time and across sectors.

These two forms of power—one political and one material—are often treated as conceptually distinct, but the reality is that major business actors in capitalist democracies often harness both simultaneously and thus have "extensive and consistent" influence over policy outcomes (Fairfield 2015). For example, threats of disinvestment from structurally powerful firms will be more effective if such firms also enjoy instrumental power, with direct access to political elites at the apex of decision making.

Throughout this book, I borrow from Fairfield's defining work on business power to both demonstrate and distinguish between the kinds of power and influence that corporate actors enjoy in Indonesia's land and resource industries. I show how changes to Indonesia's political economy in the post-authoritarian period imbued major domestic plantation and mining firms with more structural and instrumental power than at any other period in Indonesian history. This is because, first, although the contemporary Indonesian state's revenue base is remarkably diversified and no longer as dependent on oil rents as it was during the twentieth century, it is also the case that three primary commodities— crude palm oil, coal, and oil and gas—constitute major sources of foreign exchange for the Indonesian government and are drivers of the country's export income. Indonesia's agribusiness conglomerates in particular have investments that stretch across sectors, up and down value chains, and employ millions of Indonesians in both rural and urban settings, which instills such businesses with immense structural power when it comes to regulatory decisions.

Second, Indonesia's especially competitive patronage-driven democratic system widens the scope for business to exercise instrumental power, especially in the land and resource sectors. The clientelist and patrimonial ties that underpinned state-business relations during the authoritarian government were not undone by democratic reform; instead, electoral politics fragmented and decentralized such relationships (Aspinall 2013; Aspinall and Berenschot 2019; Robison and Hadiz 2004). As Aspinall (2013, 56) observes, the "flourishing of patronage . . . has been a major preoccupation of scholars working in virtually every sphere of Indonesian politics and society" in the post-authoritarian era. Like in many other emerging or semi-democracies (Svakonyi 2020; Yadav and Mukherjee 2016), in Indonesia, elected officials and state managers seek the material resources that corporate actors can supply, in turn giving business leverage over government decisions when it comes to contracts, licenses, and regulations that impact their investments, interlocking state and business interests in a symbiotic relationship. There are well-established reasons to expect clientelist relations to be ubiquitous in the cash crop and extractive industries of a patronage democracy (see discussion of the resource curse above). These are rent-rich industries, and state actors have the authority and the incentives to auction off land licenses and permits and extort private sector actors for their personal benefit (Isham et al. 2005; Kolstad and Søreide 2009). Indeed, such practices are commonplace in Indonesia (Aspinall and Berenschot 2019).

Yet, although business access to these sectors necessarily depends on the state as the "gatekeeper" of various land and export licenses, private sector actors can accumulate immense wealth over time, especially during booms, which in turn provides them a degree of autonomy from rent-seeking political and state elites and significant instrumental political power to shape regulatory decisions at the sector level. For these reasons, Indonesia's democratic political economy demands a business-centered analysis of resource nationalism, with particular attention to the different forms of power that domestic capital wields when it comes to interventions that enable or restrict foreign flows.

Determining What Business Wants

How can we determine the kinds of policy outcomes that businesses want? This is a complex question and the subject of much debate within the comparative political economy literature. Scholars working within the OEP tradition see business actors' distinct policy preferences as key to explaining regulatory outcomes. One line of argument is that business preferences for protection are determined by the sector in which they operate (Frieden 1991; Shafer 1990). From this perspective, companies in mining, cash crops, and other raw commodity sectors are more likely to demand state protection than companies in, for example, light manufacturing. This is because commodity exporters are selling a highly specific product with only limited uses and markets, which makes them vulnerable to price shocks and in more need of protection. A related school of thought argues that product inflexibility matters less than capital mobility (Haggard, Maxfield, and Schneider 1997, 38–39; Pepinsky 2008, 2009). This research argues that owners of land, natural resources, and industrial assets have different preferences to firms that derive their value from portfolio investments. In general, those firms with mobile capital will favor less state regulation, less expansionary macroeconomic policies, and an open investment regime.

These two paradigms, which derive business preferences from the nature of the industries in which they operate, have trouble accounting for intrasectoral differences and the conflict and competition that takes place between interest groups when it comes to trade or investment policy. Nor can a theory of sector-derived preferences explain why business within a sector might change their preferences over time. In Indonesia, for example, the largest producers of crude palm oil opposed a proposal in 2013 to cap foreign shareholding at just 30 percent. Yet, back in the 1990s, the most prominent domestic business actors in this sector lobbied the Suharto government successfully to close this sector to foreign investors (Lindblad 2015). In other words, even within sectors, businesses have a range of diverse, and sometimes conflicting or evolving, policy positions.

Another stream of research argues that business actors' heterogeneous trade and investment preferences are best explained by looking at the characteristics of businesses themselves, rather than the sectors in which they invest (Hamilton-Hart 1999; Milner 1988; Puente and Schneider 2020; Ramaswamy, Kroeck, and Renforth 1996). In Helen Milner's (1988) seminal study of trade policy in America and France, she demonstrates how businesses with international investments and overseas assets are more inclined to reject protectionist trade and investment policies not just abroad but at home as well. This is because, first, companies might fear retributive interventions on the part of the countries in which they invest; second, highly internationalized businesses might import to, or invest in, their home country via "foreign entities," such that their own interests would suffer under more protectionist regimes (Milner 1988, 23).

Since Milner's pioneering research, firm-centered studies of economic regulation have evolved and produced important theoretical innovations about the kinds of businesses that prefer liberalization over protectionism and the kinds of businesses that hold the critical political resources to have those preferences realized. The "new new trade theory" (NNTT) argues that firms operating within the same industry, and exporters as well, can have heterogenous policy preferences (Kim and Osgood 2019). Instead, a primary predictor of a firm's position on trade is, instead, its size and productivity (Osgood et al. 2017; Plouffe 2015). Across countries and industries, these scholars have found that "larger firms support trade liberalization and are more likely to engage in trade-related lobbying" (Kim and Osgood 2019, 405). Sarah Bauerle Danzman (2020) also makes the case that large and politically influential companies are major determinants of states' FDI policy, too, but she finds that businesses' access to credit is what determines whether they will support or oppose constraints on foreign investment. Specifically, if local debt financing costs are high and subsidized sources of credit begin to dry up, domestic business will lobby for more foreign investment and seek partnerships with multinational firms to fund their operations; on the other hand, where companies can rely on domestic financing, and especially state banks, their preference will be for protection against FDI.

This body of work serves as a critical building block for tracing the role that domestic capital plays in shaping land and resource policy. Resource nationalism in patronage democracies like Indonesia can turn on the preferences of business actors who, for reasons outlined above, enjoy either structural or instrumental power or both. Based on existing political economy studies of firms and policy preferences, we can expect that where the dominant domestic business interests are inwardly oriented with low levels of internationalization, demands for localization are likely to prevail; if the major domestic firms are internationalized and integrated into regional or global networks of capital, support for resource nationalism will be much weaker and such policies are less likely to take shape.

One major and relevant critique of OEP approaches, however, is their tendency to analytically isolate firms and their owners from political and historical contexts, in turn missing potentially important factors that shape business preferences and their distinct relationships with state actors. In middle-income countries, especially those in developing Asia, the emergence and expansion of a domestic business class is often embedded in contentious postcolonial histories and interethnic rivalries (Gomez and Lfaye De Micheaux 2017). The unequal and ethicized nature of capitalist development in countries such as Malaysia, Indonesia, and Singapore, invariably shape the nature and political influence of different kinds of business actors (Gomez and Lfaye De Micheaux 2017). Throughout the Southeast Asian region, the presence of ethnic Chinese capital has long constituted a distinct and at times politically controversial feature of each country's political economy (Dieleman and Sachs 2006; Hsiao and Gomez 2013; Yeung 2006). This is especially the case in Indonesia. Alongside factors like the size and internationalization of companies and conglomerates highlighted by OEP and NNT theorists, identity emerges as an important factor that underpins distinct businesses' preference and sources of policy power. Throughout this book, I show how the rise of pribumi mining companies with more protectionist preferences and the dominance of ethnically Chinese family-owned plantation giants with more liberal preferences reflect each group's distinct relationship with the state, both historically and in the post-authoritarian period. Over the course of the twenty-first century, the former tended toward expanding their interests in coal and mineral mining through leveraging favorable state loans and cultivating direct political relations with the state, sometimes entering politics directly; the latter turned away from the state in the post-authoritarian period, maintained more political distance, and instead tended toward internationalizing their assets. There are, of course, exceptions and nuances to this characterization of how identity and protectionist preferences intersect; the broad picture, however, is one in which the features of Indonesia's major agro- and mining businesses, including levels of internationalization and firm size, correlate with identity and help to explain patterns of protection in the mining and plantations industries.

Constraints on Big Business in the Resource Sectors

This book presents an argument about nationalist policymaking that hinges on business power and preferences. At the same time, resource nationalism is by no means purely a reflection of business preferences, nor does private capital exert absolute power over the policy process. Comparative empirical research has illustrated the ways in which corporate interests can fail to transform their agendas into policy when such policies are seen as an "electoral liability" (Fairfield 2015, 30) or when, as Pepper Culpepper (2011) argues, a particular policy problem has "political salience" and attracts the scrutiny of mass publics. Indeed, in all capitalist democracies, including Indonesia, "politicians who make economic policy operate under conditions of political competition" (Tufte 1980, xiv). If we assume that politicians' primary goal is reelection, then political elites in government will pursue the sorts of economic interventions and business deals that they feel will best serve their primary goal of career preservation and reelection (Geddes 1996). Sometimes that means appealing to (or colluding with) business interests; however, politicians also make decisions contrary to what powerful business actor groups want if it means cultivating votes and popular support.

Conflicts over resource nationalism attract public scrutiny in Indonesia, and at particular moments, government attention to popular opinion motivated a policy path that was at odds with the demands of business. I demonstrate how in Indonesia, particular resource projects were especially politically salient, such that state managers were compelled to consider the wider electoral implications of how they managed a specific foreign contract. In the Freeport case, for example, negotiations over the American company's contract attracted immense media attention. As the following chapters elaborate, Freeport was the ultimate symbol of Indonesia's history of foreign exploitation, and over the decades, the company became central to nationalist narratives about economic subjugation by neocolonial forces. The government perceived the mine, therefore, to be different to other mines and set out to ensure it would be owned and operated by a state-owned company rather than a local tycoon or oligarch. To be sure, the state's acquisition of the Grasberg mine might generate opportunities for local and politically linked business elites in the form of mining service contracts later down the track. But the decision to exclude private capital from the divestment deal was a critical and politically motivated decision on the part of the Jokowi administration.

There were also many occasions where the state did not bend to the demands of private business in the oil and gas sector, too. This was primarily due to the instrumental and structural power of the sector's SOE Pertamina. The SOE's historical domination of the upstream (and downstream) sector since the early years of political independence gave its advocates an advantage during nationalist policy debates. Although private domestic players entered the upstream sector and expanded their interests rapidly in the post-Suharto period, very few could compete with the state-owned giant's significant and increasing market share. Despite a checkered past of financial mismanagement and corruption, Pertamina's historical identity as the state's developmental engine also meant the SOE continued to benefit from broad public support.

However, although lawmakers calculated and considered public support for state over private ownership in such instances, it is important to clarify that popular forces and civil society organizations have, for the most part, *not* been a major constraint on the activities and decisions of either private business or state managers when it comes to resource nationalism. This book will elaborate how civil society enjoyed influence over the terms of decentralized resource management during the early years of Indonesia's democratic transition, helping to establish new rules and institutions for the involvement of communities at sites of corporate land use and extraction. But the commodities boom and the entrenchment of patronage-driven politics created a democratic milieu that in the second decade of Indonesia's post-authoritarian period, boosted the policy power of business actors, while diminishing the voice of civic actors with alternative and community-centered visions for extraction and land use.

Booms and Big Business

To sum up, this book conceptualizes resource nationalism as an economic policy intervention that, like all economic policies, emerges via struggles between a range of interest groups. Any theory of resource nationalism must take into account the preferences and strategies of the local business class and the nature of the largest domestic companies that operate in each sector. Such an approach is especially important when attempting to explain economic regulation in the land and resource sectors of middle-income and patronage democracies. Historically in Indonesia, colonial powers and foreign multinationals dominated the cash crop and extractive economy because local businesses lacked both capacity and capital. The contemporary period has seen a remarkable expansion by domestic business into the land and resource industries. This shift imbues domestic corporate actors with new forms of structural power to drive policy at the sector level. Meanwhile, the centrality of patronage to politics and policymaking in Indonesia gives big business enormous instrumental power by virtue of the personal connections and material resources such actors can wield.

This analytical approach also recognizes that business can hold wide-ranging preferences when it comes to foreign flows. I look to the ownership structures, internationalization, and the identities of major local businesses in order to help explain different patterns of nationalist policymaking. In Indonesia, some of the major proponents of resource nationalism were domestic resource companies with little internationalization and with superior instrumental power, who saw state protection and privilege as the primary means of business growth. At the same time, there were other Indonesian businesses that opposed nationalist regulations, especially those with large internationalized companies with significant assets and subsidiaries abroad and those with ethnic Chinese ownership as well. Such business actors engage less directly with the state and instead exhibit superior structural power, and they saw foreign capital and shared ownership structures not as a threat but as a boon for the sector and for their interests. By bringing business into the analytical foreground, this framework sheds light on the critical role that domestic capital plays in defining the terms of resource nationalism and in transforming landscapes of ownership in resource-rich countries such as Indonesia.

HISTORIES OF OWNERSHIP

To explain contemporary patterns of resource nationalism, we need to understand the roots of nationalist agitation and the evolution of ownership in each sector. This chapter lays out the genesis of nationalist thinking within Indonesia's political, policymaking, and business communities. It characterizes distinct time periods that mark the development of Indonesia's political economy according to prevailing patterns of ownership in each sector and the status of nationalist policymaking.

This historical chapter's purpose is twofold. First, it provides the foundation for the book's structural arguments about business power and resource nationalism. I maintain that ownership patterns at the sector level and the nature of the businesses that come to dominate production in each sector have implications for nationalist policymaking. Such patterns of ownership invariably emerge from historical political-economic structures and from prior government efforts to either sideline or nurture domestic capital. It is therefore critical to understand the historical context that surrounds the rise of domestic business in Indonesia's agricultural and extractive sectors. A second motivation for providing a history of ownership is that although Indonesia-focused literature is rich in scholarly accounts of the country's economic history, few home in specifically on these major primary sectors to demonstrate, compare, and explain varied patterns of ownership since colonial exploitation first began.

The chapter is divided into three parts. The first describes how Dutch colonizers and later the Japanese occupiers went about organizing foreign private and state ownership and exploitation of Indonesian land and resources. The second section demonstrates how in the wake of Indonesia's revolution, a newly independent and democratic government grappled with pressure to localize the resource-based economy while facing massive economic constraints. Under such conditions, resource nationalist efforts were statist in nature. The third and final section characterizes the authoritarian New Order government's approach to foreign investors in the land and resource industries. It shows how President Suharto courted foreign capital in the early stages of each sector's economic development while simultaneously fostering the growth of a new domestic business class in plantations, coal, and oil and gas services by compelling foreign investors to partner with or purchase from local firms. This emergent business class was concentrated around a small group of economic elites who, for much of this period, remained dependent on the state and on Suharto personally to expand their wealth. The capacity for domestic capital, therefore, to execute autonomous influence over Suharto's nationalist policy decisions was limited, except under boom conditions. Indeed, market-cycle theories of resource nationalism have much resonance during this era, in the context of a relatively strong and centralized state and a politically weak domestic business class. This dynamic would change considerably after 1998 when the New Order political economy collapsed and a democratic transition began.

Land and Resources under Empire

The Dutch colonial project was primarily a commercial one that focused on the colony's rich agricultural, oil, and mineral potential. The colonial experience of resource exploitation imbued the colony's indigenous elite and its public with a suspicion, even antagonism, toward foreign capital (Bresnan 1993). In the early postindependence years, the government struggled to increase local ownership of Indonesia's economy because the constraints on nationalist aspirations were immense: state revenue was limited and indigenous business interests were weak, capital poor, and disorganized. Instead, foreign companies and Chinese merchants continued to take the leading role in most parts of the economy, including plantations and extractives. President Sukarno eventually pursued an expansive program of statist nationalism, which saw major agricultural and mining concessions taken over by the state. But this policy path brought the president into conflict with moderate economists and other sections of society that viewed his statist programs as a threat to their own material and political interests. A mixture of internal policy conflict and economic constraints meant statist aspirations largely failed. Sukarno was forced to relinquish power, and General Suharto's new government would reopen the economy to foreign capital and aid while nurturing a domestic business class.

The Colonial Enterprise: Foreign State and Corporate Control

From the late 1700s until World War II, the colonial government and European entrepreneurs expanded into and eventually came to dominate the extraction, production, and trade of the archipelago's agricultural and mineral commodities. The Dutch created a highly stratified economy. Indigenous elites were compelled to provide land and to mobilize peasant labor for colonial estates and mining projects. Dutch SOEs and large Western companies dominated the sugar, oil, and mining sectors, while a mix of Western and indigenous smallholders were responsible for the export of rubber, coffee, and tobacco (Lindblad 2008, 19).[1] Many indigenous farmers remained outside of commercial plantations and engaged in low-scale local trading and subsistence farming. As Ian Chalmers (1997, 6) puts it, "a small, European-dominated modern sector [was] linked only tenuously to a vast, indigenous agricultural economy."

The Netherlands' exploitation of Indonesia's natural resources and the stratification of the colonial economy along identity-based lines would become a chief grievance of Indonesia's nationalist movement in the years to come. The colonial government largely failed to modernize the economy. The Dutch provided little education or training to the local population beyond a narrow slice of the indigenous elite. The colony's trade surplus was not used to benefit local development, and the vast majority of revenue flowed back to the colonial homeland (Booth 1998). Instead, the Dutch developed an economy based on primary commodity exports in which Western companies dominated enclave extractive and cash crop sectors. This section explains how the colonial political economy shaped ownership of Indonesia's plantations, oil and gas, and mining sectors, in turn motivating calls for resource nationalism in the decades that followed.

OIL AND GAS

Dutch private and state-owned companies dominated the archipelago's oil industry. The Dutch introduced the Netherlands East Indies Mining Act in 1899, which outlined that mineral rights were invested in the colonial state and that surface land rights did not confer subsurface rights to the minerals beneath (Bee 1982, 19). In other words, only the Dutch government could authorize mining activity throughout the archipelago. In addition, high barriers to entry—capital intensity and technological requirements—meant that indigenous participation was limited entirely to the provision of low-skilled labor at oil wells on Sumatra and Borneo.

The Royal Dutch company was the dominant player in the sector. It was a private enterprise but enjoyed sponsorship from the Dutch monarchy.[2] Its only serious competitor was Shell Oil Company of London. In 1907, the two firms merged, heralding the birth of Royal Dutch Shell, a company that would eventually build a global empire off the back of its assets in the East Indies. By the 1920s, Royal Dutch Shell had a near monopoly over the extraction and sale of the colony's oil. Back home, Dutch statist nationalists took issue with the privileged position this private company enjoyed in such a lucrative industry, and they demanded a greater role for SOEs. So, in 1921, the government established the state-owned oil company Nederlandsch-Indische Aardolie-Maatschappij (NIAM). The colonial government prioritized NIAM and Royal Dutch Shell in its granting of concessions such that few other Dutch or international companies could compete.[3]

Nevertheless, while the 1899 Mining Act made it difficult for non-Dutch firms to enter the market (van der Eng 1998, 307), some American companies still managed to establish a foothold in the East Indies oil sector, and by the end of the 1930s, Caltex and Stanvac had risen to prominence (Barnes 1995, 5). As table 2.1 demonstrates, on the eve of World War II, Royal Dutch Shell, Stanvac, Caltex, and NIAM controlled the majority of Indonesia's oil production.

When World War II broke out, the Netherlands East Indies was the fifth largest petroleum producer in the world, and oil contributed to 25 percent of the colony's exports (Bartlett et al. 1972, 54). To the extent that Indonesians were involved in oil extraction or production, however, it was mostly as manual laborers. Royal Dutch Shell, Caltex, and Stanvac all employed a mix of indigenous, Chinese, and Tamil labor, and Dutch, British, and American expatriates held the technical and management positions. The skills deficit of local workers compared to overseas-trained engineers and managers meant companies could justify the segregation of staff. However, for Royal Dutch Shell, segregation took on an explicitly political

TABLE 2.1. Major oil companies and production, 1940

COMPANY	PRODUCTION (MILLION BARRELS)	CONTROLLING INTEREST
NV de Bataafsche Petroleum Maatschappij (BPM)	35.3 (57%)	Royal Dutch Shell
NV Nederlandsch-Indische Aardolie Maatschappij (NIAM)	10 (17%)	Netherlands Indies Government and BPM
NV Nederlandsch-Koloniale Petroleum Maatschappij (NKPM)	16.2 (26%)	Standard Vacuum Co. (Stanvac)
NV Nederlandsche Pacific Petroleum Maatschappij (NPPPM)	Unknown	Standard Oil Co. of California and Texas Corporation
NV Nederlandsche Nieuw Guinee Petroleum Maatschappij (NNGPM)	Unknown	40% Royal Dutch Shell; 40% Standard Vacuum through NKPM; 20% Caltex through NPPM

Source: Adapted from Bee 1982, 6.

meaning and was not simply a function of the sector's skill requirements. In their revealing archival work, Joost Jonker and Jan Luiten van Zanden (2007, 316) show how the company's leadership was wholly committed to the Dutch imperial enterprise and opposed a growing movement in the Netherlands for a more ethical approach to administering the colony. Senior management encouraged expatriate staff to see themselves as part of a ruling colonial class. In an industry magazine from 1921, a Royal Dutch Shell manager warned of growing "class consciousness" among "Asian employees" and defended the superior position of its white staff and the colonial system they represented (Jonker and van Zanden 2007, 316–17). In the years to come, the indigenous elite would cast foreign oil and gas companies as agents of economic and political repression. As we shall see, the system of ownership and exploitation in the oil industry drove nationalist resolve among Indonesia's emerging economic thinkers and political leaders.

MINING

The Dutch also enabled foreign corporate domination of the minerals sector. Small-scale miners, both indigenous and Chinese migrants, had long exploited the archipelago's tin (especially from Bangka and Belitung), nickel (from Sulawesi), silver (from Java), and gold (from Kalimantan) deposits (van der Eng 2014, 7). However, it was only once the Dutch established large commercial operations for key minerals that the archipelago was transformed into a prominent global mineral exporter. From 1850, when the colonial government opened a Bureau of Mines, the Dutch began to invest seriously in the colony's coal and mineral capacity (Friederich and van Leeuwen 2017, 57).

The 1899 Mining Law that regulated the oil industry also applied to mineral mining. As was the case for oil, the law separated surface and subsoil rights to minerals and vested the subsoil rights in the Netherlands East Indies government. Under the law, the tin mining trade on the Bangka and Belitung islands became the exclusive domain of the colonial government. The Dutch state enterprise Bangka Tin Mines and a private Dutch company, Billiton Maatschappij (which later became BHP Billiton), monopolized the sector. By the 1940s, through the activities of both Billiton and Bangka Tin Mines, the Netherlands East Indies had become a world leader in tin exports (Hunter 1968, 75). The first coal mine, meanwhile, opened in 1849 in South Kalimantan and was operated by a Netherlands Indies government–owned company. While several small Dutch private ventures were set up during this period, the sector's production output only expanded significantly when Dutch-government companies opened large coal mines in Ombilin in West Sumatra (1892), and Bukit Asam in South Sumatra (1919) (Friederich and van Leeuwen 2017). By World War II, the East Indies mining sector was expanding in earnest. Table 2.2 displays the level of

TABLE 2.2.   Major mining companies and production levels, 1940

COMMODITY	PRODUCTION	COMPANY	CONTROLLING INTEREST
Tin[a]	44.4	Bangka Tin Mines	Dutch state-owned
		Gemeenschappelijke Mijnbouw-maatschappij Billiton, GMB	Joint Dutch private and state-owned
Coal[a]	2,009	Bukit Asam in Tanjung Enim, South Sumatra	Dutch state-owned
		Ombilin Coal Mining, Ombilin mine in Sawahlunto, West Sumatra	Dutch state-owned
		NV Steenkolen-Maatschappij Poeloe Laoet, in Pulau Laut, Southeast Kalimantan	Dutch state-owned
Bauxite[a]	275	Nederlandsch-Indische Bauxiet Mijnbouw Maatschappij	NIBEM
Nickel[a]	55.5	NV Mijnbouw Maatschappij Celebes in Soroako	Subsidiary of NV Billiton
		NV Mijnbouw Maatschappij Toli in Southeast Sulawesi	Associated with the private NV Oost Borneo Maatschappij
Gold[b]	2,798	NV Mijnbouw Cikotok gold and silver mine, West Java	Subsidiary of NV Billiton, part Dutch state-owned and private
Silver[b]	46,847	NV Mijnbouw Cikotok gold and silver mine, West Java	Subsidiary of NV Billiton, part Dutch state-owned and private

[a]Thousand tons; [b]Kilograms.
Source: Compiled by the author from Hunter (1968), van der Eng (2014), and Lindblad (2008).

minerals production just prior to World War II and the Dutch companies that dominated each subsector.

Although small-scale mining continued in different parts of the archipelago during the colonial period, indigenous communities were largely engaged in mining enterprises as wage laborers, alongside Chinese immigrants, often brought in by the Dutch to work the mines (Houben and Lindblad 1999). This pattern of Western domination would endure into the postindependence era and remain a contentious issue for Indonesia's economic nationalists.

PLANTATIONS

Before colonization, indigenous communities already traded commodities, like sugar, rice, cotton, coffee, indigo, and pepper, across the archipelago and to other parts of Asia. However, large-scale commercial agriculture emerged only in the nineteenth century through the expansion of Dutch and European plantation companies. The three most strategic export crops were sugar, coffee, and tobacco. The Industrial Revolution in Europe and America at the start of the 1800s stimulated rising global demand for primary commodities, so the Dutch embarked on a program to mobilize local labor and develop a "sophisticated plantation sector" in the East Indies to serve the economic needs of Europe (Dick 2002, 5).

A key turning point came in 1830 when the Dutch introduced the Cultivation System. This was a state-led program of compulsory cultivation in which Javanese peasants were compelled to produce commodities for the Netherlands government to sell on European markets (Houben 2002). The system was highly coercive and delivered benefits only to Java's three groups of elites—the Javanese aristocracy, Chinese merchants, and the colonial government—while exploiting peasant labor without fair financial compensation (van Zanden and Marks 2013, 48). The colony's export production increased rapidly, and by the middle of the 1800s, profits from East Indies plantations contributed one-third of the Netherlands' state revenue (Houben 2002, 65).

However, reformists back in the Netherlands began calling for an end to such crude programs of exploitation in the colony. Business associations and liberal economists also called for reform and demanded the government open the East Indies plantations sector to more private enterprise (van Zanden and Marks 2013). In response, the Agrarian Law of 1870 ended the Cultivation System and facilitated the expansion of foreign private enterprise into the East Indies. In essence, the law outlined that all land belonged to the colonial state, which had authority to lease those lands to private companies. Land inhabited and cultivated by "natives" was still formally state property, but this land should be leased to private plantation companies through an agreement with village heads and regional elites (Kano 2008, 282–83). Compulsory crops were phased out, but the new system did not significantly change conditions for indigenous farmers and laborers. Leases drawn up between indigenous elites and private companies, with Dutch government approval, were often remarkably unfair. Locals rarely had a sense of how much their land was worth or knew the price of commodities on the global market (Houben 2002, 66). Such leases also often included the provision of local labor to work on the plantations, thus sustaining a system of labor exploitation that delivered Western companies enormous profits.

The Ethical Policy, introduced in 1901, marked an important shift in the colonial government's approach because it ensured more funding was allocated to education, health, public works, and infrastructure. Better infrastructure and technology, together with a healthier labor population, produced a marked increase in the productivity of East Indies plantations (Houben 2002, 68). Overall, however, the colonial plantations system continued to be highly stratified and exploitative. Export-oriented cash crops were dominated by foreign plantation companies, indigenous participation was mostly limited to wage labor, and commodities were traded by giant Dutch trading houses. For Indonesia's emergent political class at the time, the plantations sector provided a clear example of colonial economic exploitation and the exclusion of Indonesia's native populations from trading their own commodities on global markets.

So, overall, in the Netherlands East Indies export-driven economy, indigenous communities primarily played the role of laborers, not owners, producers, or traders. Dutch and other foreign companies as well as Europeans and Chinese merchants benefited far more from the colonial economy than did the indigenous population. The Dutch offered little in the way of technological training and education for Indonesians working in these sectors, nor did the colonial powers invest meaningfully in manufacturing or secondary industries. In effect, cash crops and minerals worked to crowd out development of manufacturing industries—a classic case of the "Dutch disease," or the resource curse. Primary commodity sectors remained Western enclaves and skilled positions in Western companies were all held by foreign nationals. But European and Anglo-American domination would come to an abrupt halt in World War II.

From Occupation to Revolution: Reclaiming Land and Resources

Germany's occupation of the Netherlands in 1940 left the colonial empire vulnerable, and the Dutch proved incapable of defending the East Indies against invading Japanese forces. Japanese rule (1942–45) was a double-edged sword for the local population. The military engaged in violence and repression, and food shortages, high inflation, and a steep drop in imports meant that for most Indonesians, the Japanese occupation was a time of enormous suffering (Ricklefs 2008, 237). Yet, for the first time, indigenous bureaucrats and intellectuals were given authority to manage the country's administrative, political, and economic resources. When the Dutch returned to reclaim their colony at the end of the war, they found their assets, including strategic land and resource projects, taken over by indigenous groups and a population on the cusp of revolution.

Japanese Occupation

Japan's occupation of the Netherlands East Indies lasted just over three years. It was a time of great economic hardship for the local population, and the Japanese forced labor system meant tens of thousands of Indonesians died of exhaustion, illness, and malnutrition (Bartlett et al. 1972, 56). But the occupation also had a profound impact on Indonesia's nationalist movement because Japan gave emergent indigenous leaders the political and administrative resources to develop their ideas and organizations (Benda 1956, 1958). Japan's objective in World War II was to eradicate Western domination over Asia and bring Southeast Asia into Japan's "Asian Co-prosperity Sphere." The Japanese thus invoked anti-Western sentiments among their new subjects and helped mobilize Indonesia's growing nationalist movement.

The Japanese program of indigenous mobilization had geographical limits, however. It was ultimately the East Indies' natural riches that motivated Japan's swift invasion of the Dutch colony in 1942. The Japanese concentrated their political activities on Java, where there were fewer natural resources, and political institutions and education were more sophisticated. On the outer resource-rich islands of Sumatra and Sulawesi, the occupiers treated their subjects with an iron fist, and there was little effort to mobilize villagers, laborers, or local leaders. Out here, where the principal goal was resource extraction, the Japanese needed a passive, not assertive, indigenous population. Japan sought primary commodities like oil and rubber as well as cheap labor to finance the war effort. Private Japanese companies and SOEs took over the most strategic foreign-operated assets in the mining, oil, plantations, and trading sectors (Yasuyuki 1996).

Nevertheless, unlike the Dutch, the Japanese trained and used indigenous staff to manage operations at oil rigs, mines, and plantations and in doing so, supported the first early steps toward localization of the country's major resource projects. For example, by the end of March 1942, the Japanese controlled every functioning oil field in Indonesia (Barnes 1995, 6). The Japanese promoted Indonesian staff and provided training to manage the country's oil assets. The Japanese established two training schools from which the graduates went on to fill the upper echelons of Pertamina, the New Order–era national oil company, in years to come. The Pertamina motto "Learn while you work, work while you learn" was inspired by those years under Japanese occupation (Barnes 1995, 6). Minerals and plantations were also targeted for annexation by the Japanese. Private Japanese firms were brought in to exploit tin, coal, nickel, and bauxite. As Thomas Lindblad (2008, 52) notes, "Mitsubishi ran the tin mines in Bangka and Belitung, Mitsui was involved in coal and bauxite mining, Sumitomo was assigned the nickel mines in Sulawesi." The Japanese also annexed foreign- or "enemy"-owned plantations, and by 1944, all major foreign-owned estates across the various subsectors had been farmed out to twenty-two private Japanese companies (Lindblad 2008, 52). The Japanese interned Dutch plantation managers and supervisors, replacing them with Japanese officials or senior Indonesian supervisors.

As the war progressed, all the colony's strategic export sectors deteriorated due to poor management and a lack of shipping capacity with which to bring commodities onto global markets (Lindblad 2008, 53). By 1944, rubber exports, for example, were only a fifth of what they had been prior to the war (Lindblad

2008, 53). The petroleum sector stagnated as well. Back in 1939, crude production was 170,000 barrels per day (bpd); by 1946, production had dropped to just 5,700 bpd (Barnes 1995). Meanwhile, the tin and coal mining sectors that were growing quickly at the turn of the century "almost collapsed" under Japanese rule (Friederich and van Leeuwen 2017, 57). Indeed, the entire economy suffered immensely under the Japanese.

Japan surrendered on August 15, 1945, following the American attacks on Hiroshima and Nagasaki. Two days later, nationalist leaders Sukarno and Muhammad Hatta declared the independent Republic of Indonesia before the Dutch could return. However, the Dutch came back to reclaim their colony, and a revolutionary war between the Indonesian Republic and the Netherlands ensued until 1949.

Revolution and the Birth of Economic Nationalism

When the Dutch returned, they found their former colony on the brink of revolution. Indigenous intellectuals and leaders articulated their nationalist aspirations with greater confidence, clarity, and determination than had been the case prior to Japanese occupation. How had decades of foreign control and economic exploitation shaped the ideas and policy agendas of Indonesia's political and economic elites? There were three distinct ideological streams within Indonesia's nationalist movement, each associated with different organizations and political parties. The major point of distinction between nationalist groups was not social or economic but rather religious and in particular their position on the role Islam should play in an independent Indonesian state. Foreign-educated intellectuals associated with Partai Nasional Indonesia (Indonesian National Party [PNI]) and Partindo (Indonesia Party) advocated a pluralist nationalism that recognized the many religious and ethnic communities across the archipelago. Led by Sukarno, a charismatic and skilled orator, these nationalists sought a plural and multireligious basis for an independent Indonesia. Islamic nationalists, meanwhile, sought formal recognition for Islam in a future independent state and found expression through religious organizations—Muhammadiyah and Nahdlatul Ulama—as well as political parties such as Masjumi and Partai Sarekat Islam (Islamic Union Party). Finally, the Partai Komunis Indonesia (Indonesian Communist Party [PKI]) was the most secular of the nationalist groups and their objective was ultimately to overthrow the imperialist-capitalist system imposed on the native population.

Their economic visions were less distinct or well developed. Nationalist leaders in all three groups believed that economic independence was as important as political independence (G. Kahin 1952). Nationalists across the ideological spectrum shared a set of ideas about Indonesia's economy that had a socialist flavor.

The intellectuals who led these movements all expressed support for the notion that a future independent state must "control economic life and operate critical sectors of the economy" to remedy the social disparities that had become entrenched under colonial rule (G. Kahin 1952, 52). Differences would become more pronounced in the postindependence era. But until then, Indonesia's nationalist movement was united behind opposition to the laissez-faire capitalism of their colonial masters and the Western companies that controlled much of the economy. And there was widespread support for a strong role for the state in owning and exploiting natural resources.

A small but growing local business class also made important contributions to the plans for economic independence. It is important to note the growth in indigenous enterprise that took place outside of the resource industries toward the final years of Dutch rule. The Great Depression hit the colony hard. The East Indies government responded with import restrictions, which had the effect of stimulating a local manufacturing boom (Lindblad 2008). Dutch, Chinese, and a small number of indigenous enterprises opened new industrial ventures in the production of cigarettes, soap, textiles, footwear, and other manufactured goods. Much of the wealth generated by this brief emphasis on industrialization and manufacturing was captured by ethnic Chinese entrepreneurs who had access to credit and trading houses (Lindblad 2008, 31–33). However, new indigenous businesses also emerged and their productivity began to increase. This nascent business class viewed Dutch firms and long-dominant ethnic Chinese traders as competitors and hoped an independent government would support and privilege pribumi—that is, non-Chinese indigenous—enterprise.

When it became clear that Japan would lose the war, the occupying force established advisory boards to prepare the colony for independence. On them sat nationalist political leaders like Sukarno and Mohammad Hatta, alongside indigenous business figures such as Agoes Moesin Dasaad, a successful Sumatran trader, and Ahmad Bakrie, who would go on to establish one of Indonesia's most prominent family-owned conglomerates. The Japanese set up the Investigative Committee for the People's Economy in 1945, and a series of meetings and conferences followed in which businesspeople and nationalist leaders developed new ideas for an independent Indonesian economy. At such forums, Western-style capitalism was rejected by all parties.

At the All-Java Conference of Indonesian Economists in 1945, for example, Hatta "called for a socialist-type of economy based on the spirit of gotong royong" (meaning mutual help or reciprocity) (Post 1996, 629). He envisioned a system based on state-led cooperatives as a means of building a unified and coherent national economy. It was Hatta's collectivist economic ideas that inspired Article 33 in the 1945 constitution, which holds that the economy should be based on familial principles and that strategic sectors, including natural resources, should be controlled by the state for the prosperity of the people.[4] The (still small) indigenous business community supported such notions of "service and brotherhood" and of a close relationship between state and pribumi enterprise in the spirit of growing an independent economy that was no longer dominated by Dutch firms and ethnic Chinese traders (Post 1996, 629).

In the years that followed the declaration of independence and formulation of the 1945 constitution, the Dutch returned and waged war against their former colonial subjects. The revolutionary war was devastating for many parts of the economy, but these years also provided opportunities for the new republic and local business elites to pursue their vision for an independent economy.

Revolution in the Resources Sectors

When the Japanese surrendered, the newly independent government quickly moved to take over strategic parts of the economy before the Dutch could return and seize their colonial assets. In many cases, it was the republic's military that moved in to manage these assets, and as such, generals in the revolutionary army became heavily involved in the exploitation and trade of primary commodities. The army engaged in black market trading across a range of sectors in order to fund its activities during the revolutionary war.

In Sumatra, for example, Indonesian workers' groups and military leaders became the de facto owners of oil assets (Bee 1982, 8). Workers formed *laskar minyak*, or "oil fronts," often with direct military backing, and defended the annexed assets against attempts by Stanvac and Royal Dutch Shell to return to their fields (Bee 1982, 8). In the context of a Dutch blockade on Indonesia's exports, these oil fields were a useful source of revenue and petroleum products for the revolutionary war effort in Sumatra and, to a lesser extent, Central Java.

Indonesian forces claimed ownership of plantations, too. New trading companies were established to replace the Dutch-owned giants that had long dominated the trade of agrocommodities. For example, the new Indonesian government established the Central Trading Corporation to export rubber to Southeast Asia. Local military forces were "deeply involved in the firm's trading operations" to ensure the exports escaped the Dutch blockade (Lindblad 2008, 59).

The archipelago effectively had two economies during the war—the economy in republic-controlled areas and the economy in Dutch-controlled areas. Where the Dutch regained control, estates in parts of Java and Sumatra were brought back to life. It was a similar picture in the mining sector. When the Dutch took back the tin mines on Bangka and Belitung, tin mining and exports started up once more. However, resource industries in the republic-controlled regions fared poorly. Here, the formal export-led economy fell apart and a black market in commodities such as rubber and oil exploded (Cribb 1988). From a broader developmental perspective, this period was devastating for the country's export-led economy; nevertheless, local ownership (or largely military ownership) over these industries generated profits for formerly excluded indigenous actors and helped to fund their war of independence.

By 1949, the Dutch were under growing international pressure, particularly from the United States, to retreat from the East Indies. The Dutch government negotiated its withdrawal in 1949 at the Round Table Conference where the Dutch and Indonesian leadership signed the Finec Agreement (Financiele en Economische Overeenkomst [Financial and Economic Agreement]), which set the terms for decolonization. In return for political independence, the Dutch demanded significant economic concessions. This agreement "secured maximum economic and financial benefits for the Netherlands, especially the Dutch private companies operating in Indonesia," most of which were active within the resources sectors (Thee 2010, 58). Finec guaranteed Dutch and other foreign firms operating in Indonesia protection against nationalization (unless both sides agreed to such a transfer of ownership) and determined that commodity exports should continue to be directed to European markets. Most significantly, however, the agreement forced the new republic to take on the debt of the Netherlands East Indies government, which amounted to over 4 billion guilders. This burden was "unprecedented in the history of decolonisation" (Lindblad 2008, 74) and fed nationalist resentment for years to come.

Independence and Democracy: Nationalist Dilemmas

For the new republic, the question of how to repair and grow Indonesia's economy under the constraints of Finec became increasingly contentious during the years of parliamentary democracy (1950–56). Structurally, the devastated Indonesian economy relied heavily on foreign investment and needed foreign companies and aid in order to substitute for the lack of local capital, expertise, and technology and to kick-start growth. Institutionally, Finec set clear boundaries that protected foreign investors and favored Western trading partners. But nationalist sentiments and expectations for greater local control ran high. Some of Indonesia's political and economic elite advocated a moderate approach to localizing strategic parts of the economy; others demanded a more dramatic and immediate break from foreign economic control. This period was marked, therefore, by intensifying nationalist demands amid massive economic constraints.

Moderate nationalists sought compromise and advocated a slow transition toward a localized and industrialized economy. Under Vice President Mohammad Hatta, with the influence of economists like Sumitro Djojohadikusumo and Sjafruddin Prawiranegara, successive postindependence governments committed to honoring Finec and protecting existing foreign assets in order to portray Indonesia as an attractive destination for much needed foreign investment and aid (Bartlett et al. 1972, 109). According to Booth (1998, 62), such moderates "argued that changes in the pattern of ownership and control [of the economy] would have to come slowly as an indigenous entrepreneurial class emerged." This was the approach taken by the first several governing coalitions under Prime Minsters Hatta, Natsir, Sukiman, and Wilopo. The moderate approach produced positive, if not remarkable, economic outcomes. According to Lindblad (2008, 126), in the first half of the 1950s, "growth was export-driven and macroeconomic performance compared favourably with most other Third World countries."

However, these governments were always under pressure from more staunchly nationalist groups, especially from within PNI, PKI, and labor unions. Factions within the military were also growing impatient with the slow pace of economic reform and what they saw as the sustained domination of Indonesia's economy by foreign actors. These groups demanded immediate expulsion of Dutch capital and wanted more assertive state interventions to expand local ownership of the economy. Distinct and sometimes conflicting approaches to localizing the economy played out in the country's resource industries.

Popular and Statist Resource Nationalisms

The governance of Indonesia's resource sectors during this time reflected growing demand for local control, with advocates for both state ownership and popular control growing in numbers and influence. Domestic business actors, on the other hand, remained almost entirely absent from nationalist mobilization in these industries. In the plantations sector, for example, smallholders were very productive during the 1950s, but exports from the large foreign-controlled estates contributed the most to the economy and delivered much needed tax revenues for the republic (Booth 1998, 53–63). Given the economic circumstances, the government was ambivalent about engaging in an aggressive program of localization in this sector. So, as Jamie Mackie (1961, 338) explains, for most of the 1950s, "the old relationships of foreign ownership and control were not significantly modified." As the 1950s progressed, however, a form of popular resource nationalism intensified. Labor strikes became more common, and the position of Dutch-owned estates appeared increasingly precarious. There was growing number of popular nationalizations, sometimes encouraged or led by the PKI. Peasants would occupy estates, set up villages and grow their own crops, and refuse to leave, despite intermittent pressure from the central government, which feared the broader economic implications of popular takeovers (Lindblad 2008, 155).

In the mining sector during the 1950s, the government pursued a program of statist resource nationalism that was largely motivated by pressure from unions and nationalist factions in parliament. In the tin sector, for example, the government nationalized the Bangka mine and transferred the contract to a new state-owned company, PN Tambang Timah Bangka (Lindblad 2008, 165). Similar transfers took place in the coal sector. After the Japanese surrendered, the Dutch reasserted control over the Bukit Asam coal mine. But following independence in 1949, mine workers called for the government to nationalize the company. In 1950, the government set up the Perusahaan Tambang Arang Bukit Asam (Bukit Asam State Mining Company [PNTABA]) and negotiated with the Netherlands to acquire the mine. The Dutch-run Ombilin mine was also transferred to Perusahaan Negara Tambang Batubara Ombilin (which would later become part of Bukit Asam) (Devi and Proyogo 2013).

The picture in Indonesia's oil sector was very different. Oil was largely insulated from the occupations and nationalizations that took place in the plantations and mining sectors. The Indonesian government understood the necessity of oil rents for the fledgling economy and was therefore at pains not to interrupt production at foreign-run oil mines. To this end, the new government respected the "let alone" agreements that had been drawn up between the Dutch government and the three oil majors back in 1948, which provided them with a range of attractive guarantees in return for splitting profits generously with the Indonesian government (Wing, Glassburner, and Nasution 1994, 54). With Stanvac, Caltex, and Royal Dutch Shell continuing to produce and export, the sector grew rapidly during the first decade of the postindependence period and made significant contributions to state revenue (Booth 1998, 55).

At the same time, the more stridently nationalist elements within Indonesia's political elite were resentful of the let-alone agreements, Finec, and foreign oil companies' ongoing domination of Indonesia's petroleum sector. Legislators from PNI and Masjumi expressed deep suspicion of Western oil companies and accused companies of fudging financial reports and paying minimal tax (Wing, Glassburner, and Nasution 1994, 55). Legislators also pressured the government to postpone all new oil and gas concessions and development permits until the government and parliament could agree on a new petroleum law (Bee 1982, 9). But questions regarding the appropriate level of foreign ownership and the regulation of foreign companies proved divisive (Wing, Glassburner, and Nasution

1994, 55–56). Foreshadowing the fate of very similar debates in the parliament half a century later, politicians could not find common ground and the bill stagnated. Years passed and neither the parliament nor the commission could reach a resolution on the terms of the law.

A Fledgling Business Class outside the Resource Industries

The Indonesian government tried to support the growth of locally owned companies (Dick 2002, 176). Such efforts, however, took place outside of plantations and extractives, where large foreign firms and state enterprises remained dominant. The capital inputs required to compete with these existing firms was far beyond the reach of Indonesia's fledgling business elite. Instead, the state nurtured the growth of a small domestic business community in manufacturing, trade, and industry. It is worth outlining the expansion of the business elite during this time because some would go on to use their wealth to make inroads into land and resource projects decades later.

The infamous Benteng Program, introduced in 1950, was a major government effort to strengthen the indigenous business class by giving local traders preferential access to import licenses in order to undercut Dutch and ethnic Chinese domination in the lucrative import sector (van Zanden and Marks 2012, 146). However, the scheme was riddled with rent seeking and corruption. Most indigenous importers were in fact fronting for nonindigenous interests—that is, ethnic Chinese or foreign—who had more capital and better networks with which to establish an importing business (van Zanden and Marks 2012, 146). A trade in licenses developed, and political parties in government exploited the system to raise cash for their campaigns and their party's operational costs. By 1956, the program was all but abandoned.

Still and despite the failed Benteng Program, during the first half of the 1950s there was real growth in entrepreneurship and in the size of the indigenous business class more generally. The number of indigenous enterprises in manufacturing, trade, services, and banking increased, with around 500 firms being incorporated annually. Economic historians believe over 40 percent of these firms were fully owned by indigenous Indonesians, just over a third were Chinese Indonesian owned, and the rest were joint ventures (Lindblad 2008, 88–89). Indigenous conglomerates were born during this period, usually via import licenses and favorable lines of credit to which they had access through close personal relationships with political figures in government. For example, Achmad Bakrie's Bakrie and Bros. had a monopoly on the import of motorcycles, sewing machines, and radios. Hasjim Ning, another prominent indigenous businessperson, had exclusive rights to import General Motors cars Soedarpo Sastro-satomo enjoyed access to capital through his closeness to the sultan of Yogyakarta and enjoyed import licenses and contracts for military vehicles.

Yet, despite moderate growth in the size of the domestic business class, the major source of state revenue and gross domestic product (GDP) growth came from the petroleum and agricultural sectors, which remained under the control of Dutch and Western companies. Manufacturing, where more locally owned enterprises had entered the market, accounted for just 12 percent of net domestic product (Booth 1998, 58). According to Anne Booth (1998, 58), "for the 1950s, Indonesia had the lowest share of non-agricultural to total national product of any Asian country except Pakistan."

There was widespread discontent with the minor role that Indonesians played in the major sectors of their economy. Resource exports from Sumatra, parts of Kalimantan, and Sulawesi were keeping the national economy afloat. But people in the outer islands increasingly felt that Indonesia's resource-based economy had little impact on their own welfare, and instead the economic benefits flowed back to Java (Dick 2002, 180). Attempts to Indonesianize the workforce in the resource sectors achieved only modest outcomes, too. In 1957, the top Dutch trading firms and foreign resource companies increased the number of Indonesians working in lower and middle-rung positions, but management roles remained dominated by Dutch citizens (Lindblad 2008, 168–70). The republic was also engaged in a bitter dispute with the Netherlands over control of resource-rich West Irian (contemporary Papua). The republic claimed sovereign rights to all of the former Netherlands East Indies territory, but the Dutch refused to cede control of West Irian. Years of negotiations failed, and by the mid-1950s, political parties in the legislature were pressuring the government to take a more confrontational approach.

Meanwhile, divisions between the Islamic, communist, and pluralist political parties in parliament meant governing coalitions were fractious and unstable (Feith 1962). Between 1949 and 1957, Indonesia had ten different cabinets with as many prime ministers. There was growing disillusionment within the political class and the broader public because it seemed the moderate approach to Indonesia's stalling economy was failing, and the Western-liberal model of parliamentary democracy had only produced polarization and instability. Those in favor of a more nationalist economic agenda enjoyed increasing influence over government.

Guided Democracy and the Statist-Nationalist Turn

By the end of 1956, Indonesia was drifting toward a more strident and assertive economic nationalism. After years of instability, in 1957, President Sukarno

brought an end to parliamentary democracy and in April of that year, he un-
veiled his plan for "Guided Democracy"—a benevolent term for an authoritarian system of government that disempowered the parliament and transferred
unchecked authority to the president. Sukarno claimed this new system was better suited to Indonesians' cultural proclivity for consensus building and their
communitarian values.

His parallel concept of a "guided economy" constituted a program of greater
state intervention, protectionism, and a more aggressive approach to reversing
foreign control of the economy (Chalmers 1997, 15). A spate of nationalizations
began, the first of which were not officially state sanctioned. In late 1957, laborers, organized through unions affiliated with the PKI and the radical wing of
PNI, mobilized and took over Dutch-owned enterprises across a range of sectors (Cribb and Brown 1995, 78–79). President Sukarno and General Nasution,
the army commander, declared martial law and ordered a stop to "uncontrolled"
takeovers. The government confiscated the seized Dutch assets, placing them
under military management (Cribb and Brown 1995, 79). The military now exercised de facto control over strategic parts of the economy, including shipping
lines, banks, plantations, oil wells, and tin and coal mines.

All former Dutch-owned estates were seized as well. The government consolidated 542 former Dutch plantations under new SOEs, with their directors
appointed by President Sukarno. Mackie, writing in 1961, noted that plantations
were a critical part of the Indonesian economy and that "control of that wealth
[was] now for the first time in Indonesian hands" (338). Senior Indonesian plantation workers were now tasked with managing the estates. However, army officers were also attached to the regional units of these state enterprises as
supervisors. Meanwhile, most of the former foreign-owned mines were already
under Indonesian government control by the time of Guided Democracy, and
by 1958, almost all coal was being produced by Bukit Asam. The Indonesian government gained full control of all coal mining in the country when the Dutch
firm Oost-Borneo Maatschappij handed over its coal mines at Batu Panggal and
Sigihan in East Kalimantan to the state-owned Sebuku (Pham 2014, 286).

The oil sector, on the other hand, remained the domain of the same three
Western oil giants. Sukarno understood that Stanvac, Shell, and Caltex would
need to continue their operations, as local business simply did not have the capacity to meet the demands of complex oil investments. However, he asserted
greater central government control over the sector by establishing new state-
owned oil companies to manage other smaller oil wells no longer operated by
the Western majors. Sukarno decided to hand managerial responsibility of one
of the new state companies, Permina, over to the Indonesian Armed Forces
(TNI). This decision was based partly on pragmatism. Sumatra was in a state of

political turmoil owing to several regional rebellions, and security around the oil fields was tenuous. However, as Anderson Bartlett et al. (1972, 134) observed, "such an expanded role [for the TNI] fitted well with the philosophy of Chief of Staff Nasution, who saw the army as a dynamic force in nation building." Nasution appointed Colonel Dr. Ibnu Sutowo as Permina's director and gave him the task of developing Indonesia's first SOE.

Then, in 1958, the government formally nationalized NIAM's assets in Jambi and incorporated another new SOE, Indonesia Oil Mining Inc., or Permindo (Pertambangan Minyak Indonesia). NIAM had been half-owned by the Dutch government and half-owned by Royal Dutch Shell. The latter retained its share in the new company. The government, however, outlined a plan for the entire company to be Indonesianized, "with Shell providing training and technical assistance" only (Bartlett et al. 1972, 120).

In response to years of equivocation by parliament, Sukarno also exercised his emergency powers to approve Law No. 44/1960 concerning Petroleum and Natural Gas Mining. The new law established the republic's ownership of all petroleum resources and vested all oil rights in the state. It mandated that foreign companies would no longer hold concession rights, per the previous Dutch mining law, but would instead become government contractors. According to Philip Barnes (1995, 11), the law established that "all extraction of petroleum (and gas) shall be undertaken solely by the state . . . and shall be implemented solely by state owned enterprises . . . who may in turn reach work agreements with various contractors . . . where the state enterprise is unable to carry it out." The law effectively gave state enterprises ownership and operating rights to all of Indonesia's petroleum resources, while enabling foreign oil firms to remain principal operators of current and future wells. The innovative system thus helped the sector to sustain investment and productivity while still taking steps toward Sukarno's statist-nationalist objectives.

The oil sector continued to grow throughout the period of Guided Democracy, but the rest of the economy fell deeper and deeper into crisis. The takeover of Dutch firms had led to a decline in productivity (Booth 1998, 63–69). Other foreign companies left in the country were also targeted for nationalization throughout the 1960s, and hostile takeovers by pro-communist unions impacted American, British, Australian, and European firms. By 1964, almost all foreign interests had been seized by popular forces or the state (Dick 2002, 188).

Meanwhile, drought ravaged parts of Java throughout the early 1960s, ruining rice crops and leading to devastating famine. Basic goods and food were in short supply and inflation had soared to over 600 percent by 1966. The country's most productive sectors like rice, tin, and rubber ground to a virtual halt. Private investment "almost ceased" (Booth 1998, 71). Sukarno's statist nationalism delivered for many Indonesians the kind of political and emotional satisfaction that Harry Johnson (1965) spoke of in his early work on economic nationalism. But the overall economic outcomes, in a context of limited state revenue and widespread drought and famine, were deeply damaging.

Political tensions ran high throughout the period of Guided Democracy as well. The PKI was growing in strength. The party claimed more and more members and was actively organizing peasants at the grass roots. Sukarno had long expressed admiration for and interest in Marxist ideas, and throughout the 1960s he moved closer to the PKI and the communist bloc, both in terms of his ideology and his diplomatic relations. Islamic groups, particularly Nahdlatul Ulama, together with the military, increasingly viewed the president's warm relations with the PKI as a direct threat to their own influence within the government and their economic assets as well.

Tensions erupted in 1965. On September 30, a group of leftist military officials, calling themselves the 30 September Movement, killed several senior military personnel whom they alleged were part of a plot to overthrow Sukarno and disempower the PKI, with help from the Central Intelligence Agency. Major General Suharto, commander of the army's strategic reserve (KOSTRAD), took over the armed forces and proclaimed the 30 September Movement to be a communist coup.[5] Under Suharto's command, the armed forces led an anticommunist purge that resulted in the deaths of between 500,000 and 1 million people (Cribb 2001; Roosa 2020). Within two years, General Suharto consolidated his power over the armed forces, extinguished the PKI, and forced Sukarno's resignation. Under a new president and a new regime, Indonesia's resource sectors would once again be transformed into arenas of foreign control.

The New Order: Nurturing a Domestic Business Class

When Suharto came to power in 1966, the government's economic strategy turned quickly and dramatically away from the statist nationalism of Guided Democracy. The new president launched a thorough program of liberalization in order to secure aid from international financial institutions and attract much needed foreign investment. Liberalization and the fortuitous oil booms of the 1970s enabled a swift economic recovery. GDP growth surpassed most developing economies and averaged 8 percent annually between 1971 and 1981; over the same period, Indonesia transitioned from the category of "very poor" to "middle income," according to the World Bank's country rankings (Arndt 1983, 144).

During these early years, Indonesia was sometimes referred to as a "comprador state" among academics and political observers (Robison 1986, 114–16). The concept describes how Suharto promoted foreign investment and sustained an economy that served the needs and demands of foreign capital, particularly in the resource sectors. In the process, the government largely sidelined the domestic private sector, except for a small clique of business actors dominated by Chinese Indonesian tycoons and military elites. Their firms were dependent on contracts with foreign business, which were facilitated by the New Order state.

However, over the course of three decades, the Suharto government also took measures to protect domestic industry and to prioritize, nurture, and expand the private sector. The state was never completely isolated from the demands of Indonesia's small but growing pribumi business class, and the government set about generating new opportunities for the growth of domestic business at particular junctures. Such efforts largely coalesced with resource booms, and market-cycle theories of resource nationalism have much resonance with this period of Indonesia's economic history: when structural economic constraints were low—that is, when oil prices were high and the economy was stable and growing—Suharto's policy "pendulum" would swing toward nationalism and protectionism, "reinforced by the huge commodity windfall gains" (Hill 2013, 117). Just like in other sections of the economy, however, in the land and resource industries the major beneficiaries of Suharto's nationalist interventions were a narrow cohort of ethnic Chinese cronies, a select group of pribumi tycoons, and the president's own family.

Logging: Foreign Compradors Become Cronies

The logging industry was an archetypal example of how the New Order political economy functioned. Today, logging is no longer the major source of state revenue it was during the Suharto years, but the industry produced some of Indonesia's wealthiest businesspeople, and the roots of the contemporary palm oil industry's ownership structure can be traced back to President Suharto's interventions in the timber industry decades prior. Logging thus warrants particular attention in this historical chapter.

From 1967, the government offered attractive investment terms in order to entice foreign capital into the archipelago's largely untouched forests. The government granted concessions to companies from the United States, Malaysia, Korea, Japan, and the Philippines, and log exports doubled each year until 1973 (Ascher 1998, 51). By the end of 1970, the Forestry Department had issued eighty-one new logging concessions of which forty-six were for foreign companies covering 7 million ha. Foreign investment constituted 80 percent of investment in the forestry sector during this period (Barr 1998, 6). The influx of foreign companies opened up opportunities for local elites to accumulate significant wealth. Military elites often acted as silent partners for foreign investors wanting to enter the industry (Barr 1998, 6). When it came to domestic investors, Suharto distributed concessions primarily to ethnic Chinese businesses, who then partnered with military officials or acted as partners for foreign investors (Robison 1986, 187–88). Logging concessions were also used by the president to purchase loyalty and turn senior military officials (sometimes entire military units) into his clients within the New Order's emergent patrimonial regime (Ascher 1998). The president encouraged joint ventures in part because ethnic Chinese entrepreneurs could bring the business acumen that military officers lacked.

These deals were new incarnations of the type of business relationships that military officers had established with Chinese merchants and traders during the revolutionary war as a means of accessing capital to both fund the war effort and accrue personal wealth (Mackie 1991). Suharto himself was infamous for the lucrative relationships he developed with ethnic Chinese businesspeople while part of the Diponegoro military division in Semarang during and following the war. The two ethnic Chinese businesspeople who came to dominate the logging and timber products sectors were Salim and Bob Hasan, both of whom had well-established commercial relationships with Suharto dating back to the 1950s (Mackie 1991, 93).

At the same time, Suharto excluded the pribumi, or nonethnically Chinese, businesspeople from these sorts of lucrative rent-seeking opportunities. The president's goal was to neutralize sources of independent political power (Ascher 1998, 53). Instead, he promoted Chinese Indonesian business elites while maintaining a Dutch-style cultural oppression of Indonesia's ethnically Chinese minority. In doing so, the government entrenched an economically privileged but politically limp wealthy business class. The president's Chinese cronies returned the favor by financing the New Order program for industrialization as well as Suharto's personal projects. For example, tycoons in the logging sector, like Bob Hasan (chair of Apkindo, the Indonesian Wood Panel Association which operated as a downstream cartel for the industry), Prajogo Pangestu of Barito Pacific, and Sudono Salim (known also by his Chinese name Liem Sioe Liong) of the Salim Group, helped finance everything from petrochemical plants, infrastructure projects, to the Taman Mini theme park (Ascher 1998; Borsuk and Chng 2014).

These investment arrangements between foreign investors, Chinese business, and the military typified the New Order's style of capitalist development, whereby state and domestic business interests were compradors for, and subordinate to, the interests of global capital. However, as Richard Robison (1986, 115) argues, both in the forestry sector and beyond, the New Order government was creating the conditions for the growth of domestic business. Eventually, in 1984, the government proscribed further foreign investment in the timber sector completely, and this sector became the domain of domestic capital. By the early 1990s, government policy ensured that both the logging *and* downstream plywood industries were highly concentrated around a small number of companies, all of which were owned by Chinese Indonesian businesspeople with close links to Suharto (Resosudarmo and Yusuf 2006, 14). Table 2.3 displays the largest business groups in the sector and describes their relationship to President Suharto.

Plantations: The Retreat of the State

During the economic chaos of Guided Democracy, Indonesia's plantations deteriorated dramatically. From 1967, the new government initiated a series of programs, funded through international loans, to try and improve yields and revitalize the export-oriented plantation estates that had previously been the country's economic backbone (Hardjono 1994, 204). But state subsidies to the government-owned estates were poorly managed and prone to corruption. The state-owned plantation firms that now dominated the sector, known as PTPN (PT Perkebunan Negara), were often led by senior military officers who had been placed there to accumulate rent rather than to efficiently manage the enterprise. The general neglect of cash crop sectors, particularly rubber, meant Indonesia never reclaimed its once prominent position in global markets (Hill 1994, 76).

The nascent palm oil sector was an exception. The Suharto government identified palm oil as a crop with immense economic and developmental potential. In the mid-1970s, the World Bank and Asian Development Bank began funding programs to expand crude palm oil (CPO) production as a strategy for diversifying sources of cooking oil, which in the 1970s relied heavily on a limited supply of coconut oil. Palm oil expansion thus began in the 1970s, primarily through subsidies to government-owned estates. A secondary goal of palm oil expansion was to engage rural communities in the outer islands as a way to reduce poverty and provide livelihoods to transmigrants (Gaskell 2015). To that end, nucleus estate schemes were established where private companies and state-owned plantations leased a section of their concession to smallholder farmers, and by the early 1980s, according to Joanne Gaskell (2015, 39), "2% of oil-palm plantations were owned by smallholders, 28% by private companies, and 70% by the government." At this stage of the sector's development, almost none of the private companies developing palm oil plantations were foreign owned.

Palm oil plantations fed into an expanding and highly lucrative domestic CPO processing industry, which in turn fed into cooking oils for Indonesia's growing

TABLE 2.3. Ownership, concession area, and production levels of largest timber groups, 1990

GROUP	OWNER(S)	TOTAL CONCESSIONS	CONCESSION AREA	PRODUCTION CAPACITY
Barito Pacific	Prajogo Pangestu, Chinese Indonesian tycoon and Suharto crony	22	2,215,500	1,236,900
Korindo	Korean-owned	7	828,000	624,000
Djajanti	Burhan Uray, Chinese Indonesian tycoon; Sudwikatmono, Suharto's cousin and a member of the infamous "Gang of Four," was also a major shareholder	24	2,726,500	618,000
Bumi Raya Utama	Adijanto Priosoetanto and his brother Soenaryo Priosoetanto, both Chinese Indonesian businesspeople	9	1,060,000	519,000
Indo Plywood	Sudono Salim, Suharto's closest Chinese Indonesian crony; the Suharto family was also a major shareholder	2	350,000	508,850
Alas Kusuma	PO Suwandi and Ibnu Hartomo, Suharto's brother-in-law	17	2,248,000	409,340
Surya Dumai	Martias Fanigono, Chinese Indonesian businessperson	7	904,000	405,400
Kalimanis	Bob Hasan, one of Suharto's closest Chinese Indonesian cronies	3	855,000	390,000
Satya Djaya Raya	Susanto Lyman, prominent Chinese Indonesian intellectual with close ties to government and military	12	1,597,000	369,000
Kayu Lapis Indonesia	Sudono Salim, Suharto's closest Chinese Indonesian crony; the Suharto family was also a major shareholder	14	1,789,000	349,300
Raja Garuda Mas	Sukanto Tanoto, Chinese Indonesian tycoon and Suharto crony	2	259,000	340,000
Sumber Mas	Yos Sutomo, Chinese Indonesian businessperson	7	710,000	328,200
Hutrindo	Akie Setiawan, Chinese Indonesian businessperson	17	1,587,000	252,000
Others		391	37,603,000	5,780,000

Sources: Information on concessions and production capacity from Barr (1998, 12); ownership details were compiled by the author using Brown (1999), Suryadinata (2012), and a range of media articles and company reports.

population. Ownership of the CPO refining and cooking oil distribution was heavily concentrated during the Suharto years. A handful of Suharto's Chinese Indonesian cronies dominated this portion of the sector, and they benefited directly from a state policy restricting CPO exports. Three tycoons essentially controlled CPO processing: Sukanto Tanoto, Eka Tjipta Widjaja, and Sudono Salim (Borsuk and Chng 2014, 297–301). According to one report, "in 1989, [Salim] controlled 45% of the licensed capacity for fractionation and refining" (Gaskell 2015, 41), and Salim and Widjaja became the two major buyers of CPO on the domestic market by the 1990s, which meant they effectively controlled domestic prices (Borsuk and Chng 2014, 302).

By the late 1990s, the palm oil plantation sector was in the midst of transitioning from a state-owned sector geared toward rural development and the domestic market to a sector geared toward revenue generation and, increasingly, export markets as well (Zen et al. 2016, 81). The shift in priorities is reflected in the sector's ownership structure. Table 2.4 is taken from Zahari Zen et al. (2016, 81) and shows the remarkable expansion of privately owned and smallholder estates and the much slower growth in government-controlled estates. Private plantation firms were mostly domestically owned, and the sector was difficult for foreign investors to penetrate.

The surge in private investment was stimulated by state policy that granted local firms access to cheap credit (Casson 2000, 13). The principal beneficiaries of these attractive investment terms were the familiar cast of established Chinese Indonesian business elites, many of whom had amassed fortunes in the logging industry

TABLE 2.4. Area of oil palm, area growth rate, and crude palm oil production in Indonesia by mode of production

YEAR	AREA AND PRODUCTION	GOVERNMENT ESTATES	PRIVATE ESTATES	SMALLHOLDINGS	TOTAL
1980	Area ('000 ha)	200	89	6	295
	Production ('000 t)	499	222	1	721
1990	Area ('000 ha)	372	463	291	1,127
	Areal growth (%)[a]	6	18	28	14
	Production ('000 t)	1,247	789	377	2,413
2003	Area ('000 ha)	561	2,555	1,811[b]	4,926
	Areal growth (%)	3	14	15	12
	Production ('000 t)	1,716	4,778	3,257	9,750

[a]Annual compound areal growth rates, 1980–90, 1990–2003, 2003–7, and 2007–11.
[b]Including 897,457 ha in NES plasma and a balance of over 900,000 ha of individual holdings.
Source: Adapted from Zen et al. (2016, 81).

TABLE 2.5.   Palm oil ownership, 1997

COMPANY	GROUP	GROUP OWNER	TOTAL LAND BANK AREA (HA)
Salim Plantations	Salim Group	Sudono Salim, Suharto's closest Chinese Indonesian tycoon	1,155,745
Golden Agri Resources	Sinar Mas Group	Eka Tjipta Widjaja, Chinese Indonesian tycoon	320,463
Asian Agri	Raja Garuda Mas	Sukanto Tanoto, Chinese Indonesian tycoon	259,075
London Sumatra Indonesia	Napan Group	Henry Pribadi (member of the Salim family), Ibrahim Risjad (a pribumi businessperson), and Bambang Trihatmodjo (Suharto's son)	245,629
Astra Agro	Astra Group	William Soeryadjaya, Chinese Indonesian tycoon	192,375
Texmaco	Texmaco Group	Marimutu Sinivasan, Sumatran tycoon	168,000
Surya Damai	Surya Damai Group	Pung Kian Hwa (Martias), Chinese Indonesian tycoon	154,133
Duta Palma	Duta Palma Group	Surya Damadi, Chinese Indonesian tycoon	65,800
Bakrie Sumatra Plantations	Bakrie Group	Aburizal Bakrie, Sumatran tycoon	49,283
	Total		2,610,503

and enjoyed close personal relations with President Suharto. By 1998, according to Anne Casson (2000, 14), "around 69 percent of the total planted area owned by private companies was owned by just eight conglomerates." Table 2.5 displays the major private palm oil producers in 1997, just before the Asian financial crisis.

At the same time, during the 1990s, Suharto sought to significantly expand foreign involvement in the sector so as to boost productivity and increase revenue and foreign exchange, at a time when oil revenues were declining. Some sectoral growth thus came from foreign investors (McCarthy and Cramb 2009, 115–16). By the late 1990s, of all privately owned palm oil estates, about 20 percent were foreign owned (Feridhanusetyawan 1997, 28). The plan was to dramatically increase the land allocated to palm oil plantations and to offer half of this land to foreign-owned private estate companies (Casson 2000, 8). For example, before the Asian financial crisis hit in 1997, the government had already earmarked 1.5 million ha of land to Malaysian palm oil companies.

These plans, however, prompted opposition from Indonesian palm oil producers, who saw competition from foreign agrifirms as a direct threat to their own interests (Lindblad 1997, 26). In early 1997, while the investment board was in the midst of considering applications from four Malaysia investors, the Suharto government suddenly closed the sector to foreign firms entirely (Borsuk and Chng 2014, 349). According to Tubagus Feridhanusetyawan (1997, 28), "the stated reason for the ban was to prevent too much land acquisition by foreign plantation [companies], and [to] make it easier for the domestic conglomerates that are beginning to dominate the industry to purchase new land." In their seminal study of the Salim Group, Richard Borsuk and Nancy Chng (2014, 349) similarly suggest that Sinar Mas and Salim lobbied Suharto to ban foreign investment in the palm oil industry because they viewed Malaysian firms in particular as a threat to the prominent position these two firms held as the primary growers, producers, and distributors of CPO. Suharto acquiesced and closed the door to foreign capital at the behest of a small handful of his cronies.

This development is significant for two reasons. First, the introduction of a foreign investment ban was at odds with the government's, and indeed Suharto's, stated developmental and growth objectives and illustrated the degree to which domestic conglomerates, including those owned by Chinese Indonesians, had begun to execute an independent influence on nationalist policy outcomes.

The Suharto government nurtured and built this class of wealthy business elites, making them dependent on the state for patronage, privilege, and opportunity. But by the end of the 1990s, as this case illustrates, the domestic agri-conglomerates enjoyed relative autonomy from the state such that they could shape foreign investment policy in ways that contradicted the state's broader economic objectives. This case is also significant because a decade later in the post-Suharto period, as we shall see, the dominant business interests in this sector opposed nationalist demands to cap foreign investment.

Oil and Gas: Building a State-Owned Giant, Planting Private Sector Seeds

During the first half of the New Order, oil rents were crucial for Indonesia's economic recovery, and foreign capital was crucial for the industry. Oil and gas extraction is capital intensive anywhere in the world, but in Indonesia, difficult geology, terrain, and remoteness make investment particularly expensive and high risk (Barnes 1995, 57). The immense capital investments required to explore and extract oil and gas prevented any significant penetration by domestic businesses into the upstream sector. Instead, the Indonesian government carved out space in the market for its state firm, Pertamina.

Suharto took a similar approach to the previous government: the state invited foreign companies to exploit Indonesia's hydrocarbon reserves while compelling them to partner with local enterprises. The goal was to expand state control, build up the capital and technological capacity of the national oil company, and increase the SOE's participation through partnerships and contracts with foreign investors. State managers understood this strategic sector would, at least for the medium term, remain highly dependent on upstream foreign investors.

To achieve these goals, Ibnu Sutowo, Suharto's minister of mines and the director of one of the state companies, Permina, tweaked the contract system established under Sukarno's 1960 Petroleum Law. It is worth explaining this regulatory regime in some detail here because it was changed as part of the broader post-Suharto liberal reform program after 1998, and nationalist mobilization in the contemporary period has largely focused on reviving the New Order system. In 1968, new production-sharing contracts (PSCs) gave the government a share of foreign contractors' oil production, which state oil companies could then market and sell domestically or abroad. Second, under the PSC system, some of the foreign company's exploration costs could be reimbursed by the state in a "cost-recovery" system (Bee 1982, 24–25). This was an attractive system for oil companies because they could recoup many costs associated with their initial investments. But the system also outlined that once an oil company's contract expired, the state effectively owned much of the infrastructure and technology at the oil well, making it theoretically easier for a state enterprise to take over operatorship.

To establish a more powerful sectoral SOE, Suharto merged Pertamin and Permina into P.N. Pertamina (Perusahaan Negara Pertambangan Minyak dan Gas Bumi Nasional) and made Ibnu Sutowo the new director.[6] Under the 1971 Pertamina Law, Suharto granted the new national oil company immense regulatory power and control over the sector's revenue. Specifically, all foreign operators had to contract with and have their work plans approved by Pertamina. The national oil company was also given a monopoly over marketing the government's share of crude oil and gas and a monopoly over the sale of refined petroleum products on the domestic market.

Aspects of this system incentivized Pertamina to cultivate new foreign contracts. Under the PSC system, all foreign companies were compelled to pay their royalties and taxes to Pertamina. Contractors also paid "signatory bonuses" in the millions of dollars, which went straight to Pertamina (Bee 1982, 31–32). Each contract brought in new revenues for Pertamina, and the company was well placed to benefit from the oil boom of the early 1970s. Although Pertamina did not operate any significant wells of its own, the national oil company quickly became a powerful state firm in control of significant capital.

Under the PSC system and in the context of buoyant global oil prices in the early 1970s, the sector made a substantial contribution to Indonesia's remarkable economic recovery. Between 1966 and 1974, over sixty PSCs were signed (Goldstone 1977, 124). Crude output rose from 500,000 bpd in 1966 to 1.4 million bpd in 1974 (Glassburner 1976, 1106). By 1970, oil exports constituted 40 percent of Indonesia's export revenue, and the boom of 1974 brought this figure to almost 70 percent (Barnes 1995, 19).

Whereas upstream exploration and production was the domain of foreign multinationals, Pertamina helped to facilitate the entry of local companies into the oil and gas services industry. Barriers to entry are far lower in this subsector, which includes construction services, the provision of pipes, rigs, transport, and the like. According to Jean Aden (1993 92), "from 1968 to 1976, Ibnu Sutowo underwrote the growth of an Indonesian oil service sector." He did this by forcing foreign service companies to engage in joint venture arrangements with Pertamina and by awarding service and construction contracts "to young would-be businessmen" (Aden 1992, 91), many of whom had connections to the military and to either Sutowo or Suharto directly.

Pertamina also became the focal point for the New Order government's program of resource-based industrialization. Suharto and Sutowo shared a vision for Pertamina to become the engine of Indonesia's industrialization—a "national development 'company,'" much like Japan's Mitsubishi (Goldstone 1977, 125). The company invested in wide-ranging industrial projects including roads, shipping, transportation, fertilizer factories, oil trading, petrochemical plants to steel industries, as well as other development projects such as schools, clinics, and mosques (Bee 1982). Pertamina's industrial investments came to an abrupt end, however, in 1975–76, when the company went bankrupt. When oil prices dropped in 1975, Pertamina defaulted on a series of loans, and Suharto ordered the central bank of Indonesia to move in and rescue the company. The company had also developed a "notorious penchant for paying inflated prices" and was a lucrative source of kickbacks and illegal fees for senior government and military officials (Glassburner 1976, 1104). Pertamina provided off-budget funds directly to Suharto and his family as well (Goldstone 1977, 127).

Despite policymakers' efforts to reform Pertamina, the company continued to benefit politically wired business elites throughout the 1980s and 1990s. Richard Borsuk (1998), a longtime journalist of Indonesia's politics and economics, described how Pertamina established a "web of cozy supply contracts in shipping, drilling, and exploration" for Suharto's cronies and family members. The relatively small amount of crude that Pertamina pumped was consigned to trading companies in Hong Kong and Singapore controlled by the Suharto family, and "family companies also handled all of Indonesia's oil-product imports" (Borsuk 1998).[7]

A small number of Indonesians ventured beyond the oil and gas services and trading sectors and entered the world of upstream production. But Indonesian companies were limited mostly to technical assistance contracts (TACs) rather than PSCs, which covered areas with old existing wells that were abandoned by foreign oil companies. Most TACs were handed to cronies and family members. Writing for the *Far Eastern Economic Review* in 1989, Michael Vatikiotis (1989) told of how Pertamina began "farming out" upstream contracts to domestic private firms in order to bolster the domestic industry. That year, Pertamina made the first offer of equity in a foreign PSC to an Indonesian firm. Arco and BP won a PSC for natural gas exploration in the fields north of Bali, and Pertamina offered a 10 percent share to Bimantara, the company owned by Suharto's son Bambang Trihatmojo. The offer was remarkable because by law, only Pertamina was entitled to a 10 percent stake in PSCs. Several other PSCs and TACs were awarded that year to connected companies, too (Vatikiotis 1989).

The only privately owned Indonesian firm to become a serious upstream operator during the New Order was Afirin Panigoro's Medco Energi International. Panigoro leveraged his ties to the Suharto family and to senior bureaucrats in the ministry and built the company up from a small drilling services enterprise into an integrated and international energy company. Panigoro set up Meta Epsi Pribumi Drilling Company in 1980 with financial assistance from Eddy Kowara Adiwinata—the father-in-law of Suharto's daughter Siti Hardijanti "Tutut" Indra Rukmana (Aditjondro 2006, 136). This was the first oil and gas services company owned by a pribumi Indonesian businessperson. In 1992, Panigoro expanded into upstream oil and gas exploration and production with his newly incorporated Medco Energi International, which became the first Indonesian oil company listed on the Jakarta Stock Exchange. The company took pride of place as one of the country's top ten oil producers after purchasing Stanvac Indonesia from ExxonMobil in 1995 for US$88 million, most of which came in the form of favorable state bank loans.

By the mid-1990s, Indonesia's oil wells were drying up, and new exploration investment had flat-lined for years. Just as local businesses began expanding into upstream hydrocarbon production, the sector was already in decline. By this time, oil was no longer the backbone of the Indonesian economy. The Suharto government had done much to diversify sources of economic growth and state revenue, motivated by the oil price collapse of the early 1980s. Figure 2.1 shows the significant decline in the sector's contribution to GDP growth.

At the close of the New Order, the structure of the upstream sector remained much the same as it had been decades earlier in the sense that multinationals continued to dominate. In the early 1990s, there were over 300 wells producing oil

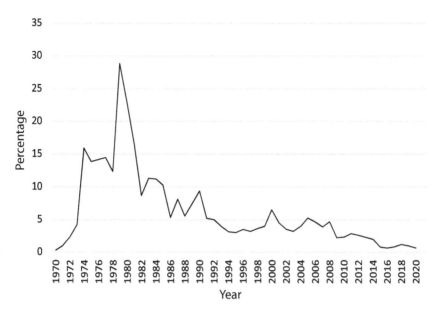

FIGURE 2.1. Oil rents (percentage of GDP)

Source: World Development Indicators (2022)

around the country—a huge increase from the early 1960s. However, the vast majority of the country's production continued to come from a handful of multinationals. In 1993, American companies Caltex, Maxus, Arco, Mobil, and Conoco accounted for 74 percent of Indonesia's oil production (Barnes 1995). Pertamina was still only a minor player in upstream oil production; indeed, its role in production had declined over the course of the New Order in relative terms (Ascher 1998, 39).

Mining: Balancing Foreign, State, and Fledgling Domestic Capital

Since the start of the New Order, the government treated the mining sector as one that could achieve a balance between attracting massive and valuable foreign investment, ensuring state control and revenue generation, and enabling participation of domestic companies in the more accessible and less capital-intensive segments of the industry. The start of the New Order was marked by a swift program of liberalization in the mining sector. But in keeping with the broader pattern of this period when commodity prices were buoyant, the government changed investment rules to privilege local businesses.

The government introduced Law 11/1967 on Basic Provisions of Mining, which together with the Foreign Investment Law of the same year, motivated an influx of foreign capital. Under the new law, foreign mining companies could enter into a contract of work CoW with the government, which set the terms for taxes, import duties, royalties, divestment, and the like. The contracts protected companies from changes in government policy, and the terms were maintained for the life of the contract. CoWs offered foreign companies a predictable and attractive investment environment. Within just a few years of the law's implementation, fifty-three new concessions were opened up for mineral exploration in copper, nickel, tin, and gold, heralding "a period of unprecedented mineral exploration activity during the next 25 years" (van Leeuwen 1994, 14).

In 1967, the government signed a "first-generation" CoW with Freeport McMoran for the Ertsberg deposit in the mountains of what was then West Irian and today known as Papua. Indonesia was in the midst of a painful political and economic transition, and the foreign company was in a much better bargaining position than the Indonesian government. The company's CoW included terms that were remarkably favorable for the company: a three-year profit tax holiday, exemption from royalty payments, no quotas on Indonesian staff, and no divestment requirements (Leith 2002).

The huge potential of the Freeport mine and the terms of its CoW motivated other companies to invest. However, the government readjusted the generous contract terms offered to Freeport. For a "second-generation" of CoWs, the government removed the tax holiday, increased corporate taxes, set royalty levels, included provisions for the employment of Indonesian staff, and obliged companies to divest 20 percent of the equity shares to Indonesian nationals (van Leeuwen 1994, 26). Although much better for the Indonesian government, these terms were still appealing to foreign companies, and new prospectors descended on the archipelago in search of copper, nickel, bauxite, and tin.

In the copper sector, according to Theo van Leeuwen (1994, 26), seven second-generation CoWs were signed between 1969 and 1972, with most exploration done by the larger foreign companies, Rio Tinto (Australian), Kennecott (American, later acquired by Rio Tinto), and Newmont (American). Several nickel contracts were signed as well. The Dutch had opened a nickel mine in Southeast Sulawesi before World War II. That mine, eventually taken over by the government in 1961, became the property of PT Aneka Tambang (Antam), the state-owned mineral mining company that Suharto established in 1968 after consolidating several smaller SOEs with interests in bauxite, nickel, and gold.

Third-generation CoWs, designed in 1976, reflected a renewed nationalist thrust in government policy. According to Robert Dickie and Thomas Layman

(1988, 93), "these contracts included . . . more stringent linkages to the local economy, including requirements to use more local labour, sourcing, equity ownership and management." The new contract terms compelled foreign firms to divest 51 percent to local businesses (state or nonstate) within ten years of production (a requirement that would be reintroduced decades later during the commodities boom of the mid-2000s). Companies were also encouraged to establish processing and smelting facilities in Indonesia as part of an effort to industrialize the minerals industry and a 10 percent tax was added to unprocessed mineral ore exports. Two factors motivated a more nationalist approach to these mineral contracts. First, by the mid-1970s, the New Order government was in a much better bargaining position than it had been in 1967 when it signed the first CoW with Freeport. The economy was growing at around 6 percent per annum, oil prices were high, mineral prices were buoyant, and other countries around the world were introducing similar regulations in response to high prices (Bhasin 2000, 67–68).

Second, this period was marked by growing public criticism of the Suharto government and popular mobilization against foreign capital. In the 1970s, much of the Indonesian population remained impoverished, and yet military elites, Chinese Indonesian businesses, and members of the president's family had acquired striking and conspicuous wealth through dealings and partnerships with foreign business (Mackie 1998a). Anti-foreign tensions culminated in the 1974 Malari affair in which violent protests broke out against the government's corruption and perceived favoritism toward foreign investors. The third-generation CoWs were designed against the backdrop of both a commodities boom and a wider mood of nationalist agitation.

Between 1984 and 1997, the fourth-, fifth-, and sixth-generation contracts were drawn up for foreign mining companies, each adjusting conditions of investment and aiming to strike a balance between attracting foreign capital and enabling local firms to gradually enter the sector. By the end of the New Order, there were a total of 12 CoW mines in the production stage and 126 in other stages of development (Bhasin 2000). The major CoW holders are listed in table 2.6.

CoWs in the minerals sector were designed for and allocated entirely to foreign investors. Other forms of mining concessions known as *kuasa pertambangan* (or mining authority [KP]) were distributed to local mining businesses. Unlike CoWs, these KPs were not insulated from regulatory changes. At the end of the New Order, reports suggested that approximately 600 KPs had been issued (Resosudarmo et al. 2012, 33). The majority of these KPs were for medium-to-small-sized mineral ventures that made only modest contributions to production and exports.

The coal sector had its own separate contract system. In this subsector, similar to the logging industry, foreign multinationals were initially invited to

TABLE 2.6. Major New Order contracts of work

CONTRACT OF WORK	COMPANY	MINERAL
First generation (1967–68)	Freeport (USA)	Copper
Second generation (1968–76)	Antam (Indonesia)	Nickel
	Pacific Nickel Indonesia (USA)	Nickel
	INCO/Vale (Canada) and INDECO (Japan)	Nickel
	Billiton (Dutch)	Tin
	BHP (Australia)	Tin
	Koba Tin (Australia, then Malaysia)	Tin
	ALCOA	Bauxite
	Kennecott/Utah (USA)	Copper
	Rio Tinto/CRA (Australia)	Copper
	Newmont (USA)	Copper
	Endeavor Resources (USA)	Copper
	OMR (Japan)	Copper
	BHP (Australia)	Copper
Third and fourth generations (1976–86)	130 contracts of work issued for gold mines, most of which went to small Australian mining ventures	Gold
	Majors included:	
	Ashton (Australia)	
	BP Minerals (USA)	
	CRA (Australia)	
	Dominion Mining (Australia)	
	Duval (USA)	
	Newmont (USA)	
	Utah International (USA)	
Fifth generation (1986–96)	Avocet (UK)	Gold
	Freeport McMoran (extension of first-generation contract of work)	Gold and Copper
	Eastern Mining Company (USA)	Gold
	Enarotali Gold Project (USA)	Gold
Sixth generation (1997)	Agincourt Resources (Singapore)	Gold and Silver
	Avocet (UK)	Gold and Silver
	Ensbury Kalteng (Singapore)	Gold
	Iriana Idenburg (Cayman Islands)	Gold
	Iriana Cenrawana (Singapore)	Gold
	Indocal (Hong Kong)	Gold
	Aperio (the Netherlands)	Metals
	Newcrest (Australia)	Gold and Silver
	Golden Arrow (Virgin Islands)	Gold
	Landsdowne Holdings (the Netherlands)	Gold
	East Asia Minerals (Canada)	Gold
	Archipelago Resources (Canada)	Gold
	Highlands Gold (Papua New Guinea)	Gold
	Woyla Aceh (Cayman Islands)	Gold

Sources: Adapted from van Leeuwen (1994) and Ministry of Energy and Mineral Resources (2011a).

invest, explore, and establish large mines; however, as the sector evolved, domestic companies came to play a larger role. The government perceived the immense potential of the coal sector and understood the capacity for local enterprises to engage in this subsector given the relatively uncomplicated extractive process and smaller up-front costs, when compared to hard-rock mineral mining (Lucarelli 2015). Prior to the boom of the twenty-first century, the New Order government was laying the groundwork for local firms to enter the coal market.

The coal sector had stagnated from the time of the Japanese occupation and only began to grow rapidly again in the 1970s. A new energy policy proposed in 1976 outlined an agenda to expand oil exports and promote coal for domestic use (Friederich and van Leeuwen 2017). The government enabled private investment, both domestic and foreign, in coal exploration using a coal contract of work (CCoW) system. These contracts were slightly different to minerals CoWs. The state-owned coal company, Perusahaan Negara Tambang Batubara (PNTB), acted as the sector's regulator in much the same way as Pertamina regulated the oil sector. Companies contracted with PNTB, which had responsibility for the overall management of the sector's operations, and it received a 13.5 percent share of each company's annual coal production to distribute domestically.

Between 1982 and 1990, PNTB signed twelve CCoWs (Friederich and van Leeuwen 2017, 59). Ten of these contracts were foreign. The two domestic companies were Tanito Harum, owned by Kiki Barki, a Chinese Indonesian businessperson, and Indominco Mandiri, owned by the Salim Group. PNTB, meanwhile, expanded its own production at the Ombilin and Bukit Asam mines in Sumatra (formerly Dutch owned). The foreign companies that signed first-generation CCoWs were responsible for a significant increase in coal production during the late 1980s and early 1990s and accounted for by far the largest proportion of coal exports (see table 2.7). These international mining giants effectively turned Indonesia into an important coal-producing country by the end of the 1990s (Lucarelli 2015).

There were nineteen second-generation CCoWs, most of which were signed in 1994. These were reserved entirely for domestic firms, but the concessions were smaller than the first generation of foreign contractors. Third-generation contracts were signed between 1997 and 2000, against the backdrop of the Asian financial crisis and tumultuous political change, and although open to foreign investors, the vast majority of these contracts ended up in the hands of domestic firms (Friederich and van Leeuwen 2017). As we shall see in the following chapter, at the turn of the century, political and economic turmoil suddenly made the Indonesian coal market less attractive to foreign capital, allowing domestic firms to make remarkable inroads into an increasingly strategic industry.

TABLE 2.7. First-generation coal contracts of work, 1981–90

COMPANY	OWNER/CONTROLLING SHAREHOLDER	YEAR OF COAL CONTRACT OF WORK	CONCESSION SIZE
Arutimin	ARCO and Utah International (USA)	1981	1,260,000
Utah Indonesia	Utah International (USA)	1981	797,200
Agip/Consol	Agip Carbone (Italy) and Consolidated Coal (USA)	1981	774,200
Kaltim Prima Coal	Rio Tinto and BP (Multinationals)	1982	790,900
Adaro	Enadimsa (Spain)	1982	148,148
Kideco	Consortium of Korean companies	1982	254,804
Berau	Mobil Oil (USA) and Nissho Iwai (Japan)	1983	487,217
Chung Hua	EMRO and Tai Power (Taiwan)	1985	150,300
Allied Indo Coal	Transfield (Australia) and Mitra Sakti (domestic)	1985	844
Multi Harapan Utama	Several including Swabara (Australia) 40%	1986	189,954
Tanito Harum	Kiki Barki (Chinese Indonesian)	1987	123,846
Indominco Mandiri	Salim Group (Chinese Indonesian)	1990	100,000

Source: Friederich and van Leeuwen (2017, 60).

The Roots of Resource Nationalism

Throughout colonial occupation, the independence era, and through much of the New Order period as well, foreign capital and multinational corporations benefited enormously from Indonesia's land and resource industries. Despite the economy's dependence on foreign investment—indeed, in many ways because of it—consecutive governments pursued a range of nationalist economic interventions to try to nurture domestic capital. In the land and resource sectors specifically, the New Order state acted as an incubator for the development of capital, compelling foreign and state companies to partner with and purchase from a small clique of business elites, usually with close ties to the regime. Cronyism and clientelism remained the organizing logic of state-business relations and underpinned the expansion of local private business into the mining, oil and gas, timber, and palm oil industries. The result was a growing but largely dependent capitalist class with limited policy power in the context of a strong state and sustained reliance on foreign investment, particularly in oil, gas, and mining.

The market-cycle theory has much explanatory power when it comes to this period of Indonesian history, with the New Order government providing more opportunities to local firms when the economy was doing well off the back of booming oil prices. To be sure, such efforts invariably favored particular sections of capital. Suharto cultivated a highly collusive system in which contracts, licenses, and concessions were distributed to business interests with close connections to the center of politicobureaucratic power—the most lucrative of which were reserved for Chinese Indonesian cronies, military generals, or the president's family members (Robison 1986). Nevertheless, by the late Suharto years, the structure of capital was gradually changing. Andrew MacIntyre (1991) even argued that in the New Order's final decade, an autonomous business class was emerging, which had begun to organize, albeit within the New Order's corporatist framework, and exert independent influence on the state's economic policies. Domestic business was playing a more prominent and directive role within policymaking networks than at the start of the New Order and was no longer as tightly anchored to the interests of senior military or politicobureaucratic elites. MacIntyre's seminal work on state-business relations did not deal specifically with the plantation or resource industries. But there were signs here too that the government was dealing with a more powerful domestic private sector. In logging and palm oil, big domestic private firms largely controlled production and these corporate actors began to exercise more policy influence when it came to foreign flows—for example, Suharto's decision to ban foreign investment into palm oil plantations in the late 1990s was at the behest of domestic tycoons.

The New Order political economy and the business groups to which that system gave rise suddenly fell apart in 1997. The Thai baht collapsed and triggered a series of currency devaluations throughout Asian markets. In Indonesia, the crisis prompted capital flight, widespread defaults on bank loans, and inflation soared. The country's GDP growth plummeted while the poverty rate skyrocketed (Hill 2000). State banks and other state enterprises were bankrupted by the crisis, and many of the Chinese Indonesian tycoons with interests in extractives and plantations found themselves drowning in debt (Borsuk and Chng 2014; Chua 2008). Suharto was forced to turn to international financial institutions, the IMF and the World Bank. These institutions made loans conditional on the dismantling of monopolies, privatization of state companies, including Pertamina, and the opening of sectors like plantations to foreign investment (Pepinsky 2009). The centralized system of patronage distribution and cronyism that had buttressed the growth of Indonesia's conglomerates and resource companies appeared to be quickly crumbling.

As the economic crisis deepened, it became a political crisis, too. The public directed their anger at those businesses and families that benefited most from the New Order political economy. Latent discontent with authoritarianism and corruption transformed into a popular movement for democratic reform (Aspinall 2005). Indonesians took to the streets to demand free and fair elections and an end to "*Korupsi, Kolusi,* and *Nepotisme*" (corruption, collusion, and nepotism). After days of violent street protests, Suharto resigned on May 21, 1998.

THE NEW RESOURCE NATIONALISM

This chapter documents the rise of resource nationalism in Indonesia during the twenty-first century. It paints a picture of nationalist mobilization and policy transformation in the wake of Suharto's fall and during the global commodities boom (2003–13). The chapter also outlines the fate of nationalist policy proposals after the boom came to an end in 2014. The chapter's primary purpose is descriptive. By tracing the genesis and trajectory of three proposed nationalist changes to investment and ownership rules in each sector (mining, plantations, and oil and gas), I set up the book's main empirical puzzle: the boom triggered new and pervasive nationalist demands across the land and resource industries, but nationalist policy outcomes were highly uneven. The subnational variation elaborated in this chapter illustrates the limits of prevailing market-cycle theories and state-centric explanations for the rise and fall of resource nationalism.

Before moving into the sectoral case studies, it is important to understand the broader policy context that characterized the early post-Suharto years. This was a time of transformative political change, and in the wake of a devastating financial crisis, Indonesia's economy underwent a major program of structural adjustment as well. After Suharto's sudden resignation, a new government set about urgently redesigning economic institutions and drawing up new investment rules across a range of sectors. Under pressure from international lenders like the World Bank and the IMF and alongside advice from more liberal-oriented economists in government, the interim president, B. J. Habibie, launched a program of economic liberalization that including lifting restrictions on foreign capital and reducing the role of SOEs in the economy (Rosser 2001). The IMF forced bankrupt Indonesian banks and firms to relinquish their assets to finance spiraling debts, and those assets were then often snatched up by foreign banks and corporations. These changes generated a diffuse but also palpable public resentment toward foreign capital. Many of the IMF's loan conditions caused economic hardship for ordinary Indonesians, as state budgets were constrained, credit dried up, and prices rose when subsidies were taken away from basic goods, including petrol (Robison and Rosser 1998).

The collapse of Suharto's centralized regime also unleashed new demands for greater local control over political and economic decisions, especially in the regions that were far from the country's bureaucratic and economic centers on Java. Pro-democracy activists called not only for competitive and fair elections but also for decentralization of the political system. Such demands were especially strong in the resource-rich parts of the country. After decades of domination by the central government, district administrations wanted to have more control over, and derive more benefits from, natural resource projects (McCarthy 2004; Resosudarmo 2005). These demands were appeased by a series of laws that decentralized a significant degree of authority, political and economic, to district government for a range of business licenses and permits and that channeled a greater share of resource revenues from the central government to district and provincial governments (Laws 22/1999 and 25/1999).[1]

The decentralization of authority over land and resource governance had significant consequences for the structure of ownership in land-based resource industries, especially the mining industry, because district heads were given freedom to issue mining licenses with little oversight by the central government. Oil and gas contracts, however, remained the responsibility of the central government. Although licenses for plantations remained tied to the central National Land Agency as well, local governments were given new rights to issue a range of other business and land use licenses relevant for palm oil companies. As this chapter will show, resource nationalist demands that surrounded new sectoral bills were in some instances a reaction against decentralization and the resultant explosion of concessions and companies (both foreign and domestic) that were approved by local authorities.

It was against this backdrop of liberal economic reform and decentralization that Indonesia experienced the twenty-first century's global commodity boom. In the mid-2000s, the price of coal, minerals, palm oil, and oil—Indonesia's major commodity exports—began to rise. This fortuitously timed boom would help drive economic growth for the next decade while also motivating lawmakers to rethink the rules surrounding ownership and control of strategic land and extractive projects. This chapter details how the mining sector experienced the most nationalist policy intervention. The government introduced new and increasingly restrictive rules for foreign capital as part of a new mining law introduced in 2009 and a revised version that was introduced in 2020. When it came to plantations, the government bent to the IMF's demands for complete liberalization of the foreign investment rules. In the decades that followed, demands to reverse this intervention through two new sectoral bills largely failed despite lobbying by parliamentarians and sections of the domestic business community to include caps on foreign investment. Finally, in the oil and gas sector, attempts to revise the 2001 Oil and Gas Law and enshrine privileged access for Pertamina, the state-owned enterprise, to expiring foreign contracts produced an extended period of policy conflict. Parliament and government lawmakers were unable to agree on either the terms of investment for foreign companies or the privileges that SOEs and domestic firms should enjoy. During these boom years, Indonesia was often painted in the foreign press as an extreme case of resource nationalism; the picture that emerges in this chapter is one of significant subnational variation, which was distinct from historical patterns and difficult to explain using prevailing market-cycle paradigms.

Mineral and Coal Mining:
A Slow Nationalization

In an interview in June 2014, PDI-P politician Sonny Keraf explained that "the nation is sacred," and this sacred quality gives the government of a nation a special right to exploit its mineral wealth. He continued, "We as a nation decide who can come here and use our resources and under what rules. Boom or no boom, we don't care. If you don't like our conditions, then just leave." As the former deputy head of parliamentary Commission VII on energy, mineral resources, and environmental affairs, Sonny had been a key figure in the design of, and debates over, Law 4/2009 on Mineral and Coal Mining (the 2009 Mining Law). His remarks to me captured well the mood of public debate over this law, especially in the years following the law's implementation. One of the major goals of the 2009 Mining Law was to enable local ownership of Indonesia's mines. Many industry analysts cast the new and more nationalist regulatory framework as a response to rising commodity prices, as had been the case historically, and so they believed Indonesia's policy pendulum would swing back toward a liberal pro-foreign investment regime when prices dropped, and the state would again start courting foreign investors.

However, resource nationalism persisted beyond the boom. In this section, I demonstrate how, as commodity prices soared, nationalist mobilization in the mining sector rose in tandem. A consensus grew among a wide range of state and private sector actors that the time had come for foreign-owned mines to be incrementally handed over to local companies. Once the boom ended in 2013, incoming president Joko Widodo (Jokowi) faced a more challenging set of economic circumstances, but the nationalist momentum endured. In 2020, the government penned another new mining law. This new law was introduced amid the global pandemic that emerged in 2020, which brought about immense economic uncertainty and constrained sources of state revenue.[2] But the revised law upheld the most nationalist aspects of the old 2009 law, and heavily favored the country's domestic mining companies.

Booming Mines, Rising Nationalism

The Asian financial crisis and Suharto's resignation dampened foreign interest in Indonesia's mining sector. First, the political transition brought uncertainty, which spooked investors, and many reneged on the contracts they were in the process of negotiating before Suharto stepped down. Second, Suharto's fall was accompanied by an outpouring of demands for greater regional autonomy from the central government. In the resource-rich parts of the country like Kalimantan and Sumatra, communities demanded more control over their mining commodities and more equitable distribution of resource rents (Resosudarmo 2005). The Habibie government (1998–99) responded with Law 22/1999 on Regional Governance, which stated that the "regions shall have the authority to manage national resources located in their areas and shall be responsible to conserve the environment in accordance with the laws and regulations." However, no clear detail was offered in terms of how each sector should implement this broad directive. Such legal ambiguity, combined with growing restiveness in some of the resource regions, made existing foreign investors anxious and potential investors ambivalent. For example, between 1997 and 1999, foreign investment in Indonesia's mining sector averaged US$946 million annually; between 2000 and 2003, that figure shrunk to US$60 million (Khaliq and Noy 2007, 24).

Nevertheless, the mining sector bounced back quickly. As global commodity prices began rising from 2003, so too did the volume of exports leaving Indonesian shores. According to a report by USAID (2013, 7), the country's "bauxite exports rose fivefold between 2008 and 2011, while copper concentrate exports increased eleven-fold, and exports of laterite nickel ore increased eightfold in the same period." Coal exports grew at a remarkable pace, too. In 1996, Indonesia produced approximately 50 million tons of coal; by 2010, that figure had risen to just over 210 million tons (Indonesia Investments 2018; Lucarelli 2010, 31). A large portion of Indonesia's coal and minerals were destined for China and India, whose rapid industrial growth spurred global demand and sent prices soaring.

The boom helped drive impressively high gross domestic product growth levels in Indonesia, which averaged 6 percent between 2005 and 2011 (Tabor 2015, 4).

Rising demand for Indonesia's mining commodities, skyrocketing prices, and the vaguely worded directives in the regional autonomy laws all motivated lawmakers in the Ministry of Energy and Minerals to propose a new legal framework for the sector. The result was the 2009 Mining Law. The new law, which replaced the law that had governed the sector since 1967, made two crucial changes to the old system: first, the central government delegated much of the responsibility for mining licenses to district and provincial heads, which was in line with the broader program of decentralization.[3] Under the old system, only the central government had the authority to issue contracts and mining permits. Second, the law overhauled the long-established CoW system, which regulated the activities of foreign mining companies. The government decided to replace CoWs with a simple licensing system in which all mining ventures, whether large or small, foreign or domestic, received licenses.

To recall, the old contract system protected foreign companies from any change in government regulations during the life of their large long-term mining projects. With licenses, however, any changes in Indonesian laws or regulation would be applied to all license holders. The new law included an article obliging foreign companies to divest, though it was worded in the most general terms. Article 112 (1) stated that all foreign-owned mining companies had to begin divesting shares to local entities within five years of starting production. Companies were required to first offer shares to the central government, then to the regional government where the mine was located, and then to SOEs, regional-owned enterprises, and finally to private domestic companies.[4] The portion of divested shares was not specified, nor was the procedure for determining the share price. These sorts of details would be worked out by the ministry in future regulations. But the intention was to provide a legal obligation for the incremental takeover of foreign mines by local entities, starting first with the state.

When the law's details were revealed, it appeared initially to be an expression of a statist resource nationalism. But it was widely understood that the state and state-owned mining companies like Bukit Asam or Antam would not have enough capital to buy the foreign divested shares that would be up for sale in the coming years. Indeed, in the late 1990s and early 2000s, when first-generation coal contractors were obliged to sell their shares to Indonesian parties, they found it impossible to find willing buyers. For example, an American embassy report on the coal sector in 2000 described the lack of state interest in several major coal divestment deals:

> In 1999 . . . KPC offered a 30-percent share in the company at the government's agreed price of US $175 million. State mining companies—PTBA

for coal, PT Aneka Tambang for miscellaneous mining and PT Timah for tin—objected to the high price of KPC shares. . . . In another case, PT Arutmin Indonesia was obliged to divest 31 percent of its shares. In 1999, Arutmin offered 24 percent of its stock, valued at US$40 million, to local investors without success. Kideco Jaya Agung is required eventually to divest 30 percent of its shares. In 1999, Kideco was to have sold 23 percent, but received no response from buyers. (Embassy of the United States of America 2000, 11)

To be sure, these were the crisis years, and the government and SOEs were immensely credit constrained. But with no recent history of the state or state firms buying into expensive foreign mines, industry insiders viewed the new divestment regime in 2009 as a potential boon for the country's growing number of private domestic mining companies.[5]

It is important to note that divestment had long been a requirement for foreign miners in Indonesia. Throughout the Suharto era, as discussed in chapter 2, there were several generations of CoW and coal CoW (CCoW), and each generation laid out guidelines for the terms of divestment. Most of the mineral CoW required some level of divestment to local parties, but the precise details were negotiated on a case-by-case basis. For example, Freeport McMoran's first-generation contract for the Grasberg gold and copper mine signed in 1967 had no divestment obligations. Meanwhile, Newmont's fourth-generation contract, signed in 1986, required majority divestment by the twentieth year of operation. The first and second generation of CCoWs mandated foreign companies divest a majority (51 percent) of their shares after ten years. Third-generation coal contracts (1997–99), on the other hand, required just 5 percent divestment within fifteen years in a bid to attract capital into the sector at a time of crisis (Lucarelli 2010, 27). In essence, the Indonesian government tweaked the terms of each generation in order to suit the economic conditions of the time; however, once signed, each contract was protected from regulatory changes.

The new law gave the state power to set divestment terms for the industry at any point in time. Indeed, numerous implementing regulations and amendments followed the 2009 Mining Law, and with each iteration the divestment regime became increasingly nationalist. First, Government Regulation No. 23/2010 (GR 23/2010) ruled that foreign companies had to divest at least 20 percent of their business by the fifth year of production. Then, in 2012, the government shocked the foreign mining industry with Government Regulation No. 24/2012 (GR 24/2012), which compelled foreign companies to divest a minimum of 51 percent by the tenth year of production. In addition, the government confirmed that existing foreign contracts would have to be renegotiated to reflect the new divestment terms. In other words, foreign mining companies would have to sign up for the new divestment regulations, whatever the terms of their current contract. The intervention made international headlines. Industry analysts and foreign companies criticized what they viewed as a radically nationalist turn in Indonesia's investment regime. In interviews, foreign firms and diplomats of investor countries privately referred to the regulation as a "watered-down nationalization" of foreign assets. International business analysts and economists warned that such an aggressive foreign divestment framework would undermine the sector's long-term growth and hurt perceptions of Indonesia's investment climate.

Nationalism beyond the Boom

In the years that followed and as commodity prices cooled, the government struggled to revise foreign mining contracts and bring them in line with the new law. Few agreed to sign up for the new system. Instead, some companies threatened, or even took, legal action against the Indonesian government (van der Pas and Damanik 2014). Another major sticking point in these negotiations was the government's pursuit of an industrializing form of resource nationalism. The 2009 Mining Law included provisions to compel companies to process their nickel, copper, and bauxite ores on Indonesian shores prior to export (Warburton 2017a, 2017b). But few foreign companies had processing facilities or wanted to invest in building them. The government tried using processing requirements and export bans as a tool to compel companies to accept the new divestment requirements, but negotiations continued to make little progress.

So, in September 2014, as he approached the end of this final term in office, President Yudhoyono (2004–14) decided to offer foreign companies relief in a bid to fast-track and complete some of the contract negotiations. A new government regulation (GR 77/2014) made foreign companies' divestment obligations contingent on the type of mining activities they carried out. It was a complex calculation. For example, companies engaged in mineral processing only needed to divest a maximum of 40 percent; companies engaged in the more capital- and technology-intensive underground mining only had to divest a maximum of 30 percent. The goal was twofold: first, the new policy was designed to break the stalemate with the largest foreign companies and, in particular, with Freeport McMoran, which was planning an $18 billion investment in a complex underground section of its Grasberg mine. Negotiations over the company's divestment obligations had stalled for years, and the company was refusing to sign off on the new terms given the scale of the investment on which it was about to embark. Second, the new schedule for divestment also aimed to encourage companies to invest in downstream processing facilities (Junita 2015; Warburton 2018).

However, this regulation had only a brief life span. Two years later, in 2017, the new administration of President Jokowi introduced another amendment to the divestment regime. Government Regulation No. 1/2017 outlined that all foreign companies with a mining license had to divest their shares in stages and reach 51 percent Indonesian ownership by the tenth year in production. In other words, it resurrected the divestment regime the Yudhoyono government had introduced in 2012 and then revised in 2014. The government also introduced an accompanying regulation that stated foreign companies currently holding CoWs would not be allowed to export their mineral ores unless they transitioned from a contract to a mining license, as laid out under the terms of the 2009 Mining Law. The new divestment terms would apply from the date a company transitioned from its CoW to its new license.

What made this regulation particularly perplexing for the industry, and indeed for analysts of resource nationalism, was that it was introduced in the context of relatively low commodity prices (Busch 2017). From 2013, the global price of coal, copper, gold, and most other minerals experienced a significant decline, which hurt Indonesia's trade balance. When Jokowi took office, the Indonesian government was facing serious revenue shortfalls. Yet the nationalist trajectory was sustained. Overall, between 2009 and 2017, the rules governing foreign companies' divestment obligations changed four times. Each iteration (with one exception) set the sector on a more nationalist path.

Three years later, in May 2020, the Jokowi administration and the national parliament quite suddenly rushed through parliament an entirely revised version of the 2009 Mining Law, with little input from civil society, economists, or academic analysts and almost no public debate. The new law outlined that contracts held by the major mineral and coal companies would now enjoy automatic renewal for two ten-year periods, and concession size limits were lifted, too. The law also made the central government responsible for licensing, effectively reversing the decentralized management of mining permits outlined in the 2009 law. The new law also specifically mentioned a 51 percent divestment rule, elevating this detail from its previous status as a lower-level government regulation, which are much easier for ministries to change or overrule. However, no time period for reaching 51 percent local ownership was stipulated, which effectively meant the details of divestment would (again) be left to the government's discretion. Still, the decision to enshrine the 51 percent divestment rule into law was remarkable.

These revisions were tabled and passed through parliament at the height of the COVID-19 pandemic and at a time when Indonesia's economy was on the brink of a technical recession—its quarterly growth rates in May were the worst since 2001 (Orji 2020). When the virus brought the world to a standstill in early 2020, Indonesia's exports decreased by 30 percent (Rajah and Grenville 2020). Yet, even though aspects of the law were clearly intended to encourage investment like enabling larger concession sizes, the deteriorating economic situation did not prompt a reversal of the law's nationalist flavor. The picture that emerges suggests, therefore, that the Indonesian government's nationalist push cannot be explained in terms of market cycles or a shift in state power vis-à-vis foreign capital.

Plantations: Opening the Door to Foreign Capital

While Indonesia was slowly closing its doors to foreign miners, the lucrative plantations sector remained open to foreign-owned companies. Like the coal and minerals sectors, the global agribusiness industry enjoyed steadily increasing prices during the first decade of the twenty-first century. Growing demand for agrocommodities from China, India, and parts of Europe motivated a new wave of FDI into the agricultural sectors of many developing, middle-income, and high-income countries. This influx of foreign capital caused consternation in some countries (Fullerton 2012; Oliveira 2013; Perrone 2013).

In Indonesia, as foreign investors moved into the booming palm oil sector during the early 2000s, nationalist demands gained little traction with policymakers in government. Throughout 2013 and 2014, the Indonesian parliament was negotiating a new law to govern the plantations sector, and nationalist protagonists lobbied the government to cap levels of FDI in land concessions for agriculture. By that time, new divestment requirements and caps on foreign investment had increased for mining, oil and gas services, and horticulture (Patunru and Rahardja 2015). Yet, notwithstanding the broader mood of nationalism in other industries and despite a history of shutting foreign firms out of commercial plantations, the demands of nationalist advocates largely failed to generate policy change when it came to the rules governing ownership and investment in this sector.

A Nationalist Proposal Fails

At the turn of the twenty-first century, Indonesia's plantation sector underwent a program of liberalization following a long history of protectionism and anti-foreign policies (explained in chapter 2). The Asian financial crisis forced the Indonesian government to throw its agricultural industries open to foreign capital. In 1998, the IMF issued Indonesia a letter of intent that outlined conditions for a $43 billion bailout package. That letter committed the government to a series of conditions, including lowering taxes and export restrictions on forestry and agricultural products, such as logs, timber, and rattan (Gellert 2005, 216). The letter of intent also required removal of any restriction on foreign investment in palm oil plantations.

Initially, the government tried to contest the IMF conditions. During the early stage of the crisis, Suharto "surrounded himself with identifiably 'nationalist' policy makers" and resisted many of the IMF's demands (Pepinsky 2008, 444). However, as the crisis deepened and agribusiness tycoons like Eka Tjipta Widjaja, Sudono Salim, and Bob Hasan spiraled into debt, the nationalist position advocated by parts of the Suharto administration was severely weakened (Basri and Hill 2008; Rosser 2001).

Shortly after the government changed foreign investment rules for plantations in 1999, Malaysian agrifirms swept in quickly, buying up new concessions and taking over plantations owned by debt-ridden tycoons (Borsuk and Chng 2014). As Paul Gellert (1998, 81) explains, the financial crisis and devaluation of the rupiah from Rp. 2,500 to Rp. 8,500 meant that palm oil exports were "more lucrative than ever," which in turn made the sector especially attractive for foreign investors and, thus, a target of international lenders like the IMF and World Bank. The government sustained an open foreign investment regime throughout the decade and a half following the crisis, and Indonesia's palm oil sector experienced strong growth and levels of foreign investment increased remarkably during the boom years (figure 3.1). Although FDI volumes presented in figure 3.1 are for the entire agricultural sector, the vast majority of foreign inflows are directed to oil palm plantations.

Foreign capital now played a crucial role in a sector that had previously been almost entirely controlled by Indonesian companies.[6] Over 85 percent of all FDI in Indonesia's agricultural sector between 2008 and 2016 was channeled into palm oil (Prakasa and Oxfam 2016). Most of Indonesia's other agricultural subsectors were dominated by locals. For example, in rubber and cacao, independent smallholders account for over 85 percent of production, and foreign companies play almost no role (Arifin 2013). It is only the lucrative palm oil industry that has attracted sizable foreign investments. According to one analyst, by 2004, 60 percent of Indonesia's palm oil plantations were held by foreign investors (Jiwan 2013, 52). Ten years later, in 2014, one report claimed that foreign investors held over 5 million of the total 8 million ha of dedicated palm oil lands (Adnan 2014).

Against the backdrop of high crude palm oil prices and surging FDI, the Ministry of Agriculture began working with parliament to develop a new plantations law in 2014. The decision to revise the old law (Law 18/2004 on Plantations) was made initially in response to a 2010 Constitutional Court decision, which found that parts of the 2004 law criminalized smallholders and farmers for en-

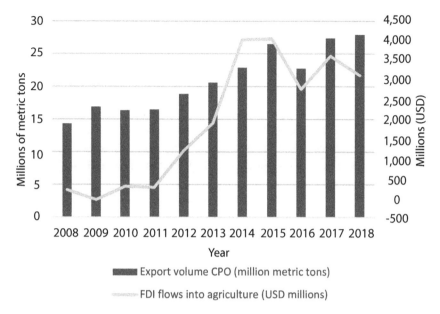

FIGURE 3.1. Export volume of crude palm oil and FDI, 2008–18

Source: Bank Indonesia (FDI flows) and Indonesian Statistics Agency (BPS)

tering company lands and was, therefore, unconstitutional. The decision forced the law back to parliament for revision. During parliamentary deliberations, a coalition of legislators from various political parties took the opportunity to propose a cap of 30 percent on foreign ownership of plantation companies (HukumOnline.com 2014). The bill would apply to the entire plantations sector. However, the proposed cap clearly targeted the palm oil subsector where foreign capital constituted a far greater share of investment than, for example, rubber or cacao. Press coverage of the bill focused almost exclusively on the impact it would have on palm oil. One international media outlet described the bill as follows: "Ostensibly, the intent is to allow smaller local [palm oil] players to participate in a sector presently dominated by large companies, many of which are listed giants from Malaysia and Singapore. Under possible new legislation, existing foreign players would be given up to 5 years to pare down their shareholdings" (*Nikkei Asian Review* 2014a). Like the divestment clause in the 2009 Mining Law, this article in the bill contradicted the 2007 Investment Law, which protected foreign investors from caps, restrictions, or divestment. The proposal, if it were realized, would also conflict with the Foreign Investment Board's Negative Investment List, which at the time determined the sectors where foreigners could invest and specified how much equity they could hold in a company operating in that sector. The list stipulated foreigners could own up to 95 percent of an agricultural company, conditional on recommendation from the Ministry of Agriculture.

Foreign press linked the plantations bill to other anti-foreign interventions emerging in other sectors (Adnan 2014; Beckmann and Rakhmatillah 2014; McBeth 2014b; Zadek et al. 2014). Headlines warned that the resource nationalist character of the 2009 Mining Law and its implementing regulations was now spreading from the mining to the plantations sector (McBeth 2014; *Nikkei Asian Review* 2014b; Reuters 2014; Taylor and Supriatna 2014). There was some truth to such analyses: those who worked on the plantations law explained in interviews that inspiration had indeed come partly from changes in the mineral mining sector.[7] Parliamentary Commission IV had also introduced a new law on horticulture earlier in 2014, which included a similar cap on foreign investment. Legislators felt the same sorts of caps on foreign capital should be applied to plantations where foreign ownership—at least in the palm oil sector—was in fact much higher.[8]

Although parliamentarians initially proposed the cap on foreign investment, the clause reflected a broader nationalist thrust in the Ministry for Agriculture's policy goals as well. The ministry laid out a strategic plan for 2009–14 that emphasized food and agricultural independence and prioritized local produce over imports (Ministry for Agriculture 2009; Patunru and Rahardja 2015). The minister at the time, Suswono, was a senior member of the Partai Keadilan Sejahtera (Prosperous Justice Party, PKS), an Islamic party known for taking a nationalist position on resource issues generally and whose faction in parliamentary Commission IV supported the foreign investment cap.

Nor was the 2014 bill the first effort by the ministry to facilitate more local ownership in the palm oil sector. In 2013, a ministerial regulation outlined that all foreign palm oil companies collaborating with farmers' cooperatives should divest a minimum 30 percent of their shares to the cooperative after fifteen years (Ministry of Agriculture Regulation 98/2013 on Plantation Licensing). The government's intention was to empower local farmers and redistribute more of the commercial benefits from the palm oil industry to smaller-scale farmers. By most accounts, however, there was no attempt to enforce the new policy. The Palm Oil Farmers Association (Apkasindo) publicly complained that the regulation was essentially redundant because farmers had no means and no knowledge of how to buy such shares (Kontan 2013). In interviews, the industry peak body, Gabungan Pengusaha Kalapa Sawit (Association of Palm Oil Companies, GAPKI), along with other stakeholders active in the industry, had limited knowledge of the regulation and showed little understanding or concern for its consequences.[9] Moreover, by 2014, the ministry's energy was focused on the content of the new plantations law and on restricting FDI through an alternative legal mechanism.

In the end, however, when the plantations bill was signed into law in September 2014, the paragraph outlining a 30 percent cap on foreign investment had, quite suddenly, been dropped despite strong support in parliament and, at least initially, the backing of the minister. Instead, the final version of the law outlined in the most general terms that foreign investment levels would be detailed in future government regulations.

An Unsuccessful Second Attempt

The following year, in 2015, parliament began deliberating a separate bill for the palm oil sector. This was a newly inaugurated parliament (2014–19) that began its term after the 2014 Plantations Law was finalized. Several key advocates for the cap on foreign investment in the plantations law were reelected, and they turned their attention to designing a separate bill that would specifically govern the palm oil subsector. There were several justifications for the initiative: first, legislators argued that the country's most lucrative export sector was unique and it faced a plethora of complex regulatory challenges associated with permitting, land conflict, labor, and downstream industrialization that necessitated a separate law. Second, protagonists argued that a new bill was necessary to "protect against foreign influence" (Julianto 2016).

One of the bill's most vocal supporters was Firman Soebagyo, the deputy chair for parliamentary Commission IV (2014–19) and a member of Golkar. He appeared regularly in the press throughout the bill's deliberation speaking of the need to regulate against the domination of Indonesia's land by large conglomerates and to prevent the expansion of foreign ownership in the palm oil sector. At a public event in March 2017, Firman stated that "there are certain parties that hold a big monopoly over land. This is the legacy of history, and the result of the [Asian] financial crisis when lots of Indonesia's land was sold out" (Brapetky 2017). He went on to explain that he had "requested the government to place limits on foreign shareholding in the palm oil industry" because troubled Indonesian companies were selling down their shares to foreign investors. Firman made public promises that a new sectoral bill would place a cap on foreign shareholding in Indonesian palm oil companies and thus accomplish what the 2014 Plantations Law had not.

Firman and other nationalist advocates also framed the bill as a necessary tool for undermining the Indonesia Palm Oil Pledge (IPOP), which was signed in 2015 by the largest palm oil producers (Mongabay 2016). Firman argued that the pledge, which committed signatories to achieving zero deforestation in their supply chains, was a boon for big palm oil but killed small and medium-size domestic companies that would be unable to meet the high sustainability standards set by the pledge. IPOP was, in the eyes of nationalists, a foreign attack on Indonesia's middle-rung domestic enterprises.

GAPKI supported the idea of a sector-level law (Julianto 2016). In 2017, GAPKI's chair, Joko Supriyono, stated publicly that the association backed much of the bill's contents and that as Indonesia's most strategic sector, palm oil needed its own distinct legal umbrella (Supriyanto and Sandi 2017). Indeed, parts of the draft appeared to be written by major industry actors themselves. For example, sanctions for companies found to have neglected their environmental impact responsibilities were significantly reduced, and the bill provided all sorts of fiscal incentives to companies, too. The bill removed limits on concession sizes and also restrictions on companies expanding into precious carbon-rich peat lands (Jong 2017).[10] There was no indication, however, that GAPKI had changed its mind about the cap and divestment requirements.

The government agreed with parliamentarians' assertions about IPOP, and eventually it convinced signatories to abandon the initiative entirely (Arshad and Fogarty 2016). But once again, the government did not support legislators' demands that a cap be placed on foreign ownership in this most strategic export sector. Nor was the coordinating Ministry for the Economy keen to introduce a law that, it argued, dealt with issues already covered in existing laws, including the 2014 Plantations Law (Susanto 2018). Despite being included in the parliament's list of "priority legislation" (*prolegnas*) for the 2014–19 term, the bill was never signed into law, and at the time of writing in 2022, the draft continues to sit in the prolegnas with seemingly little momentum behind it. Thus, against the backdrop of both price booms and price deflations, the commercial plantations sector continued to welcome, rather than constrain, foreign capital.

Oil and Gas: A State of Nationalist Ambiguity

Nationalist demands in this sector revolved around revisions to a sectoral law that was established in the wake of the Asian financial crisis: the 2001 Oil and Gas Law. As one part of the broader package of economic reforms rolled out by the new post-Suharto government, this law removed Pertamina's regulatory powers and the downstream monopoly it had enjoyed throughout most of the New Order period (explained in chapter 2). The law, which had been shaped in the context of significant intervention by the IMF and the World Bank, was immensely unpopular among sections of the political and bureaucratic elite. Several years after the law's implementation, Pertamina's management and their allies in government and parliament began lobbying for revisions that would reinstate Pertamina's regulatory role and, most importantly for our purposes, would provide the national oil company with privileged access to take over expiring foreign oil and gas contracts.

The boom had complex implications for the sector and for nationalist agendas. Although the boom meant oil prices were rising during the first decade of the twenty-first century, Indonesia's production volumes were dwindling fast, in turn putting both the sector and the government's budget under pressure (*Financial Times* 2008). There was, therefore, resistance to nationalist proposals among more liberal-oriented industry experts and bureaucrats, who continued to argue in favor of encouraging foreign capital as a means of expanding and propping up the struggling industry. In response, both the Yudhoyono and Jokowi governments neither entirely rejected nor fully realized nationalist demands; instead, they prevaricated, leaving the industry in a state of regulatory ambiguity.

The Statist Nationalist Backlash

Nationalist mobilization in the oil and gas sector was largely a backlash against the dramatic program of liberalization the Indonesian government pursued in the wake of the 1997 Asian financial crisis. Understanding the nature of that reform process is critical for understanding the nationalist policy conflicts that emerged in the years that followed. The IMF's bailout package for Indonesia was contingent on a set of reforms that included restructuring Pertamina, which for decades had functioned as the industry regulator, an oil producer, and as the country's major downstream petroleum distributor (chapter 2). The World Bank was also pushing the government to transform Pertamina into a purely commercial entity, rather than the industry regulator, so it could compete with private companies "on equal footing" (World Bank 2000, 20).

Such proposals were initially met with fierce opposition from Pertamina and conservative bureaucrats within the Ministries of Energy and Mining and SOEs. Opponents tried to mobilize members of the legislature to prevent the reform program from becoming law.[11] But then in 1999, PricewaterhouseCoopers (PwC) performed an independent audit of Pertamina, and several damning sections of the report were leaked to the media. The public learned that from April 1996 to March 1999, Pertamina had unaccounted losses of US$5 billion due to "embezzlement, illegal commissions, price mark-ups on procurement contracts, gross inefficiency and incompetence" (ICIS News 1999). PwC's audit revealed the extent to which Indonesia's national oil company had been "pillaged by the Suharto's and their cronies" (*Jakarta Post* 2000).

The report's findings discredited the efforts of statist nationalists and their campaign to stop slated reforms to the state-owned giant and bolstered support for reform and liberalization of the sector. In response to the report, President Abdurahman Wahid[12] (1999–2001) appointed Baihaki Hakim, former president of Caltex Pacific Indonesia, as the new CEO of Pertamina, and industry veteran Purnomo Yusgiantoro as minister and gave them both full authority to implement PwC's and the World Bank's recommendations. In 2001, a new oil and gas law was introduced, which reorganized the sector and shifted the locus of power away from Pertamina. The new law removed Pertamina's regulatory responsibilities, denying the company access to much of the on- and off-budget revenue streams it had enjoyed for decades. An independent body was established to take over Pertamina's regulatory tasks: the Badan Pelaksana Kegiatan Usaha Hulu Minyak dan Gas (Regulatory Body for Upstream Oil and Gas Activities, BP Migas). BP Migas was quasi-independent. It was a nonprofit state-owned legal entity entirely separate from Pertamina. BP Migas formally sat outside of the executive branch of government, though the legislative and executive arms of government had control over the appointment of its director.

Under the new law, the production-sharing contract (PSC) system (chapter 4) remained the same, but Pertamina no longer signed and monitored upstream companies' contracts (Wolf 2009, 33). Instead, all foreign and private companies' contracts, operational reports and plans, taxes and fees were managed by BP Migas (HukumOnline.com 2010). Even Pertamina now had to have its contracts and work plans approved by BP Migas. The law also liberalized the import and distribution of petroleum products and the rules around refining, storage, and transport, which meant in theory Pertamina no longer had a monopoly over downstream sales. The reality, however, was that the company managed to retain its dominance over the retail of petroleum products due to its sprawling infrastructure across the archipelago (PricewaterhouseCoopers 2016). This was where the company was able to maintain its revenue flows following the sector's restructuring process.

Pertamina's corporate strategy from 2004 onward, after being formally incorporated, was to acquire stakes in existing blocks and take over expiring foreign-operated blocks. This was a less risky strategy than investing in exploration activities, which required immense capital with no guarantee of reward. Under the terms of Government Regulation No. 35/2004, which was an implementing regulation for the 2001 Oil and Gas Law, Pertamina must engage in tenders and make applications to take over or participate in operation contracts in the same manner as private companies. This system, since its inception, irked many within Pertamina. Senior managers argued the government should offer formal assistance to Pertamina in order to help expand its share of the country's upstream oil and gas resources. The SOE's leadership maintained that government support should come in the form of "privileges or special rights" to expiring foreign blocks (RMOL.Co 2011). Pertamina wanted a right of first refusal. Under this system, an expired contract for a foreign-operated block would be offered first to Pertamina and the company would then decide whether it wanted to run the block, engage in a joint operating contract with the existing or new operator, or sell down its 100 percent share to other companies.

Successive Pertamina CEOs and senior management lobbied for this kind of system. Former CEOs Widya Purnama (2004–6), Ari Soemarno (2006–9), Karen Agustiawan (2009–14), and Dwi Soedjipto (2014–17) all publicly supported the idea of having a right of first refusal (Damayanti 2010; *Energia* 2014; *Oil and Gas Financial Journal* 2007). The company's leaders made regular appeals to the government by pointing out Pertamina's poor production levels relative to the multinational giants operating in Indonesia, like Chevron and ExxonMobil, and implored the government to enshrine a first right for the SOE to take over expiring foreign contracts.[13] Furthermore, proponents argued, if Pertamina was to compete in terms of size and profits with other state oil companies like Malaysia's Petronas or Brazil's Petrobras, then it would need more in the way of direct government support (Detikfinance 2013b).

Pertamina's leaders worked behind the scenes and leveraged a network of loyalists in the bureaucracy and the parliament in an endeavor to realize their goal of a first right. This approach reflected an established set of practices the company had employed during the New Order. For decades, the company had been a central cog in Suharto's patrimonial political regime, and it had built up a web of loyal clients throughout the state that it continued to mobilize in the post-Suharto era in service of its nationalist agenda. This network lobbied behind the scenes to convince lawmakers in the ministry and the parliament and the bureaucrats in the oil and gas regulator BP Migas to support the company's bid for specific oil and gas blocks and to support its formalized right of first refusal.[14] A former chair of the parliamentary Commission VII on energy and natural resources stated in an interview that Pertamina had staunch supporters in the parliament and bureaucracy, and although small in numbers, "they bark[ed] the loudest."[15]

Still, this strategy achieved little during the Yudhoyono years. Draft regulations on Pertamina's first right were kicked around the corridors of the Ministry for Energy and Mineral Resources for years but were never formalized. For example, in June 2009, the ministry drafted a regulation that according to Minister Purnomo Yusgiantoro (2000–9), outlined the state oil company's privileged right to expiring foreign contracts. The director general for oil and gas at the time, Evita Legowo, also stated publicly that the draft regulation was complete and simply awaited the minister's approval (Detikfinance 2009). However, the regulation never came to be and seemed to disappear from the ministry's agenda after President Yudhoyono won his second term in office in 2009.

By 2012, nationalist protagonists refocused their energy on achieving legal changes via a different avenue. That year, a coalition of thirty public figures and intellectuals together with twelve civil society organizations brought a case to the Constitutional Court. Indonesia's second largest Islamic organization, Muhammadiyah, spearheaded the case, but representatives from Nahdlatul Ulama, the largest Islamic organization, were also participants (Habir 2013). Pertamina-affiliated actors from the company's labor union (Federasi Serikat Pekerja Pertamina Bersati [FSPPB]) formed a key part of the coalition, and prominent economists like Kwik Gian Kie and Rizal Ramli also gave evidence against BP Migas. Although Pertamina did not formally participate in the case, it was widely understood that sections of the company's leadership had endorsed, if not financed, the initiative.[16]

The plaintiffs claimed BP Migas had undermined state control over natural resources, as mandated by Article 33 of the constitution. The regulator had instead "opened the door to liberalisation" (*Tempo Magazine* 2012), they argued, and was acting in the interests of foreign companies, rather than in the interest of the nation (HukumOnline.com 2015). In a decision that stunned the industry, the court found in favor of the plaintiffs and ruled the regulator be dissolved immediately. The court based its decision primarily on Article 33 of the constitution and found that "BP Migas's statutory functions were insufficient to constitute state 'control' of the sector" (Butt and Siregar 2013, 168). The majority also argued that the 2001 Oil and Gas Law undercut state control by denying state actors the capacity to directly appoint "state agencies or corporations in exploiting oil and gas reserves. . . . [Instead] the Law required them to go 'through the proper competition and market mechanism'" (Butt and Siregar 2013, 113). The court's decision clearly favored the statist nationalist position and supported Pertamina's claim to special dispensations. The government quickly set up an interim regulatory body, SKK Migas, that would perform the functions of the now defunct BP Migas. Parliament, meanwhile, now had the task of drafting a new oil and gas law.

Nationalist Tensions and Regulatory Stalemate

Efforts to revise Indonesia's oil and gas law were wracked by conflict and competing interests. Deliberations in parliament dragged on for years, and at the time of writing in early 2022, the government and parliament had still not agreed on the law's final form. In interviews, legislators and legal advisers working on the bill said that two points of contention dominated the years-long debates in Commission VII: Pertamina's privileged access to expiring foreign contracts and the question of what form a new regulator should take, including whether BP Migas's regulatory responsibilities should be returned to Pertamina, which would mean resurrecting the New Order system.[17]

Between the court's decision in 2012 and the end of President Yudhoyono's period in office in 2014, no progress was made. The sector during this time became the subject of a major corruption investigation. In 2013, the Corruption Eradication Commission (KPK) named the minister for energy and mineral resources, Jero Wacik, and the head of SKK Migas, Rudi Rubiandini, along with the head of Commission VII, Sutan Bahtoegana, as suspects in several corruption cases involving bribes taken during oil and gas tenders with both foreign and domestic firms (Berita Satu 2013). Speculation included rumors that Indika Energy, one of the country's major domestic coal mining companies, was involved in the scandal. The investigation derailed the parliamentary deliberations over a new oil and gas bill.

In 2014, the new Jokowi government and the new parliament inherited the task of revising the sector's regulatory and investment architecture. In 2015, the Ministry for Energy and Mineral Resources tried to offer some clarity for current and potential investors with Ministerial Regulation No. 15/2015. The regulation stated that Pertamina had the right to "request" an expiring work area. If the existing foreign contractor wished to extend the contract, the ministry, together with SKK Migas, would evaluate both companies' proposals and a decision would be made based on "national interest." The regulation also stated that if the government decided to extend the foreign company's contract and reject Pertamina's proposal, then Pertamina would be offered a "maximum" 15 percent participating interest in the block.

The regulation left Pertamina's advocates unsatisfied. The language did not clarify whether Pertamina did in fact now have a legally binding first right to an expiring foreign-operated block and outlined only a maximum, rather than minimum, participating interest. The head of Commission VII in parliament at the time, Kardaya Warnika, stated in the press that the new regulation "gave no legal certainty to Pertamina that it would be given control of expired foreign-operated oil and gas blocks" (*Tempo* 2015). Pertamina leadership was not convinced by the 2015 regulation either and, in response, began articulating the state company's demands for greater privilege with increasing confidence and conviction. In Pertamina's 2016 annual report, for example, the company wrote,

> The amendment of the laws for oil and gas is expected to return oil and gas from being market commodities back to strategic commodities controlled by the state to uphold energy independence and sovereignty. The amendment will strengthen Pertamina's position as the national oil company (NOC) to represent the state in controlling strategic oil and

gas resources and infrastructure. As a representative of the state, Pertamina should be prioritized in managing domestic oil and gas blocks and encouraged to expand to overseas blocks. The priority includes the right of priority to new blocks offered, the right of priority to existing contracts and the right of priority to expiring contracts.

But the statist nationalist campaign in support of Pertamina's privilege did not compel the government or the parliament to finalize the law in the SOE's favor. Importantly, in other sectors, the government had been comfortable formalizing similar sorts of privileges for state-owned enterprises. In the electricity sector, for example, the 2009 Electricity Law gave the state-owned provider, Perusahaan Listrik Negara (PLN), a right of first refusal to supply electricity, taking precedence over private and commercial entities (Tharakan 2015). Yet, successive governments were ambivalent about embracing nationalist demands in the country's oil and gas. The result was perpetual legal ambiguity.

Booms, Busts, and Nationalist Variation

Each of Indonesia's strategic commodity export sectors enjoyed a remarkable boom in the mid-2000s. Conventional theories of resource nationalism predict that booms will trigger a nationalist response from state bureaucrats. The logic is that market shocks like a boom alter the power balance between states and foreign firms, giving states the upper hand and leaving foreign firms more vulnerable to policy interventions and contractual changes. In these nationalist conflicts between states and foreign firms, bureaucrats are often cast as shortsighted, myopic, and even corrupt. When faced with cross-country variation, meanwhile, studies have identified weak rule of law and governments' ideological leanings as the main drivers of nationalist change and the reason for why booms can generate very different policy paths around the world. In other words, the source of nationalist change and variation is traced back to the state: weak state institutions and the myopic bureaucrats that inhabit them.

In many ways, Indonesia would appear to confirm such characterizations of a resource nationalist state. Laws are routinely revised and replaced, corruption is pervasive throughout many parts of its political economy, and the country's history of colonial exploitation and foreign control of export industries has imbued politicians, policymakers, and the public with a palpable antagonism toward foreign capital. Indeed, as commodity prices rose throughout the first decade of the twenty-first century, new nationalist demands intensified.

But as this chapter has documented, there was much variation at the sector level. State managers were frequently ambivalent about the consequences of nationalist change, and nationalist demands were met with very different sorts of policy responses. In the mining sector, calls to reduce the role of foreign investors were channeled into law, and new regulatory pressures squeezed out many of Indonesia's foreign miners and made the sector far less attractive to new overseas investors, too. Despite tumbling commodity prices from 2013 onward, the Indonesian government maintained the nationalist position. In Indonesia's plantations sector, nationalist advocates opposed the monopolization of plantation land by giant conglomerates and foreign investors and argued local capital needed more protection from the state. But despite years of lobbying by parliamentarians, nationalist demands were largely disregarded by state managers and policymakers and the sector remained open to almost 100 percent foreign ownership. In the oil and gas sector, meanwhile, statists often seemed on the verge of policy victory; however, the government's ambivalence about reinstating Pertamina's privileges led to protracted policy conflict and ambiguity, both during the commodities boom and extending into the postboom period.

The distinct nationalist trajectories described in this chapter provide a striking indication that resource nationalism in Indonesia is not tethered to global prices, as market cycles predict. Nor can these outcomes be attributed solely to the actions of a more confident state flexing its muscle and exerting its new bargaining power over foreign firms. Instead, in each sector, nationalist demands met with very different policy results: some demands were discounted, some were acted on, and some were pursued with vigor well beyond the boom. As the following chapters will demonstrate, these distinct nationalist outcomes must be understood in the context of an increasingly assertive and politically influential class of domestic resource firms, whose regulatory preferences shaped the form and fate of nationalist change.

4

THE RISE OF DOMESTIC BUSINESS

Why, facing similar sorts of nationalist demands, did Indonesia's government take different policy paths across the country's strategic commodity industries? This chapter compares mining and plantations and makes the case that domestic business interests played a decisive role in determining the distinct nationalist trajectories of laws and regulations in each sector. I shift the analytical focus away from the state as the primary locus of resource nationalism and in doing so, demonstrate the expanding policymaking power of Indonesia's domestic business class. Drawing on concepts developed in the new wave of firm-centered comparative political economy research discussed in chapter 1 (Bauerle Danzman 2020; Fairfield 2015), this chapter provides an empirical account of Indonesian business actors' instrumental and structural power in the mining and palm oil industries, illustrating how such policy power grew against the backdrop of a resources boom and a new democratic political economy characterized by increasing electoral costs and widespread clientelism.

To substantiate the argument, I draw on a range of data, including on the ownership of major extractive and palm oil contracts, together with the public statements of industry associations and major firms, interviews with representatives of peak bodies and companies, industry consultants, and senior bureaucrats and politicians who were heavily involved in negotiating the sectoral laws described in chapter 3. I show how many prominent business elites of the Suharto period used these sectors to rebuild the wealth they had lost during the Asian financial crisis. Many still had enough capital (and political connections) to acquire relatively cheap coal or plantation oil licenses, and the decentralization laws designed to give regional governments greater control over land and resource industries in fact provided these businesses with new and ready access to concessions and licenses at the local level. As a result, new and lucrative relationships formed between powerbrokers and businesspeople in the regions and major business actors in Jakarta; the former became rich, but it was most often the latter who had the capacity to acquire the land and source the capital necessary to make long-term investments in mining and plantation concessions. As commodity prices soared in the mid-2000s, so too did private sector profits. In the first decade of the twenty-first century, extractives and plantations also became increasingly central to the state's foreign exchange and export revenue. The top tier of domestic business elites, thus, came to enjoy more policy power than at any previous point in these sectors' development.

To be sure, business was not entirely unconstrained in its capacity to determine the fate of the country's strategic resource projects. This chapter highlights the heated debates among state managers about the terms of investment in both sectors, and there were parts of the 2009 Mining Law and 2014 Plantations Law that domestic firms opposed, in particular around limits to concession size and ownership concentration. The next chapter also details how, in particular contexts, broader developmental concerns and politicians' sensitivity to public opinion drove nationalist interventions that favored state-owned over private business. Overall, however, this chapter's main contention is that in the mining and plantations industries, nationalizing efforts largely prevailed or failed contingent on the preferences of major domestic business interests. This observation suggests a critical shift in the relative power of state and private capital in these sectors such that local business has evolved from its largely dependent status to an increasingly powerful and decisive policy actor. The rest of this chapter is divided into two main sections: the first on mining and the second on plantations. Each section begins by detailing the entry and/or expansion of domestic enterprise into coal, minerals, and palm oil during the post-Suharto period, and then moves on to explain growing business policy power against the backdrop of the boom and Indonesia's evolving democratic setting. Finally, each section traces the role that business actors played in nationalist debates over each sectoral law.

A Nationalist Force: Indonesia's New Mining Giants

Indonesia's mining sector, and in particular the coal subsector, gradually began evolving toward greater domestic ownership during the early 2000s boom. When coal prices began rising after 2004, a handful of local business elites had already managed to buy into several strategic foreign-operated mines, and their investments quickly began to turn a profit. As the boom took off, local miners enjoyed new and immense wealth, and with that wealth came structural power and political influence. Indonesia's emerging mining giants became influential advocates for greater localization of the mining sector, beyond just coal and into precious minerals like gold and copper. This section traces the rise of Indonesia's miners, elaborates their close—indeed often direct—connections to the world of politics, and demonstrates their role as advocates for resource nationalism both during and after the boom.

Changing Patterns of Ownership: The Rise of Domestic Coal Giants

Historically, the mineral, coal, and energy industries were the terrain of foreign investors because they required capital investments of the sort that domestic players were unable to provide (chapter 2). During the New Order, Indonesia's tycoons mostly built their empires in the timber, tobacco, property, food, retail, and finance industries (Carney and Hamilton-Hart 2015; Mackie 2003). But a shift began to take place in the late 1990s, and despite the Asian financial crisis—in fact, in some ways *because* of the crisis—domestic ownership of Indonesian mines expanded rapidly in the post-Suharto period.

The coal sector experienced the most dramatic shift in ownership structures. The growth of a domestic coal industry is crucial to Indonesia's story of resource nationalism. After the financial crisis in 1998, Indonesian businesses began competing fiercely for the spoils of an industry that at the turn of the century became far more accessible to domestic capital. First, the decentralization of resource management as part of Indonesia's democratic reforms made operations increasingly difficult for foreign investors, with unpredictable and overlapping regulations and taxes between local and central authorities emerging across the country. Some foreign investors decided to sell down or sell out to local players. Against this backdrop, between 1997 and 2000, the government offered a third-generation CCoW, and with little foreign interest, the majority of the 114 contracts offered during this period went to domestic companies (Lucarelli 2010, 27).

Most importantly, in the early 2000s, the largest foreign-owned coal concessions—including BP and Rio Tinto's Kaltim Prima Coal (KPC), New Hope Mining's Adaro, BHP's Arutmin, and Korea-based coal company Kideco—all entered the period in which they were contractually obliged, under the terms of their CCoWs drawn up during the New Order period, to begin divesting to local parties. These divestments were, according to their contracts, scheduled to take place around the time the financial crisis broke out or in the years that followed. State-owned companies were poorly positioned to acquire these major mines given the impact of the crisis on the state budget and the program of SOE privatization that was being pushed by international lenders at the time. Domestic businesspeople were also struggling to pay off massive debts. Divestment deals were, therefore, initially hard for foreign miners to finalize.

For example, although KPC should have begun divesting shares to local firms in 1996, the government was forced to delay divestment for five years because there were no buyers able to meet the agreed-on share price (*Tempo Magazine* 2002). Arutmin and Kideco similarly struggled to attract buyers when they tried to divest shares because the price was too high for local business (Embassy of the United States of America 2000, 11). Such delays became the object of media attention and public critique. The hardship inflicted on the public by the IMF's austerity measures and liberal reforms generated anger with foreign intervention and foreign capital, in turn putting pressure on the government to speed up the divestment of foreign mines and compel multinational companies to let local firms in and, in the words of a *Tempo Magazine* report (2002), ensure that finally "the output of the mining sector delivers prosperity to the indigenous community."

With pressure mounting on the government to finalize these divestment deals, a small handful of New Order tycoons were eventually able to leverage state banks loans and pool resources from their remaining assets to buy into major coal concessions. Aburizal Bakrie was one of the primary beneficiaries of foreign coal divestments. Bakrie is the son of one of Indonesia's most successful indigenous entrepreneurs (mentioned briefly in chapter 2). Bakrie expanded the family business, Bakrie Brothers, during the New Order and it became a sprawling conglomerate with interests in property, media, infrastructure, and agribusiness. He had a close relationship to senior figures within Suharto's government and within state-owned enterprises, too, which during the New Order ensured access to profitable contracts in oil and gas services, infrastructure, and plantations (Robison and Hadiz 2004, 60). Bakrie became chair of the Indonesian Chamber of Commerce (KADIN) in 1993 and held the position until 2003, making him one of the most influential pribumi businesspeople of the Suharto period and early democratic period, too.

Following the financial crisis, Bakrie's companies fell deep into debt. But within a few years, the tycoon was making a comeback through inroads into the resources industries and especially coal. In 2000, Bakrie established a new company, Bumi Resources, and via a series of favorable divestment deals, Bumi acquired Indonesia's largest and most lucrative coal mines. First, in 2001, BHP Billiton sold 80 percent of its equity in the Arutmin coal mine to Bumi for US$148 million. To finance the purchase of Arutmin, Bakrie borrowed US$100 million from the largest state bank, Bank Mandiri (Tse 2001). Under the terms of its contract, BHP was obliged to divest only 31 percent, but the company was ready to leave the Indonesian market. Coal prices at the time were sluggish, and decentralization had made mining operations in the region much more precarious, with local actors occupying and looting coal from the company's concession.

Then, in 2003, Bumi took over KPC, the largest coal mine in the world. Although the details remain murky, the media reported that BP and Rio Tinto sold their shares for far below market price, at US$500 million (*Financial Times* 2016), even though the government had earlier agreed to the price of US$822 million (*Tempo Magazine* 2006). As chair of KADIN, Bakrie was able to arrange it so that he became the formal consultant on the divestment negotiations between KPC and the government. He then used that position to offer KPC a down payment of US$40 million to secure exclusive rights to bargain with the firm for a period of six months, during which time he secured a loan from Credit Suisse First Boston (*Tempo Magazine* 2006). The bank viewed the deal as an excellent one, based on both the value of the mine and an understanding of Bakrie's privileged access to bargain with Rio Tinto, BP, and the government over the shares. After years of failing to find a domestic buyer and under increasing pressure from the government, the foreign firms finally agreed to sell despite not meeting the expected market price. On the cusp of the coal boom, therefore, and with the help of state banks and political connections, one of the major pribumi tycoons of the Suharto era had managed to acquire two of the country's—indeed the world's—largest coal mines, purchases that in the years that followed propelled him to the top of Indonesia's rich list.

Other major foreign coal mines were acquired by prominent New Order–era Indonesian tycoons. Kideco, for example, was initially owned by Samtan, a Korea-based company. An Indonesian firm, Indika Inti Corpindo, won the tender to buy a majority stake in Kideco when Samtan was obliged to divest in 2003 under the terms of its contract. Indika Inti Corpindo was a subsidiary of Indika Energy, established in 2000 by Sudwikatmono, Suharto's cousin and business partner, together with Wiwoho Basuki Tjokronegoro, founder of the Tripatra Group, an energy services company. During the New Order, Sudwikatmono was a member of the infamous "Gang of Four," which included three others of the president's most prominent business cronies—Sudono Salim, Djuhar Sutanto, and Ibrahim Risjad. Sudwikatmono held shares in several Salim-owned firms and his own businesses spanned banking, film, cement, property, and wheat. His companies had for decades enjoyed special access to government and foreign contracts because of his family connection to Suharto. But he suffered during the financial crisis and was forced to sacrifice many of his assets to the state in order to pay off enormous debts. The struggling tycoon, however, managed to rebound by entering the coal sector. Sudwikatmono merged his remaining assets with Wiwoho's in 2000, and the pair established Indika Energy. Together, they were able to leverage enough capital to purchase Kideco's shares for US$140 million, with little competition from other buyers (*Tempo Interactive* 2012). Sudwikatmono's son Agus Lasmono has run Indika since 2010, together with Wiwoho's son-in-law Wishnu Wardhana.

Adaro is another prominent international mining firm bought out by a familiar cast of New Order–era business elites. Until 2001, Adaro was 50 percent owned by the Australian company New Hope Mining, 10 percent was owned by America's Mission Energy, while the remaining 40 percent was owned by Sukanto Tanoto, one of Suharto's ethnic Chinese cronies whose interests were primarily in pulp and paper and oil and gas services. After the financial crisis in 1998, Tanoto's stake in Adaro was taken over by Deutsche Bank to finance his unpaid loans (Lim 2007). The bank then sold Tanoto's shares to PT Dianlia Setyamukti, a company owned by Edwin Soeryadjaya, the son of another prominent ethnic Chinese tycoon, William Soeryadjaya of the Astra Conglomerate (Sentana 2005). In 2005, New Hope and Mission then sold their remaining shares to Saratoga Investama Sedaya, a joint venture by a group of high-profile Indonesian businesspeople: Edwin Soeryadjaya, Theodore Permadi Rachmat, Garibaldi Thohir, Benny Subianto, and Sandiaga Uno (*Forbes* 2007). All these men were affiliated with Astra. William lost control of Astra in the mid-1990s after a series of risky and, ultimately, devastating business decisions by his other son, Edward. Edwin, however, was determined to rebuild the Soeryadjaya empire (*Forbes* 2007). Saratoga's Adaro purchase was the means through which he would do it. The businesspeople listed above either own Adaro personally or through companies they control, and they remain the majority investors in 2020 with 64.77 percent of the company's shares.[1]

So just prior to the coal boom, foreign investors had begun to exit the Indonesian coal market and domestic business elites were moving in. The boom was, thus, fortuitously timed for Indonesia's coal miners because it came on the heels of a spate of domestic takeovers. Coal brought some of the country's wealthiest tycoons back from the brink of financial disaster and reestablished their position as key economic actors in the post–New Order political economy. The divestment rules that enabled some of these takeovers had been established years, even decades, earlier by the New Order government (chapter 2). This flurry of coal acquisitions by local businesses was, therefore, in part the product of prior state efforts to nurture and support the entry of domestic business into the coal industry in the long term; however, the financial crisis also enabled this ownership shift, with foreign firms opting to leave what had become an uncertain and volatile market and in a context where coal prices were relatively depressed at the turn of the century.

Beyond coal, other mining subsectors also experienced important ownership changes during the post-Suharto period. In the nickel mining sector, for example, decentralization of resource licenses outlined in the regional autonomy laws prompted a wave of investment by new Indonesian companies. Once dominated by Canadian company Inco (which was acquired by Brazil's Vale in 2006) and the SOE PT Aneka Tambang (Antam), the minerals boom saw smaller local companies begin producing and exporting the majority of the country's nickel ore (Ministry for Energy and Mineral Resources 2011a). Indonesia produced just over 3 million tons of nickel ore in 2000, all of which came from Antam (Indonesian Mining Association 2002); by 2013, Indonesia exported 60 million tons of nickel ore, which was around 60 percent of production worldwide (*Nikkei Asian Review* 2017), and of this 60 million tons, Antam produced 11 million (Antam 2013) with the rest coming mostly from medium-size and small companies around Sulawesi and Maluku that had been set up during the boom. (Vale, the major Brazilian mining firm operating in Sulawesi exports primarily processed nickel matte rather than raw nickel ores.) For example, in Southeast Sulawesi, a center of Indonesia's nickel industry, Antam was responsible for extracting and exporting the vast majority of the province's nickel ores in the late 1990s and early 2000s; by 2011, district governments had issued nickel mining licenses to 112 companies, the majority of which were small-to-medium-size local enterprises (Ministry for Energy and Mineral Resources 2011a).

So when the 51 percent divestment requirement was introduced in 2012, the trend toward local ownership was already well underway in most mining subsectors, with almost all tin, thermal coal, and nickel production coming from domestically owned companies (World Bank 2015, 41). Between 2002 and 2009, over 75 percent of coal exports came from the six largest companies and all but one, Banpu, were majority owned by Indonesian businesses (table 4.1).

One mining subsector, however, remained stubbornly in foreign hands. In the precious minerals subsector, American, Canadian, British, and Australian companies continued to dominate exploration, exploitation, and export of Indonesian gold and copper well into the post-Suharto period and during the boom. Patterns of ownership here have long reflected an international trend whereby companies from wealthy regions—North America, the United Kingdom, and Europe—dominate global metal and mineral markets, with a handful of emerging-economy mining companies growing over the past two decades (Kooroshy, Preston, and Bradley 2014). Barriers to entry are much higher in hardrock mineral mining than they are in coal or nickel, with larger up-front capital investments and complex technologies required to excavate through hard rock and often deep underground. Coal, on the other hand, is generally extracted from soft rock, requires less complex methods, and thus has lower barriers to

TABLE 4.1. Major coal companies in Indonesia by production levels, 2019

COMPANY	OWNERSHIP	PRODUCTION (TONS)	YEAR OF DOMESTIC TAKEOVER
Kaltim Prima Coal	Bumi Resources (Bakrie Group—Aburizal Bakrie)	60,932,422	2003
Arutmin		26,441,907	2001
Adaro Indonesia	Adaro Energy (Saratoga Capital—Edwin Soeryadjaya, Theodore Permadi Rachmat, Garibaldi Thohir, Benny Subianto, and Sandiaga Uno)	51,639,864	2005
Kideco Jaya Agung	Indika Energy (Agus Lasmono Sudwikatmono, Wiwoho Basuki Tjokronegoro)	34,553,086	2003
Berau Coal	Sinar Mas Group (Widjaja family)	32,351,267	Originally joint Indonesian-foreign venture; in 2015, majority shares were bought by Sinar Mas
Borneo Indo Bara	Golden Energy Mines (Sinar Mas Group—Widjaja family)	28,310,274	2006
Bukit Asam	Bukit Asam (SOE)	28,079,881	1950
Indominco Mandiri	Indo Tambangraya Megah (Banpu, Thai energy company)	12,440,475	—
Antang Gunung Meratus	Bara Multi Sukses Sarana (joint venture between Tata Power of India and a local firm with unclear beneficial ownership)	9,676,249	1996
Indexim Coalindo	PT Indexim Investama (ownership unclear, but the president director is Guatama Hartato, who also holds senior positions in Gajah Tunggal firms, owned by Suharto-era tycoon Sjamsul Nursalim)	9,206,561	—
Multi Harapan Utama	Ownership unclear, but reports suggest the firm is majority owned by the Risjadison Group (Risjad family) and the Napan Group (Pribadi family)	9,131,253	1996
Bayan Resources	Low Tuck Kwong (Singaporean-Indonesian businessperson)	31,900,000	Acquired a range of concessions between 1994 and 2007

Sources: Production figures from the Directorate General of Mineral and Coal Mining (2019); ownership information from Orbis (2020), and domestic takeover date established using various media sources and Orbis data.

entry. The extraction of nickel ore is much the same. One longtime member of the foreign mining community in Indonesia commented in an interview that Indonesian companies were known in the industry as "surface scrapers," meaning they lacked the capacity to engage in precious mineral extraction.

By the mid-2000s, however, the wealthiest Indonesian businesspeople were increasingly looking to foreign-owned gold and copper mines as their next investment frontier. Acquiring shares in existing projects was viewed as the ideal means of entering the sector rather than via riskier and costly exploration projects. The 2009 Mining Law was thus being deliberated at a time when the country's tycoons and politically influential business players were enjoying unprecedented profits from the commodities boom. As the ministry began designing regulations to compel foreign divestment, nationalist advocates within Indonesia's mining industry routinely emphasized that local firms were *sudah mampu* or "capable now," and so it was finally time for Indonesia to take back the mines from foreign companies. Business elites and politicobusiness actors within extractive interests began circling around foreign contracts for precious gold and copper mines and lobbying for regulations that would enable access to shares. Their lobbying power intensified as Indonesia's democracy evolved.

Miners' Instrumental Power

The instrumental power of domestic mining interests increased dramatically in the post-Suharto period, enabled by the country's democratic transformation at the end of the 1990s and early 2000s. More specifically, the financial costs of electoral politics meant that political parties needed to partner with, and provide leadership positions to, wealthy business elites in order to underwrite their political activities (Mietzner 2015). The boom sent private sector profits soaring and gave business actors with resource investments new influence within policy-making circles. The reverse was also true: politicians could use their positions to extend their own private business interests or those of their allies into these rent-rich industries. During fieldwork in the resource-rich provinces of East Kalimantan and South Sumatra, it seemed that every politician I met had their own coal mine. And at the national level, it was common for politicians and senior bureaucrats to have investments in some kind of extractive venture. As a result, during the post-Suharto period, Indonesia's political parties became littered with politicobusiness elites with interests in the mining sector.

One of the most prominent examples was, of course, Aburizal Bakrie. Throughout all the divestment deals Bakrie secured and during Indonesia's crisis and democratic transition, Bakrie was chair of KADIN and was also a senior member of the Golkar party. Despite defaulting on his $1.7 billion in loans after the financial crisis, Bakrie enjoyed immense influence at KADIN, Golkar, and in government circles, and he continued to maintain assets and personal networks that, as we saw above, helped him engineer favorable loans, lines of credit, and access to licenses and contracts at below market price (*The Economist* 1999; Latul 2011). The coal boom also helped Bakrie establish his political career. In 2004, he (at least formally) stepped down from his role in the family business to take up a position in Yudhoyono's first cabinet as the coordinating minister for the economy, and then in 2005, he moved to coordinating minister for people's welfare. In 2009, he was elected chair of Golkar, a position that can only be gotten with the distribution of immense amounts of money to party leaders. Bakrie's position at the helm of Indonesia's largest political party from 2009 to 2016 was secured by his personal wealth, a large portion of which was derived from the coal boom.

A major figure in the Yudhoyono administration and chair of Partai Amanat Nasional (PAN) (2010–15), Hatta Rajasa had direct interests in the mining sector, too. Prior to entering politics at the end of the New Order, Hatta was a businessperson with investments in the oil, gas, and coal mining service industries through his Arthindo Group. Hatta was an avid proponent of the divestment obligations, and he played a prominent role in economic planning more generally during President Yudhoyono's second term.[2] Key ministries within Hatta's portfolio were held by elites who not only shared Hatta's vision for a locally owned mining industry but also had personal investments in the sector. For example, Gita Wirjawan was made trade minister in 2011 and, unlike his more liberally oriented predecessor Mari Elka Pangestu, supported more stringent divestment obligations. For example, Gita told the press in 2014 that "strategic sectors [like mining] must be free from foreign control. . . . The idea of economic nationalism is based on limiting the amount of foreign ownership within the country" (Dwiarto 2014). Gita was also a successful businessperson. He started out as an investment banker and then in 2008 established his own company, Ancora Group, with subsidiaries that invested in transport, infrastructure, mining services, and oil and gas services (Detikfinance 2008; *Jakarta Post* 2008). Ancora also purchased shares in other established Indonesian resource companies, including Bakrie's Bumi Resources (Detikfinance 2008). Two of Ancora's shareholders, Robert and Rafael Nitiyudo, went on to establish Indotan, the firm that in 2020 took over Newcrest's divested shares in the Nusa Halmahera Minerals gold mine (table 4.2).

Major coal firms also exhibited superior instrumental power by cultivating direct relationships with political actors at the center of state power. Indika Energy, the owner of the third largest coal producer Kideco Jaya Agung, had a close working relationship with President Yudhoyono during his decade in power, with members of Indika sitting on the Partai Demokrat board and making generous campaign donations as well (PWYP, unpublished; Warburton 2017b).

Wishnu, son-in-law of Wiwoho, the company's cofounder together with Sudwi-katmono, stepped down from his leadership role at Indika in 2017 to directly manage Yudhoyono's son's political campaign in Jakarta's gubernatorial elections that year.

Businesspeople behind the major coal company Adaro also entered politics directly. The company's youngest owner-director, Sandiaga Uno, transitioned to a career in politics. He took up a leadership position within Gerindra in 2015 and stepped down from his role as director at Adaro. In 2017, he ran as Gerindra's candidate for vice governor of Jakarta alongside Anies Baswedan and won. As well as defeating the incumbent, Basuki Tjahaja Purnama, the pair defeated former President Yudhoyono's son, Agus Yudhoyono, whose campaign had been managed by Wishnu of Indika. Sandiaga then went on to run for vice president alongside Prabowo Subianto in 2019, but the pair failed. More broadly, Gerindra, Prabowo Subianto's political party, is bankrolled by his brother, Hashim Djodjohadikosumo, another Suharto-era tycoon whose array of business interests include coal, energy, and palm oil (Aspinall 2015a).

The instrumental power of mining tycoons reaches into regional politics, too. Decentralization incentivized new personal business ties between national economic elites and local powerbrokers in government who now held the rights to distribute permits and licenses, generating enormous wealth for both sets of actors. Having allies in resource-rich local governments is an invaluable asset for business elites at the national level, and in many instances, decentralization ironically helped to expand the assets and wealth of national extractive elites. For example, Prabowo Subianto, chair of Gerindra and a former commander of Indonesia's Special Forces during the Suharto years, owned several mining concessions through his company, Nusantara Group, with one particularly lucrative coal mining license in East Kutai district, East Kalimantan. Prabowo acquired this concession by developing a close relationship with East Kutai's district head, Isran Noor. In 2012, after London-listed Churchill Mining deposit far beyond initial expectations, Noor revoked the company's permit and then transferred the rights to Nusantara Group (Mattangkilang 2012). Isran Noor, who then became governor of East Kalimantan in 2018, has maintained a close political relationship with Prabowo. Hatta Rajasa also cultivated close business relations with Nur Alam, one-time governor of Sulawesi Tenggara. While Hatta was minister for transport (2004–7), Nur Alam's contracting companies received considerable access to infrastructure projects across the country. Hatta also channeled investment and infrastructure projects into the province and helped fund Alam's electoral campaigns; Alam, meanwhile, provided land licenses and mining permits and ensured PAN's candidates won office all around the province (Warburton 2014).

Another example involves Aburizal Bakrie's firm Bumi Resources, which attempted to buy into Newmont's Batu Hijau copper and gold mine in 2008 when the company was contractually obliged to divest. The company's contract mandated that it first offer shares to the central government and then the local government. When the central government declined, the company entered into negotiations with the district government. But it soon became clear that the regional government had struck a deal with Bumi and that Aburizal Bakrie had arranged to finance a consortium of regional government-owned enterprises as a means of ensuring access to Newmont's shares at below market price (Alfian 2010; *Jakarta Post* 2012).

Jokowi's victory over Prabowo and Hatta in 2014 (and over Prabowo and Sandi in 2019) did not shift or undercut the instrumental power of domestic miners. Senior members of Jokowi's executive, just like Yudhoyono's, had direct connections to the domestic mining industry and lobbied the president to continue taking a hard line on foreign divestment. Luhut Pandjaitan, for example, played a key role in the development of mining regulations during Jokowi's first term in office. The former military general also had significant interests in the coal sector through his company, Toba Sejahtera. Luhut helped fund and organize Jokowi's political campaign (Power 2016) and was appointed coordinating minister for politics, law, and security (2015–16), then coordinating minister for maritime affairs and investment (2016–). Luhut was a strong supporter of the majority divestment regime and was particularly assertive when it came to enforcing Freeport's obligation to divest its majority equity share (Lubis 2015; Tempo.co 2017). During Jokowi's second term, the president also developed a close relationship with Erick Thohir, a media mogul and the brother of Garibaldi "Boy" Thohir, Adaro's CEO and major shareholder. Erick served as campaign manager for Jokowi's 2019 reelection bid, and such a role usually includes making or organizing donations to the campaign budget. When Jokowi won, Erick was rewarded with the position of minister for state-owned enterprises.

In sum, Indonesia's emergent democratic political economy was marked by a new and more intense overlap between private sector mining interests and public office. The cost of competitive election campaigns at the local and national levels motivated closer and closer ties between business elites and political actors, and the booming resource sectors were an attractive investment with, especially in coal, fast and ready access to rents. New domestic mining magnates had direct channels to the politicians making regulatory decisions in the sector, and those in office often had their own private coal or mineral investments. At the same time, decentralization had, in many instances, not only given district heads new power over land and mining concessions but also provided national economic elites with wide and easy access to a range of new state actors at the local level who often welcomed new sources of capital from national businesses. The interlocking and symbiotic relationships between domestic private business and political office intensified over the course of the democratic period, with significant implications for sectoral regulations, including resource nationalism, and for the transformation of ownership.

Private Nationalization of Indonesia's Mines

Prior theories of resource nationalism suggest booms induce myopia among bureaucrats, who seek short-term gains from rising prices by changing foreign contracts and tightening foreign investment rules to benefit the state and vested interests. This picture resonates, to an extent, with the experience of Indonesia's mining sector during the boom; however, such a framework does not capture the shifting power relations between private capital and state actors during this period. Senior bureaucrats were often deeply concerned, even ambivalent, about changes to the sector's foreign investment rules. However, the political connections and instrumental power of the country's private mining giants outlined above helped to push sectoral laws and regulations down a persistently nationalist path. The result was a slow but steady nationalization of the country's mining sector in favor of private domestic business interests.

The new divestment restrictions were initially not part of the government's plan for the 2009 Mining Law. In the first version of the bill drawn up by the Ministry for Energy and Mineral Resources, there were no divestment obligations for foreign companies. Instead, according to the earliest (publicly available) iteration of the draft law, foreign companies making new investments in the mining sector would be compelled to partner with SOEs and majority-Indonesian-owned companies (Dewan Perwakilan Rakyat 2006; Investor Daily 2007). Senior bureaucrats involved in the early stages of the bill's design were careful to emphasize this point in interviews, too.[3] They described how the ministry opted for a regulation that supported joint operations and ventures between foreign and domestic businesses because it was a way of ensuring engagement with local companies, encouraging skills and technology transfers, while still offering foreign investors an assurance that they would maintain control over their mining ventures for the life of the contract. The ministry did not indicate it would be legislating for new divestment obligations. Divestment was not on parliamentarians' list of demands for the new law either. Between 2005 and 2008, public records of debate in the parliament and coverage in industry publications and mainstream media barely mentioned divestment.[4] Instead, the ministry and the parliament were focused on articles of the law that dealt with value adding, royalties, and the transition away from contracts to a licensing system (Lagaligo 2008; Majalah Tambang 2007).

In fact, the law's content came as a surprise to senior members of the bureaucracy in other economic ministries. Even some ministers had little prior knowledge of the divestment clause and were perplexed as to why it was inserted into the law so late in the negotiations. In an interview, Mari Elka Pangestu, then minister for trade, said she was shocked by the outcome because her ministry had not been consulted during the drafting of Article 112, and the divestment clause had not been widely deliberated.[5] To recall, Article 112 clashed directly with the trade ministry's 2007 Investment Law, which protected foreign investors from nationalization and forced divesture and prevented attempts to limit the duration of foreign investment in any enterprise.

The government had consulted mining companies and the industry peak bodies that represented the interests of the country's biggest miners, both foreign and domestic, such as the Indonesian Mining Association (IMA) and Indonesian Coal Mining Association (ICMA). According to one senior member of the Ministry for Energy and Mineral Resources, these associations had, after negotiations with the government, initially expected the new law would outline 20 percent divestment after ten years.[6] The firms and business association representatives interviewed for this study did not view the 20 percent figure as prohibitive, and they accepted the figure and decided to "live with it."[7] Many were surprised, however, when the 51 percent rule was introduced. A senior member of the Indonesian mining industry stated that when it came to designing the implementing regulations, "We [industry representatives] were all consulted by the ministry on the most appropriate divestment requirement, and we all said 20 percent. Everyone was happy with this. Then, overnight, no one knows why, this shot up to 51 percent. We all assume powerful domestic businessmen were in the mix here. Lobbying by groups like Adaro and Bumi is *very* effective."[8]

The divestment rules dovetailed with the interests of private domestic enterprise and those politicians with their own mining sector interests. The coordinating minister for economic affairs and close ally of President Yudhoyono, Hatta Rajasa, was a prominent advocate for the 2009 Mining Law and for the divestment obligations. He was also viewed by industry as a key representative of the interests of domestic private capital.[9] One senior manager in a large domestic mining firm explained, "The government is preparing an environment where well-connected local businessmen can take a majority share in existing projects, taking projects midway."[10] Similarly, one foreign expatriate who had operated a gold mining company in Indonesia for over two decades stated in an interview that "there is a strong belief in the foreign mining community that changes to the laws in Indonesia are being driven by the country's domestic conglomerates, who are waiting in the wings to benefit from the divestment laws. . . . Their plan is to slowly take over the projects that foreigners have set up."[11]

Members of government also believed the ministry's divestment rules reflected private sector demands, and a view within certain parts of the government with close industry connections that Indonesian businesses finally, and for the first time in the country's history, had the capacity to take over complex foreign mines. A former senior bureaucrat from the Ministry of Energy and Mineral Resources made a candid statement in a confidential interview that he was convinced the 51 percent rule introduced in 2012 came from senior members of the executive, in particular Hatta, who were close to and doing the bidding of the most prominent Indonesian business actors.[12] One former minister with an economics portfolio during the Yudhoyono government referred to the divestment regime as part of a plan to "give locals a 'leg up'" in a sector where foreign capital had dominated for decades.[13] Another industry expert working for a foreign embassy in Jakarta described the process as a "slow nationalization" of Indonesia's mining industry for the benefit of the biggest private business.[14] A senior representative from a major foreign mining company suggested that senior policymakers, politicians, and local mining tycoons came to view Indonesia's experience of the coal boom in 2007–8 as an example of what should take place throughout the entire mining sector: "Local capitalists had successfully taken over the majority of the big foreign-operated coal mines. People asked, well, why can't we do the same for hard-rock minerals?"[15]

Then commodity prices began to tumble in 2013. By the time President Jokowi took office in 2014, the boom was well and truly over. Nevertheless, few in government called for rolling back divestment obligations or for creating more conducive conditions for foreign companies or investors. Rather than appeasing foreign investors in response to low prices, as the market-cycle theory predicts and as had been the pattern throughout much of Indonesia's economic history, the nationalist mood persisted. Senior cabinet ministers continued to emphasize that Indonesians were able to run complex mining projects and that they would do it with better contributions to state revenue and community welfare (Bisnis Indonesia 2014; *Jakarta Post* 2015).

Indeed, it appeared that domestic businesses were unperturbed by the slump in commodity prices and were well placed to begin taking advantage of the new rules and buying into the gold and copper sector. That year, Medco Energy, owned by Indonesian businessperson and one-time PDI-P politician Arifin Panigoro, acquired 82 percent of Newmont's Batu Hijau mine (as described in the introduction to this book). Coordinating minister for maritime affairs at the time, Rizal Ramli, told the press that he approved of this acquisition that would see one of the country's largest mines put in the hands of an indigenous businessperson (Syahrul 2015). State officials argued that foreign companies like Newmont were more troubled by low commodity prices than the Indonesian government or Indonesian firms (Cahyafitri 2015b; *Jakarta Post* 2015). In an interview in 2014, a Newmont representative suggested that the company's main concern was the constant and fraught negotiations over divestment with the Indonesian government, and this was no doubt part of the company's calculation to leave the market entirely in 2016, combined with financial strains. Medco, on the other hand, was able to finance the major acquisition by borrowing from three state-owned banks, reportedly after some pressure from Jokowi—the president watched the Newmont acquisition carefully, hoping it might constitute a model for transferring the Freeport mine (discussed in the following chapter) into Indonesian hands in the near future (Budiartie, Teresia, and Nasrillah 2016).

Indika, meanwhile, struck a deal with Australian gold and copper miner Nusantara Resources to buy into its Awak Mas gold project in South Sulawesi. To bring the company's CoW in line with the new divestment requirements, Nusantara Resources revised its contract with the government in 2018 and then in 2019 entered into an agreement with Indika to take a 40 percent interest in its local subsidiary PT Masmindo Dwi Area by 2021, with the expectation that Indika would then increase its share in the project to 51 percent by the tenth year of production (Nusantara Resources 2020). In line with that agreement, Indika became the largest shareholder in Masmindo by taking 28 percent interest in 2020. But in late 2021, rather than just increase Indika's shares in Masmindo, Nusantara Resources shareholders agreed to a takeover by Indika's company subsidiary, Indika Mineral Investindo (Warta Ekonomi 2021). With this acquisition, Indika became the sole owner of both Nusantara Resources and Masmindo and had officially diversified into the precious mineral sector.

Various Chinese Indonesian tycoons, like Eka Tjipta Widjaja, Robert Hartono, and Johan Lensa, entered the gold and copper industry through acquisitions and foreign divestment deals (Dunia Energi 2015; Reuters Staff 2015; Sender 2011; Teguh Hidayat & Partners 2012; *Tempo Bisnis* 2012). Two formerly foreign-owned gold mines, Nusa Halmahera Minerals (NHM) and Indo Muro Kencana (IMK), were sold to less high-profile businesspeople with links to established tycoons: NHM was bought by Indotan, which has links to Gita Wirjawan, the former trade minister in the Yudhoyono government and owner of Ancora Group.[16] IMK was originally pursued by Indika as part of the firm's expansion into hard-rock minerals; eventually, Straits Resources, the Australian owner of the mine, sold to a firm owned by a Singaporean citizen named Enk Ee Tan. Mr. Tan sits on the board of, or owns, several companies associated with the Gajah Tunggal Group, owned by Singapore-based Chinese Indonesian tycoon of the Suharto era Sjamsul Nursalim.[17] The transformation of ownership of some of the country's major mineral mines is displayed in table 4.2.

TABLE 4.2. Ownership changes in Indonesia's major mineral contracts

COMPANY	OWNERSHIP	MINERAL	YEAR OF DOMESTIC TAKEOVER
Freeport Indonesia	Inalum (Indonesian state-owned) 51% Freeport McMoran (USA) 49%	Gold, copper	2018
Amman Mineral (formerly Newmont)	MedcoEnergi International (Arifin Panigoro)	Gold, copper	2016
Agincourt Resources	Astra International (United Tractors, which is majority owned by Jardine Matheson, Singapore—Hong Kong)	Gold	2015—EMR (Australian), Martua Sitorus (Chinese Indonesian tycoon of the agribusiness giant Wilmar), and Michael Hartono (Chinese Indonesian tycoon of Djarum) purchase Agincourt from G-Resources (Hong Kong) 2018—Astra International takes over
J Resources Bolaang Mongondow (formerly Avocet, UK)	J Resources Asia Pasifik (owned by Chinese Indonesian businessperson Johan Lensa and his son Jimmy Budiarto)	Gold	2010
Tambang Tondano Nusajaya (formerly Archipelago, UK)	Archi Indonesia (Rajawali Group, owned by Chinese Indonesian tycoon Peter Sondakh)	Gold, silver	2010
Nusa Halmahera Minerals (formerly Newcrest, Australia)	Antam 25% (Indonesia state-owned) Indotan 75% (Indotan is owned by Wachjo Romo "Robert" Nitiyudo, a low-profile Indonesian businessperson. He and his son have shares in Ancora, a resource firm owned by former trade minister Gita Wirjawan)	Gold	2020
PT Indo Muro Kencana (formerly Straits Resources, Australia)	Indomuro Minerals (owned by a Singaporean, Enk Ee Tan, who is linked to the Gajah Tunggal Group, owned by Chinese Indonesian tycoon Sjamsul Nursalim)	Gold	2015
Vale Indonesia	Vale (Brazil-based multinational)	Ferro nickel	—
Antam	Indonesian state-owned	Gold, bronze, nickel	—
Timah	Indonesian state-owned	Tin	—

Sources: Ownership information from Orbis (2020); domestic takeover date established using various media sources and Orbis data.

In 2020, the Indonesian government revised the 2009 Mining Law. The changes locked in the nationalist trajectory of prior regulations and reflected the expanding policy power of the country's mining giants. The content of the new law heavily favored CCoW holders. First, revisions outlined that existing CCoWs would be automatically renewed twice, rather than going up for tender at the end of the contract. This change directly benefited several giant coal producers, including Adaro and Indika, whose contracts were approaching expiry within the next two years. Importantly, the 2020 revisions also elevated the 51 percent divestment rule to the status of law; until now, that figure was outlined only in a lower-level government regulation that can be revised or rescinded at the ministerial level.

The revisions to the 2009 law were rushed through parliament quickly with little public deliberation (a process I elaborated on more in the final chapter). In the words of Faisal Basri, an economist and industry analyst, the only reason to pass the revisions with such urgency was "saving those six corporations that control 70 percent of national [coal] production" from renegotiating their contracts (*Jakarta Post* 2020). Another source from a national anti-corruption organization stated that Adaro, and specifically Boy Thohir, "wrote some parts of the law himself. . . . It was designed to secure *his* contracts."[18] Prior to the revisions, expiring contracts would have been returned to the state and put up for a tender, providing other firms and the state-owned coal miner Bukit Asam with an opportunity to compete and potentially expand their assets. In an interview, a representative from Bukit Asam expressed frustration that not even the state miner had been involved in deliberating this aspect of the law.[19] The provision outlining an automatic twenty-year extension of existing CCoWs foreclosed the opportunity for the state to retender, reallocate, and potentially take over these huge concessions.

In summary, the pattern of domestic takeovers in the mineral mining sector after the introduction of the 2009 Mining Law demonstrates how major private domestic interests began diversifying into, and slowing taking over, precious mineral mines. By 2021, for the first time in Indonesian history, local firms, most of them private, owned all major coal *and* mineral mining assets in the country. The sector had undergone a slow nationalization, led primarily by a private sector with expanding instrumental power and deep political connections at the national and local level, too. What transpired in Indonesia's mining sector challenges the notion that resource nationalism is contingent on external market prices, and compels a less state-centered account of nationalist change. Instead, in Indonesia's mining sector, a business-driven form of resource nationalism emerged and was sustained beyond the boom, underpinned by a growing and well-capitalized domestic business class that was buoyed by the boom and then viewed the commodity downturn as an opportunity to acquire the interests of troubled foreign operators.

Liberal Bulwarks: Indonesia's Agribusiness Firms

Whereas Indonesia's mining giants lobbied for more shares in foreign-owned mines, local agrifirms appeared to become bulwarks against nationalist demands. In the past, the Suharto government had imposed restrictions on foreign investment in plantations and in palm oil specifically, and such interventions directly benefited the president's Chinese Indonesian business cronies. But the open and liberal ownership regime imposed on the plantations sector by the IMF in 1999 was never reversed. Foreign investors, especially from neighboring countries, flowed freely into the palm oil sector in those early postcrisis years, establishing a complex regional network of private capital and generating an explosion in the volume of crude palm oil (CPO) production. The conglomerates that came to dominate this sector also chose to domicile parts of their business overseas and became far more internationalized than they were before. The nationalist demands of a coalition of legislators and middle-sized businesses were rejected by the Indonesian government in 2014, in part because the country's largest and most structurally powerful firms embraced rather than opposed foreign investment.

Changing Patterns of Ownership: Foreigners Reenter the Plantations Sector

As discussed in chapter 2, Indonesia's plantations sector was first the domain of Dutch and multinational companies. The sector came under the control of Indonesian state-owned companies in the postindependence period (chapter 2). But by the late 1980s, President Suharto had opened significant tracts of land for private enterprise, distributing licenses for forestry and palm oil to his allies in the military and to his Chinese Indonesian business cronies. The structure of the plantations sector shifted to one dominated by private firms and smallholders, with SOEs playing a minor role in production and export of the country's commodities like timber and rubber. Palm oil followed this same pattern, with most of the CPO production coming from private firms by the late 2000s (figure 4.1).

During the 1980s and 1990s, the government was highly interventionist and closed the palm oil sector to foreign investors (Fane 1996; Lindblad 2015). However, the Asian financial crisis and subsequent intervention from international financial institutions changed the investment rules in Indonesia's plantations

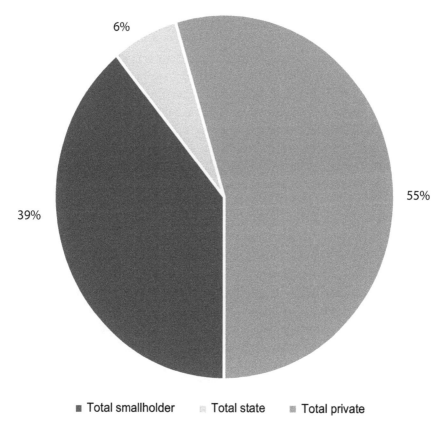

6%

55%

39%

■ Total smallholder   ■ Total state   ■ Total private

FIGURE 4.1. Proportion of palm oil production by type of enterprise, 2017

Source: Indonesia Statistics Agency (2017)

sectors. Under pressure from the IMF, in 1999 economic policymakers lifted all trade and investment restrictions on the plantations sector. At the turn of the century, the sector's regulatory regime was the most liberal it had been since the early Suharto years.

Once restrictions on foreign investment in the palm oil industry were removed, foreign investors took advantage of the new reforms, opening up concessions and buying up bankrupt and struggling domestic companies (Casson 2000; Jiwan 2013). Malaysian, Singaporean, and to a lesser extent, American companies entered the market with enthusiasm, "both because of Indonesian companies' urgent need for capital and the increasing limitation on expansion through land conversion within Malaysia" (Cramb and McCarthy 2016, 48). According to Rob Cramb and John McCarthy (2016, 16), "the Malaysian state took the opportunity to facilitate oil palm investment in Indonesia by both government-linked companies such as Sime Darby and Tabung Haji Plantations and politically well-connected private corporations such as Kuala Lumpur Kepong and IOI Corporation."

Many Indonesian companies, including the largest conglomerates, suffered unmanageable debt in the wake of the crisis and were forced to sell off part of their assets to the Indonesian Bank Restructuring Agency (IBRA), which was set up with the IMF to manage the unfolding banking crisis. IBRA then sold some of these assets on to foreign buyers or, alternatively, facilitated local companies to enter into joint ventures and mergers (Jiwan 2013, 52). The largest and most controversial case involved the Salim Group, which was forced to sell 180,000 ha of palm oil plantations to IBRA. In 2001, the agency then sold those assets to Kumpulan Guthrie, a major Malaysian palm oil company (Bresnan 2005, 220–21).

How did the influx of foreign capital alter the ownership structure of the palm oil industry in the years that followed? Precise figures on foreign ownership are difficult to obtain and estimates vary widely. In fact, even trying to differentiate between foreign and domestic enterprises is remarkably difficult in this sector. Helena Varkkey (2012, 351) suggests that through joint ventures with Indonesian partners and subsidiaries, Malaysian and Singaporean investors control over two-thirds of Indonesia's palm oil plantations. Sawit Watch, an Indonesian NGO, claims that after taking into account holding companies and foreign takeovers of small Indonesian companies, around half of Indonesia's palm plantations are in foreign hands (Viva 2010). APKASINDO, the palm oil farmers association, claims 40 percent of palm oil concessions are foreign owned, while the body representing both foreign and domestic companies, GAPKI, estimates 30 percent of the industry is foreign owned (Harian Ekonomi Neraca 2013). Even if we take the most modest estimate to be accurate—GAPKI's 30 percent figure—the proportion of foreign investment was larger than in any other plantation sector and much larger than it had been during the New Order period.

The structure of the sector is, at one level, extremely fragmented. According to GAPKI, the number of smallholder palm oil farmers has exploded in recent years, from 142,000 in the early 1990s to 2.3 million in 2015 (GAPKI 2015). In addition, in 2017, government records indicated there were 1,779 large enterprises across the country (Indonesian Statistics Agency 2017). However, much of Indonesia's palm oil lands are concentrated in the hands of a relatively small number of firms. In terms of the land under corporate control, figure 4.2 illustrates that private firms control just over half of the land licensed for palm oil production. Within that 55 percent, the largest twenty firms control over half of the total land for production. In other words, despite having over 1,700 large companies and a huge number of smallholder farmers, land and production is dominated by a relatively small number of large and structurally powerful firms.

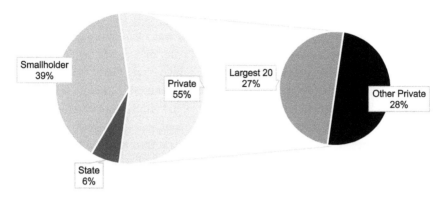

FIGURE 4.2.   Palm oil land ownership by business type

Source: Director General of Plantations, "Indonesia Plantations Statistics: Palm Oil 2015–17"

Multinational and foreign giants loom large within the top layer of Indonesia's CPO producers, with Malaysian and Singaporean firms in particular playing an important role. Kumpulan Guthrie (which would later merge with another Malaysian giant, Sime Darby), for example, entered Indonesia in 1995 through a modest joint venture with a local business; liberalization after the crisis then allowed the company to swiftly acquire twenty-five local palm oil companies, all reeling from the financial crisis (Teoh 2013, 29–31). By 2002, Guthrie had over 300,000 ha of land accrued primarily through local acquisitions, including a significant portion of Salim's palm oil holdings.

The story of Astra's foreign takeover is also an illustrative case. Astra was, in many ways, a national corporate champion during the New Order. William Soeryadjaya and his brother enjoyed close ties to senior members of the Suharto administration, which helped to grow their small trading company into the country's only major actor in the auto business industry and the sole trader for Toyota in Indonesia. In the 1980s, William expanded into timber and palm oil, like many other tycoons. But in the early 1990s, William's son Edward made a number of risky business decisions, mostly in the banking sector, and the company's debts eventually became unmanageable (Borsuk and Chng 2014). In 1993, William was forced to sell Astra, and a range of government-owned firms and Suharto cronies, like Salim, Prajogo Pangestu, and Eka Cipta Widjaja, bought into and took over the conglomerate. Then, when the financial crisis hit years later, the firm's debts exploded once more, hitting US$2 billion by 1998 (Borsuk and Chng 2014). IBRA took over, and in 2000 sold a 40 percent stake to Singapore-listed but Scottish-owned conglomerate Jardine Matheson.

Jardine has always been controlled by one family, the Jardines and their descendants, and the firm is run with limited regard for the norms of corporate

governance and transparency (Hughes and Bland 2014). But Jardine managed
to turn Astra around, and in 2004 the company was again making a profit due
primarily to a boost in motorcycle sales and palm oil exports. By 2014, Astra
was again Indonesia's largest listed company (Hughes and Bland 2014), with investments in cars, banking, toll roads, coal, and palm oil. Although Edwin Soeryadjaya had long held hopes of buying back his family's crown jewel, Astra
International is now among the most profitable companies with Jardine's sprawling conglomerate, and so the palm oil giant Astra Agro remains majority foreign owned.

Another palm oil behemoth is Singapore-listed multinational Wilmar International, one of the world's largest agribusiness conglomerates. The firm began
as a joint venture between Martua Sitorus, a Chinese Indonesian businessperson from Medan, who had relatively humble origins, and Kuok Khoon Hong,
son of one of Malaysia's wealthiest tycoons, Robert Kuok. The pair established
Wilmar in 1991 with Kuok's capital and Sitorus's local connections (Teoh 2013,
35). The firm opened its Indonesia business with just one small palm oil plantation on Sumatra but then expanded rapidly after 1998. In 2007, Wilmar merged
with the Kuok Group's (Malaysia) plantation, edible oils, and grains businesses.
The sprawling conglomerate not only produces CPO but is also among the largest diversified agribusiness trading companies in the world. Wilmar owns a
number of large tracts of plantation land today and is among the top ten palm
oil firms by land size in Indonesia (table 4.3). These foreign firms carved out a
prominent place for themselves in Indonesia's now liberalized palm oil sector.

However, at the same time, most of the Indonesian conglomerates that dominated the palm oil industry prior to the Asian financial crisis ultimately survived
and then thrived in the post–New Order economic environment. As Christian
Chua (2008) documents in his book *Chinese Big Business in Indonesia*, many of
Suharto's Chinese Indonesian cronies weathered the financial crisis, and despite
strong anti-Chinese sentiment among the pribumi business elites and the wider
population at the end of the New Order, the Indonesian government needed these
dominant firms to survive and to help prop up the fragile economy. Several of
Suharto's cronies managed to keep their plantation concessions obtained in the
decades prior through their connections to the former president, and those concessions would prove central to rebuilding their business empires in the democratic era. Table 4.3 illustrates how the Salim Group and Eka Tjipta Widjaja's
Sinar Mas remain among the country's top plantation owners and palm oil producers, just as they were during the latter half of the New Order.

Indeed, the palm oil sector provides a powerful illustration of the continuity
between Suharto-era and contemporary conglomerates. The list of names that appears in table 4.3 is remarkably similar to the lists in tables 2.1 and 2.3 in chapter 2,

TABLE 4.3. Major palm oil firms and their owners, 2016

COMPANY	TOTAL HECTARES PLANTED	GROUP	OWNER
Golden Agri	485,606	Sinar Mas (PT SMART)	Eka Tjipta Widjaja (Chinese Indonesian)
IndoFood Agri	336,675	Salim Group	Anthony Salim (Chinese Indonesian)
Astra Agro	297,862	Astra International (taken over by Jardine Cycle and Carriage in 2001 and 2005)	Jardine Matheson Group (Singapore–Hong Kong)
Sime Darby	247,412	Permodalan Nasional Berhad (entered Indonesia in the late 1990s)	Malaysian government
First Resources	207,575	Eight Capital	Fangiono family (Chinese Indonesian)
Wilmar International	198,466	Wilmar International	Established by William Kuok (Malaysian) and Martua Sitorus (Chinese Indonesian)
Eagle High Plantations	171,931	Rajawali Corporation	Peter Sondakh (Chinese Indonesian)
Asian Agri	160,000	Royal Golden Eagle (Raja Garuda Mas)	Sukanto Tanoto (Chinese Indonesian)
PT Perkebunan Nusantara IV	158,550	Indonesian state-owned	Indonesian state-owned
Makin Group	140,000	Gudam Garam	Susilo Wonowidjojo (Chinese Indonesian)
Musim Mas	130,000	Musim Mas Group	Bachtiar Karim (Chinese Indonesian)
Sampoerna Agro	130,000	Sampoerna Strategic Group	Sampoerna family (Chinese Indonesian)
KL Kepong	109,251	—	Malaysian private equity group and state-owned companies
Goodhope Asia Holdings–Agro Indo Mas	99,340	Carson Cumberbatch	Sri Lankan private holding company
Dharma Satya Nusantara (DSN)	90,000	Triputra	Winarto Oetomo, Theodore Rachmat, Liana Salim, and Subianto families
Genting Plantations	76,065	Genting Group (entered in 2005)	Tan Sri Lim Goh Tong (Malaysian)
Bakrie Sumatera Plantations	61,662	Bakrie Global	Aburizal Bakrie
Anglo-Eastern Plantations	60,860	Genton International (entered late 1990s)	Genton International, a private company domiciled in Hong Kong, owns the controlling share
Sipef Group	46,169	Sipef Group	Belgian group, Ackermans van Haaren, owns controlling share
Austindo Nusantara Jaya Plantation	45,605	Austindo Nusantara Jaya	George Tahija

Sources: Company list and planted area sourced from Hawkins et al. (2016); ownership compiled by author using company reports and Orbis data (2020).

which displayed the largest logging and palm oil firms of the 1990s. Despite experiencing what seemed at the time to be crippling debt brought about by the financial crisis, these tycoons (with some exceptions) held on to most of their plantation concessions and the palm oil boom that took off in the early 2000s helped ensure they maintained their position at the top of Indonesia's rich lists for years to come. As we shall see, however, unlike in the mining sector, the country's agri-giants were not strong advocates for reinstating the nationalist limits on foreign investors they had once advocated for.

Structural Power of Big Palm Oil

The plantations sector is, in many ways, similar to the mining sector in that it is marked by an overlap between public office and private corporate interest. Some of the politicobusiness elites discussed in the previous section on mining have significant interests in the agribusiness sectors, too. Aburizal Bakrie's company, Bakrie Sumatera Plantations, for example, is a prominent palm oil producer. Prabowo also owns several companies with investments in plantations (Aspinall 2015a). Jokowi's allies and financiers Luhut Pandjaitan and Surya Paloh similarly have a number of palm oil plantations (Sukirno 2013). Indeed, much like coal, the palm oil boom of the twenty-first century attracted so much interest that it is difficult to find a politicobusiness elite without a palm plantation somewhere across the archipelago.

However, most of the major companies in this sector do not have the sorts of direct, formal links to government of the nature that characterized the mining sector. To recall, owners of both Adaro and Indika stepped down from their roles as directors of these companies to become involved in formal politics—Sandiaga Uno was elected deputy governor of Jakarta in 2017 and then ran for vice president in 2019; Wishnu Wardhana of Indika became the campaign manager for former president Yudhoyono's son in the 2017 gubernatorial election in Jakarta. Aburizal Bakrie, a major political figure during the Yudhoyono presidency, owned the country's largest coal mines. And Erik Tohir, the brother of Boy Tohir, one of Adaro's major shareholders, led Jokowi's campaign team in his bid for reelection in 2019 and then became minister for state-owned enterprises. The directors and owners of Indonesia's agri-giants do not engage in the same level of direct political activity, nor demonstrate such transparent political ambition.

Instead, the largest domestic palm oil companies enjoy superior structural power. Big business enjoys a unique and privileged policy position in all capitalist societies (Culpepper 2011; Lindblom 1977). To recall, when businesses enjoy structural power, they need not form direct personal relations with politicians or state officials, nor do they enter politics directly; instead, to the extent that a government depends on private investment for growth and public welfare—which in turn governments rely on for legitimacy and popular support—then economic policy decisions will be structured and conditioned by the demands of prominent capitalist actors. Comparative studies have found that large firms with cross-sectoral conglomeration enjoy the most superior structural power (Bauerle Danzman 2020; Haggard, Maxfield, and Schneider 1997; Schneider 1997).

Indonesia's agri-tycoons control vast material resources earned through their diversified, multisectoral conglomerates. A brief look at their groups' assets and ranking provides an indication of the extent to which the country's palm oil giants dominate Indonesia's economy more broadly. Table 4.4 reveals that throughout the 2000s and across the entire economy, groups with massive palm oil plantations—Astra (Jardine), Salim (Anthony Salim), Sinar Mas (Eka Tjipta Widjaja), Wilmar (Kuok and Sitorus), and Royal Golden Eagle (Sukanto Tanoto)—consistently rank in the country's top ten largest conglomerates by revenue.

A second and equally important source of these firms' structural power is the fact that they ran the most productive firms in a sector that had evolved into the

TABLE 4.4. Conglomerate rankings, 2008–16

CONGLOMERATE	NAME	2008	2009	2010	2011	2012	2013	2014	2015	2016
Jardine/Astra	Henry Keswick	1	1	1	1	1	1	1	1	1
Salim	Anthony Salim and family	2	2	2	2	2	2	2	2	2
Wilmar International	Martua Sitorus Kuok Khong Hong	–	3	3	3	4	4	5	35	53
Sinar Mas	Eka Tjipta Widjaya and family	3	4	4	4	3	3	3	3	3
Djarum	Budi Hartono	4	5	5	5	5	5	4	4	4
Bakrie	Aburizal Bakrie	7	6	6	7	7	10	10	9	9
Gudang Garam	Susilo Wonowidjojo	5	7	7	9	9	8	8	7	7
Lippo Group	Mochtar Riady	8	9	8	7	8	7	7	6	6
Philip Morris International	Philip Morris	6	8	9	6	6	6	6	5	5
Royal Golden Eagle	Sukanto Tanoto	9	10	10	10	10	9	9	8	8

Sources: Globe Asia conglomerate rankings by revenue (USD).

backbone of the Indonesian export economy. Consecutive post-Suharto Indonesian governments at both the national and regional levels embraced the global demand for palm oil that exploded in the twenty-first century (McCarthy 2010). Palm oil is one of Indonesia's most important earners of foreign exchange—for example, in 2014, exports were valued at US$17.3 billion (Aurora et al. 2015). As a single commodity, its exchange earnings far outweighed those earned from other agricultural subsectors and also mining subsectors like copper, gold, bauxite, or nickel.

As investment skyrocketed in the first decade of the 2000s, state managers saw an opportunity to transfer some of the developmental burden in rural areas to the private sector, which in turn expanded the political and policy clout of the largest agrifirms. Commercial plantations incorporate and include—though often "adversely"—a large slice of the rural poor (Borras et al. 2012; McCarthy 2010). According to Janice Lee et al. (2014), between 2000 and 2009, the most rapid oil palm expansion in Indonesia was among smallholders, with annual growth rates of 11.12 percent, far higher than government estates (0.37 percent) and private companies (5.45 percent), indicating high levels of local and domestic engagement with the industry. This expansion took place in concert with private companies, who set aside land for and purchased palm fruit from smallholders as part of the state's various nucleus estate schemes (explained in chapter 2).

Over time, the state slowly reduced its role in the sector and designed a regime in which smallholders depended on private companies for land, resources, and profits (Cramb and McCarthy 2016). According to analysts of agrarian change in Indonesia, toward the end of the New Order and into the democratic period, the state retreated from its once interventionist role in the industry, facilitating both the flow of foreign and private funds, and transferring responsibility for nucleus estates and smallholder welfare over to private plantation companies (Cramb and McCarthy 2016; Pramudya, Hospes, and Termeer 2017). By 2016, the sector employed approximately 3.2 million people in the upstream segment, with some analyses estimating that the palm oil industry supported 5 percent of Indonesian households, or approximately 12.8 million people in 2016 (Hawkins et al. 2016, 8). Palm oil firms had thus become fundamental to the government's economic growth and rural development strategy.

In an interview, a prominent businessperson with interests across the palm oil and energy sectors offered a revealing observation about the distinct source of policy power and the very different relationship these conglomerates have with the state, compared to domestic mining magnates, observing that "because of how powerful they [agriconglomerates] are, the government cannot just approach them directly to discuss a new policy," whether regarding taxes, concession limits, or foreign investment. Major business actors in this sector have a more indirect influence over such state interventions, and that influence stems largely from the size and critical weight of their investments.

Sustaining a Liberal Regime

The structural importance of big agrifirms to the Indonesian economy gave their policy preferences enormous weight, and their preference was *not* for a more nationalist regime with caps on foreign capital. In 2014, the impetus for nationalist change came primarily from the political elite, rather than the business elite. The plantation bill's emphasis on local ownership was the work of parliamentary Commission IV on agriculture, forestry, food, and maritime affairs. Within that commission, nationalist advocates came from a range of political parties. Partai Demokrasi Indonesia-Perjuangan (Indonesian Democratic Party-Struggle [PDI-P]) played a leading role in pushing for a more nationalist approach to land investments.[20] But parliamentary records also highlight strong support from one of the major Islamic parties, the Partai Amanat Nasional (National Mandate Party [PAN]) (Dewan Perwakilan Rakyat 2014, 75). Deputy chair of Commission IV, Herman Khaeron of Partai Demokrat (Democrat Party [PD]), also made impassioned public statements about the critical need to curb foreign ownership of Indonesia's plantations and "protect the nation's natural resources for the people" (Info Sawit 2014). In a parliamentary media publication, Khaeron explained that the 30 percent limit on foreign investment was necessary "because we want our community's livelihoods and their aspirations be realized by the government, and for the government to ensure the Indonesian people's prosperity" (Buletin Parlementaria 2014). Nationalist advocates wanted the cap to be retroactive, too, which would force plantation firms to sell down foreign-owned shares that exceeded the 30 percent limit.

Beyond these political actors, it was also the case that medium-sized companies supported regulatory limits on foreign investment in hopes that more land would be made available through the divestment of foreign holdings in the major listed palm oil firms. For example, APKASINDO, which represents smaller and medium-sized plantation farmers, expressed frustration at the encroachment of foreign investors into Indonesia's farming land, and in 2013, the secretary general told the press that "it would be best if foreign companies were no longer given licenses, because land is becoming less available, while the Indonesian population continues to grow" (Baihaqi 2013).[21]

In an interview, a representative from GAPKI explained the competition between different types of local businesses: "Since liberalization and decentralization, the largest firms have gotten larger because it's easy for the big companies to buy concessions and licenses . . . and smallholders have done very well, too. . . . But middle-sized companies have suffered because they can't compete and buy land at the same rate as the big firms. This is why they try to find a way [the 30 percent cap] to take something from them."[22] But nationalist advocates were unsuccessful. Unlike in the mining sector, the most ardent proponents of foreign divestment in the plantations sector were not aligned with the interests of the most powerful business actors.

The palm oil sector's peak body, GAPKI, and the largest palm oil companies within it began a countercampaign. GAPKI's membership includes some of the country's large foreign-listed and foreign-owned firms. But on this matter, it was not only acting on behalf of its foreign members but also on behalf of prominent domestic companies that also opposed the bill. GAPKI warned the government that a cap on foreign ownership and forced divestments would deter future investors, devalue the price of Indonesia's land, and reduce CPO production.[23]

Importantly, a foreign investment cap of 30 percent could potentially hurt Indonesian business elites, many of whom had established and listed their businesses outside of Indonesia and who invited foreign shareholding and partnerships in their agribusiness ventures. The proposed legislation could negatively impact major Malaysian and Singaporean companies in Indonesia, like Sime Darby and Wilmar, as well as Indonesian companies with majority or large foreign ownership, like Astra Agro Lestari or the Rajawali Group's Eagle Plantations, owned by Peter Sondakh, in which Malaysian company Felda held a 37 percent stake (Global Business Guide 2014; Hermansyah 2017). Observers thus questioned how the proposed cap would work in practice, given the challenge of identifying foreign investors and deciding which companies it would affect (McBeth 2014b).

One industry insider revealed in an interview that the Ministry of Agriculture could only confidently ascertain the ownership of 30 percent of the private companies operating in the sector.[24] The rest are "gray," and many use a system whereby an Indonesian company holds the plantation license but is backed by Malaysian or Singaporean money. It is also common practice for an enterprise to begin with majority local ownership and to have a well-connected Indonesian businessperson at its helm; but once the Indonesian leadership has helped facilitate the licensing process, their shares will be bought out by the foreign partner.[25] Farmers associations and NGOs claim that Malaysian investors favor this model. McCarthy and Cramb (2016, 445–46) explain that "interlocking ownership structures" are useful for all parties because by working with Singaporean and Malaysian companies, Indonesian businesses can "upgrade their position within global value chains by accessing technologies and thereby improving their productivity"; meanwhile, Malaysian and Singaporean companies get access to land and cheap labor.

An expert at the Centre for International Forestry Research (CIFOR) with de-cades of experience working on Indonesia's palm oil sector explained in an inter-view that nationalist sentiment comes almost entirely from the parliament and a small handful of medium-sized firms, and such sentiments do not have much traction within the industry more broadly and among the companies that domi-nate it: "It's true that much of the industry is Malaysian owned—often through shares, not whole ownership—but Malaysian money and technology is usually welcomed; they have far greater technical expertise. . . . Indonesian farmers' and companies' yields are still so much lower than the yields in Malaysian planta-tions. This undercuts any strong or widespread anti-foreign or anti-Malaysian sentiment."[26] Against this backdrop, prominent domestic business elites with palm oil investments had no strong desire to limit foreign ownership—many even opposed it on the grounds that foreign capital offered opportunities for business expansion and technology transfers. The effect was that there were few powerful business elites backing or resourcing a nationalist campaign.

Members of the executive heeded the warnings of GAPKI and the corpora-tions with the largest palm oil holdings and were reluctant to disrupt foreign in-vestment flows and potentially alienate domestic investors, as well as harm large numbers of smallholders and rural laborers. Although initially in favor of the cap, the minister for agriculture at the time, Suswono, was ultimately pres-sured by more senior members of the executive to reject the parliament's pro-posal. Local governments also came out and opposed any attempt to limit the flow of foreign money. The head of the District Government Association (Ap-kasi), Isran Noor, for example, expressed concern that forcing divestment or plac-ing limits on foreign investment would impact district governments' income and local livelihoods (Republika 2013). In the end, as one senior parliamentar-ian who worked on the bill described, after drawn-out discussions with the Min-istry of Agriculture, it was decided that the nationalist path was too risky: "Investments in palm oil are big and a lot of it comes from outside, and if the foreign money leaves, there may not be enough local capital to replace the big guys."[27] Those "big guys" did not favor more localization. Instead, structurally powerful actors connected to the sector blocked nationalist proposals.

So in the wake of the Asian financial crisis, the sector became marked by highly integrated networks of regional capital. Investors from Singapore and Malaysia entered Indonesia to buy up struggling firms or to strike up partnerships with lo-cal players in order to secure access to land and cheap labor. Liberalization had been a boon rather than a burden for the country's major agribusiness conglomer-ates, and domestic business actors viewed nationalist protection as neither neces-sary nor desirable. Groups like Salim, Sinar Mas, Wilmar, and Astra all had either significant foreign ownership or invested in Indonesia from their firms that were domiciled abroad (detailed more in chapter 6), and hence their preference was to keep the sector open rather than closed to foreign capital. The situation was very different in the mining sector, where the precious minerals subsector remained an enclave of Anglo-American capital—until the introduction of resource nationalist policies pushed by domestic mining interests. Here, high-profile Indonesian businesspeople and politicians vied for access to and control over lucrative mines operated by foreign multinationals and used their instrumental power to push for favorable divestment deals.

Business Power and Nationalist Trajectories in Indonesia

The cases of Indonesia's mining and palm oil sectors show how resource booms do not just shift bargaining power between foreign capital and host states; instead, booms can induce competition and change the relative power of domestic firms and foreign ones and between different sorts of domestic firms, too. Where resource nationalism prevails, such policies are not always easily traced back to myopic, protectionist bureaucrats—programs for nationalization rest on advocates in both the state *and* domestic business class.

This chapter mapped the preferences of the major business actors in each sector and demonstrated how those preferences gave rise to distinct kinds of nationalist campaigns and policy outcomes. Indonesia's mining sector was subject to an assertive set of nationalist interventions during the boom. Despite strong opposition from multinational mining companies, widespread international criticism, and regardless of tumbling commodity prices from 2013 onward, the Indonesian government maintained the nationalist position. A new class of domestic extractive companies are central to the story of resource nationalism in Indonesia's mining sector. The coal boom gave Indonesian businesses a new source of significant capital, and they began to pursue the new frontier of mineral mining that was once reserved for Anglo-American and multinational firms. Further, as Indonesia's democracy evolved during the two decades since Suharto's fall, the top layer of the political class developed tight connections to wealthy financiers with major mining interests, or they themselves came to hold significant personal investments in the mining sector and especially in coal. The state's commitment to resource nationalism in this sector was inextricably linked to and bolstered by domestic private interests and therefore persisted despite volatile commodity prices. A business-driven form of resource nationalism thus prevailed both during and after the boom, helping to lock in the trend toward nationalization.

Indonesia's plantations sectors, and the palm oil sector specifically, were not subject to such nationalizing interventions. For the sector's biggest domestic players, nationalism was neither a necessary nor attractive policy regime for the growth of their businesses. Integrated flows of foreign and domestic capital conditioned their preferences against resource nationalism—a stance that broke with historical patterns in this sector. When the palm oil industry argued against foreign investment caps in the 2014 plantations bill, executive government listened and the parliament's and minister's proposals to limit foreign investment was thrown out in the final stages of the bill's deliberation and remained off the table in the years that followed. The sector's major firms and business associations were liberal bulwarks rather than nationalist advocates. So, unlike in many other countries around the world, Indonesia's plantation sector has remained more open to foreign ownership than its mining sector.

This chapter demonstrated the value of bringing domestic firms into the analytical foreground when studying and explaining subnational patterns of resource nationalism. In Indonesia, the domestic private sector played a critical role in shaping nationalist trajectories. Throughout Indonesia's history, many of its extractive and plantation industries lacked a strong domestic private sector presence; today, these industries are dominated by local businesses with unprecedented structural and instrumental policy power. Each sector's major business actors either advocated for or blocked nationalist interventions, and in doing so, they helped determine the fate of nationalist demands.

STATE CAPITAL AND CONSTRAINTS ON PRIVATE POWER

This chapter outlines the conditions under which state capital, rather than private capital, drove and benefited from nationalist change. In the mining and palm oil sectors, the boom years gave domestic private companies new levels of structural and, in many cases, instrumental policy power. But private business did not always win regulatory battles over foreign ownership, and the government excluded private business from some of the country's major resource contracts. This chapter looks first at the case of the 2001 Oil and Gas Law, showing how competing interests between rising private businesses and the sector's major SOE, Pertamina, generated nationalist tensions and legal ambiguity; however, in practice, Pertamina was able to secure several major expiring foreign contracts, establishing the firm as the dominant upstream producer for the first time in Indonesia's history. The second focus of this chapter is the statist exception to domestic private firms' control over the mining sector—the establishment of a state-owned holding company to take over Freeport McMoran's infamous gold and copper mine in Papua province.

This chapter identifies two distinct but related factors that supported state over private domestic capital in these instances. The first constitutes the place of state-owned enterprises in Indonesia's contemporary political economy. SOEs have maintained a central role within certain sectors, including oil and gas. One of the most remarkable features of Indonesia's postcrisis economic adjustment during the early the 2000s was the fact that despite heavy intervention from the IMF and World Bank, the government pursued only a limited program of privatization of state assets. Throughout the Suharto years, the government invested huge amounts of money into expanding SOEs in a range of sectors. Pertamina was arguably the state's most important SOE during that time. The company was the backbone of the government's developmental activities, and revenue from oil exports was directed via Pertamina into a range of other SOEs and industrial projects (Hertzmark 2007; Robison 1986). After the crisis, the Indonesian government pledged to international lenders it would embark on incremental privatization of state-owned firms. But that incremental approach meant that even two decades into the post-Suharto period, many SOEs remained partially or fully state owned. In his assessment of the state sector's evolution during the democratic period, Kyunghoon Kim (2018) shows how by 2016, across telecommunications, banking, and construction, the largest firms were all SOEs. As Jamie Davidson's (2015, 2021) work on roads and infrastructure also illustrates, the historical centrality of state capital to developmental planning in Indonesia means that consecutive governments in the democratic era have continued to see SOEs as a strategic vehicle for channeling investment and meeting certain developmental targets that are more difficult to meet through private investment alone. As a result, some SOEs—and in particular Pertamina—wield immense policy power of their own.

When it came to revising the 2001 Oil and Gas Law, statist advocates seeking privilege and power for Pertamina came up against supporters of a more business-oriented resource nationalism, who sought dispensations for what was a growing number of Indonesian tycoons and politicobusiness elites now investing in upstream oil and gas. This chapter emphasizes how the growth of domestic and often politically connected private upstream businesses complicated statist ambitions for the law, and the sector's sustained dependence on the technical expertise of foreign multinationals also gave lawmakers pause. Importantly, however, while the 2001 Oil and Gas Law had still not been revised at the time of writing in 2022, over the course of the boom and postboom period, Pertamina enjoyed a series of victories in its effort to take control of the country's major upstream oil and gas projects. Those victories were a direct result of the firm's superior economic and political resources. Pertamina's senior managers leveraged the firm's deep and historically rooted connections into the state bureaucracy and mobilized a wide range of actors in support of a campaign to acquire strategic blocks, often against the recommendation of senior bureaucrats working within economic ministries.

The second factor that supported state over private nationalization in particular cases is political. Specific statist victories in oil and gas, and in the mining sector too, can be traced back the government's calculations about political risk and public opinion. Indonesia's competitive democratic milieu means voter behavior matters to incumbent politicians. Drawing on notions of political salience

(Fairfield 2015) and Pepper Culpepper's (2011) concept of "loud politics," this chapter demonstrates how Indonesian lawmakers and politicians perceive a public preference for state ownership over private domestic control, and these perceptions guided their decision-making process when it came to politically sensitive resource projects. In general, politicians interviewed for this study sensed strong public support for economic nationalism, such that rules and regulations that constrain or exclude foreign capital are expected to track well with the public. When it came to several key cases, however, the Jokowi government believed there was a strong popular preference for state ownership of especially valuable and high-profile oil and gas and mining projects, and the president sensed an opportunity to generate political credit for supporting state over private sector interests, while also keeping strategic projects from being owned and controlled by any one group of local tycoons. Democratic politics thus incentivized Indonesia's elected leaders to pay heed to the preferences of voting publics, in turn steering resource policy down nationalist paths that under certain circumstances, benefited state capital over the interests of big domestic privately owned resource companies. These two factors—the sustained power of SOEs within the oil and gas sector and the political salience of specific extractive resource projects—are important caveats to this book's central thesis about the rising policy power of domestic private business in Indonesia's land and resource sectors.

Nationalist Competitors: The Rise of State and Private Oil Firms

In the oil and gas sector, competing nationalist visions from the major state-owned company and rising private domestic firms produced extended policy conflict over the terms of a new sectoral law. This increased competition was a direct result of how patterns of production and ownership were changing in incremental but important ways during the democratic era. First, Indonesia was running out of oil. The oldest wells were drying up, and new wells were in much more difficult-to-reach parts of the country or, more commonly, the sea. This meant that when foreign-operated contracts approached expiry, some foreign firms were choosing to abandon their investments in Indonesia. Pertamina saw the exit of foreign firms as a strategic opportunity, and as the company began acquiring old foreign wells, its production performance and profitability improved remarkably.

Meanwhile, at the same time, an unprecedented number of domestic private players entered the upstream sector, seeking access to these old wells, too. These local private sector interests opposed regulatory concessions that favored Pertamina. The twenty-first century was thus marked by increasing competition between state and private domestic capital over the spoils of a shrinking industry. Competition led to sustained legal ambiguity; however, Pertamina's superior structural and instrumental power meant that in the race to acquire strategic blocks, Pertamina emerged victorious. By 2022, debate over a new oil and gas law had faded into the background, with few contentious contracts left to compete over.

Changing Patterns of Ownership: Pertamina's Comeback and New Private Competition

The state-owned oil giant made a remarkable comeback in the post-Suharto period. Under the leadership of Karen Agustiawan (2009–14), Pertamina doubled its revenues and profits. The company won the bid for several strategic fields that boosted its share of the country's oil production. For example, after becoming CEO in 2009, Agustiawan successfully managed the purchase of a controlling share in BP's North West Java Onshore block, and under Pertamina's operatorship, the block's daily production levels increased (McBeth 2013). Agustiawan then engineered the takeover of the West Madura block in 2011, which had been run by Kodeco Energy, a Korea-based oil and gas company, since 1981.[1]

The company's contribution to Indonesia's production levels increased in turn. At the start of the twenty-first century, Pertamina was producing around just 182,000 barrels of oil per day (bpd) (Hertzmark 2007, 22); by 2015, Pertamina was producing 520,000 bpd (Rigzone 2015). According to one report, in 2012 Pertamina's profits had improved 18.4 percent on the year prior, and in 2013 it became the first Indonesian company to make the Fortune 500 at 122nd place (*Jakarta Post* 2014). These impressive gains were due in part to booming oil prices. However, Agustiawan's leadership also improved the company's efficiency and turned Pertamina into a serious oil and gas operator. The notion that Pertamina could and therefore *should* be given unique access to expiring foreign contracts was thus becoming more legitimate and more feasible.

Pertamina was highly dependent on expanding its domestic assets. Unlike other national oil companies such as Brazil's Petrobras, China's CNOOC, or Malaysia's Petronas, Pertamina had marginal interests and investments abroad. Under Agustiawan, Pertamina laid out a plan to "go international." In 2014, Pertamina's international exploration and production arm was established, PT Pertamina Internasional Eksplorasi dan Produksi (PIEP), and by 2016, the company had acquired minor assets in Iraq, Malaysia, and Algeria (Pertamina 2016). Overall, however, in the two decades following the end of the New Order, the company's business strategy was focused principally on expanding its domestic assets and it needed, and hence demanded, government assistance in order to achieve that goal. A first right of refusal for expiring blocks would give the SOE a major advantage and help it to dominate the country's oil and gas production.

Meanwhile, domestic firms were, for the first time, starting to make their mark in the upstream sector and Pertamina found itself up against new sorts of domestic competitors. During the New Order, local entrepreneurs in the oil and gas sector were active almost exclusively in services, which meant they provided materials and service contracts to Pertamina and foreign oil and gas producers. The services subsector was less capital intensive and less risky than upstream exploration and production and hence better suited to Indonesia's relatively small class of capitalists. That system continues to the present day, with local businesses dominating the oil and gas services industry, and there have long been regulatory limits on the involvement of foreign firms in this subsector. But in the post-Suharto period, domestic capital ventured into the upstream sector, generating competition between statist advocates and a small but growing number of Indonesian private players who sought a business-oriented brand of resource nationalism.

Only one Indonesian company had made significant inroads into upstream production during the Suharto era—Medco. Arifin Panigoro (mentioned earlier as the purchaser of Newmont's mine and introduced in chapter 2) established Medco in 1980 to supply oil and gas pipelines and drilling services to the big foreign oil and gas companies. As described in chapter 2, Panigoro used his personal connections to Suharto and the director general for oil and gas to acquire service contracts with foreign companies. In 1992, Medco moved into upstream production by acquiring exploration and production contracts from an American company, Tesoro; in 1995, the firm acquired Stanvac's Indonesia operations. With these acquisitions, Medco began a successful transition into the upstream sector. Medco continued to expand rapidly during the post-Suharto period. In 2008, for example, the company was producing approximately 42,000 mbbls (one thousand barrels of oil); by 2016, that figure was over 60,000, and in 2021, the company was producing over 120,000 mmbls (Medco 2021). Medco had become by far the largest and most profitable private domestic upstream oil and gas company.

While at the early stages of Medco's expansion the firm relied on Pertamina contracts, in the post–New Order era Pertamina also became a competitor. In 2019, for example, Medco announced its intention to compete with Pertamina in a tender to enter the Corridor block, one of Indonesia's most strategic natural gas concessions. ConocoPhilips's PSC for Corridor was expiring in 2023. In a statement to the press, Medco's president director Hilmi Panigoro stated that the firm respected that the government would be offering Pertamina the first opportunity to take over the PSC, but the firm expressed its desire for a tender process that would allow all local companies to compete for the block as well (Dunia Energi 2019). Ultimately, the government decided to extend the contract of ConocoPhilips but reduced the foreign firm's share and increased Pertamina's share from 10 to 30 percent (Sulaiman 2019).

Another prominent player in the domestic oil and gas scene was Energi Mega Persada (EMP). EMP was part of the Bakrie Group and owned by Aburzial Bakrie. Like Medco, the company established its foothold in the upstream sector by farming into existing blocks when foreign operators farmed out and by taking over expiring foreign contracts. For example, the Japanese company Japex had operated the Gebang block in North Sumatra since 1985 as part of a joint operation agreement with Pertamina. When Japex farmed out in 2006 due to declining reserves, EMP moved in. EMP also took over the Bentu gas block in Riau in 2006 from Spectre Resources, an American company that had operated the block since 1993 (Kurniawan 2015). However, EMP never reached the efficiency or productivity of Medco, and in 2015, the company produced just 11,454 bpd and 218 million standard cubic feet per day of gas (Kurniawan 2015).

Other tycoons expanded into oil and gas in the early 2000s. Sukanto Tunoto, the Suharto-era Indonesian Chinese tycoon who had made his fortune in forestry and agribusiness, established a petroleum exploration and production company in 2003, Pacific Oil and Gas. The following year, the company purchased a 25 percent share in the Jambi Merang block from Canadian company Repsol.[2] In the coming years, Pacific Oil and Gas engaged in joint operation agreements with Pertamina and several Chinese firms. Meanwhile, Indika Energy, the integrated energy company with subsidiaries working in coal mining (discussed in chapter 4) and oil and gas services, also ventured into upstream production. One of its subsidiaries, Indika Multi Daya Energi, was established in 2013 in order to purchase a 10 percent participating interest in Total's Bird's Head production sharing contract in Papua.

In another example, Patrick Walujo established Samudra Energy in 2005 with funding from his private equity company, Northstar Group. Walujo was a rising star in Indonesia's business community in the mid-2000s, having advanced through the ranks at Goldman Sachs and won several awards for his entrepreneurship (*Wall Street Journal Indonesia* 2014). Walujo married the daughter of prominent Suharto-era Indonesian Chinese tycoon Theodore "Teddy" Rahmat of the Triputra Group, Saratoga Capital, and Adaro Energy. In 2010 Samudra Energy purchased a 20 percent stake in Husky Oil's Onshore & Offshore Madura Strait Area in the Madura Straits block (*Offshore Energy Today* 2010). Canada's Husky Oil continued to operate the block and maintained a 40 percent interest, while CNOOC also had a 40 percent interest. The deal came as part of Husky's contract extension. Pertamina had expressed interest in either taking over or taking an interest in this contract. However, the government extended Husky's contract and arranged for Samudra Energy to farm into the project. It was precisely this sort of deal that would have been adversely affected had Pertamina been given a formal first right of refusal.

Competing Policy Powers and Regulatory Stagnation

Pertamina's enjoyed major advantages in the policy realm. First, the company had superior structural power—it produced more oil than any other national firm, and it was unique in its integrated model of having major upstream interests while also dominating downstream refining and distribution. And as Pertamina's performance improved during President Yudhoyono's period in power, its leaders' arguments in favor of providing the company more privilege began having resonance in policymaking circles.

Domestic private players could not compete with Pertamina's structural advantages. These companies' market share in the oil and gas sector remained minor compared to the foreign multinationals like Exxon Mobil and compared to Pertamina, though Medco was becoming an exception. However, these smaller private ventures in upstream oil and gas were owned by some of Indonesia's wealthiest tycoons and politicobusiness elites which, like in the mining sector, endowed them with instrumental power they could wield when it came to certain contract decisions and debates over important sectoral regulations. It is impossible to map fully, and with certainty, the personal and financial relationships between these oil and gas companies and those in public office. Some, such as Aburizal Bakrie or Wishnu Wardhana, had clear links to the executive during the Yudhoyono era. Other domestic petroleum producers like Pacific Oil and Gas were owned by tycoons whose empires stretched across the Indonesian economy. These sorts of companies opposed enshrining in law a direct advantage for Pertamina to the expiring foreign contracts they were all pursuing. For example, in an interview, a representative from Medco explained that the company opposed further privileges for Pertamina without enshrining privileges for private domestic companies, too: "We work with Pertamina on some blocks, but we compete with Pertamina, too, and we wanted the new law to ensure we also have rights to expiring foreign oil and gas blocks. . . . Competition is very intense for these expiring foreign blocks."[3]

Throughout the period of debate over the new oil and gas law, KADIN's leadership also lobbied against a legal privilege for the SOE. As the voice of the private sector and with members who were active in upstream oil and gas, KADIN wanted any legal revision to ensure that local companies were given more participating interests in the country's oil and gas blocks. KADIN explicitly and publicly opposed any formal privilege for Pertamina, instead emphasizing that Indonesia's domestic private sector should play a larger role in oil and gas exploration and production (HukumOnline 2010). The Indonesian Petroleum Association (IPA), which represents both domestic and foreign companies operating in Indonesia, was similarly opposed to the notion of new legal privileges for the SOE. In an interview, a representative of IPA spoke at length about the years-long legal process that had gone almost nowhere and had become increasingly politicized:

> All this talk of Pertamina and priority for contracts has been damaging. There's now talk of a draft Permen [ministerial regulation] or Perpres [presidential regulation] on contract extensions. This is redundant, actually. The government already has the power, at the end of a contract, to decide who gets a contract. That is exactly where the power should lie. *If the government decides Pertamina should be the one to be awarded a project, so be it.* . . . But of course, the question of contract extension is going to be important; there are so many different interests, both domestic and foreign, involved in or interested in these incredibly profitable contracts, and so it is made into a political football.[4]

The government was deeply divided on what to do about Pertamina's demands and how to manage and balance those demands with what private domestic business wanted and what they also felt the sector needed. There were many senior bureaucrats and industry experts who doubted the state-owned company's capacity to take over the country's most strategic foreign contracts and feared the consequences for the broader investment climate. The directors general for oil and gas, Evita Legowo (2009–11) and Wiratmaja (2011–17), stated routinely that their priority was sustaining investment, increasing production, and ensuring there was no interruption to Indonesia's oil and gas supplies—in other words, the priority was *not* expanding Pertamina's assets but sustaining the country's overall production levels (Detikfinance 2009; RMOL.Co 2011). In an interview, Jokowi's minster for energy and mineral resources (2014–16), Sudirman Said, also expressed concern about falling oil production, and he did not believe the government's priority should be formalizing a right of first refusal for Pertamina.[5]

From this perspective, we can see that Ministerial Regulation No. 15/2015, which the ministry argued had met Pertamina's demands, was in fact intentionally ambiguous and was designed to provide the state with discretion when choosing how to award expiring oil and gas contracts. Indeed, when pressed by journalists, the director general for oil and gas Wiratmaja Puja admitted that this regulation gave Pertamina a first right in spirit rather than in the letter of the law. In one report, Wiratmaja stated that under the regulation, "Pertamina will be prioritized, but the government does not have to choose Pertamina. The existing investor's contract can be extended, and other companies can also apply. The principle here is that prioritizing Pertamina must not become a disincentive for other investors" (Dunia Energi 2015). The goal was clearly to try to appease statist nationalist demands without granting formal privileges to the national oil company over and above foreign firms, or indeed domestic firms. So the regulatory framework remained in a state of ambiguity.

In the eyes of statist protagonists, the government's response to their demands for localization was *setengah hati*, or half-hearted (CNN Indonesia 2015). The half-hearted nature of statist nationalist reform was in part a result of those bureaucrats who argued against policies that would favor Pertamina over other overseas investors, which they believed the sector desperately needed if Indonesia was to meet the country's rising oil demand. The expansion of domestic capital into upstream oil and gas also generated opposition to Pertamina's first right of refusal and lobbying by KADIN, and domestic oil entrepreneurs complicated efforts to finalize the new oil and gas law.

Pertamina's Public Campaigns

Yet, despite failing to change the terms of the sectoral law, in practice the state-owned company was in fact given privileged access to several major blocks—at times despite anxiety and opposition coming from senior state bureaucrats. Beyond the company's structural economic advantages described above, Pertamina had unique instrumental power, too. Pertamina benefited from a long history of deep connections to the bureaucracy (described in chapter 2). Nationalist proponents associated with the company leveraged long-standing networks within the Ministry of Energy and Mineral Resources to lobby members of executive government and parliament as well to back their proposal to help expand Pertamina's reach across the upstream sector.[6]

Alongside this well-established "backdoor" strategy, nationalist protagonists ran high-profile public campaigns in support of the state oil company. Public opinion was a useful instrument for Pertamina's advocates. Complex negotiations over oil and gas contracts are not a major priority for Indonesia's voters compared to, say, inflation or health care, but the sustained public campaign for Pertamina's first right, and the involvement of major Muslim organizations in particular moments of that campaign, helped to raise public interest in the fate of specific blocks.

During the boom years, under President Yudhoyono, a loose network of Pertamina-affiliated organizations, industry commentators, and think tanks mobilized to shape public debate on the issue of Pertamina's right of first refusal.

For example, Pertamina's union, the United Federation of Pertamina Employees (FSPPB), and an associated group, the Solidarity of Retired Pertamina Employees (SPKP), regularly appeared in media reports and organized public seminars and workshops criticizing the state for failing to adequately support its national oil company. Another prominent actor in this network was the industry think tank Indonesia Resource Studies (IRESS), headed by outspoken commentator Marwan Batubara, a former legislator for Partai Keadilan Sejahtera (PKS) (2009–14). Marwan was among the most often-quoted industry analysts, and his institute was staunchly loyal to Pertamina. Although there was nothing on the public record, several industry sources believed IRESS was partly funded by sections of Pertamina and former Pertamina staff in order to influence public debate in favor of the company's interests.

Kuturbi, a former Pertamina bureaucrat and member of parliament (2014–19), was another prominent supporter of Pertamina's first right. Kuturbi had been an expert staff for Pertamina's board of commissioners from 1977 to 2006 and had a PhD from the Colorado School of Mines, where many bureaucrats in the energy and mining sector obtained their graduate education. After retiring from Pertamina in 2006, he became an industry commentator and consistently argued against the liberalization of Indonesia's oil industry. He eventually entered politics via the Nasdem party, won a seat in parliament (2014–19), and sat in the commission responsible for revising the oil and gas law. In an interview, Kuturbi explained that he entered politics to defend Pertamina and to lobby for the company's rights in the new law: "Pertamina must be offered all [expiring] contracts, and Pertamina should be doing all community relations when it comes to joint projects. Foreign companies shouldn't be so integrated into our community and society. And they should not own our natural assets and then use those assets to make profits and leverage our assets to borrow from banks. Pertamina should be the company that does this."[7]

Many of the organizations and individuals that were publicly lobbying for Pertamina, including Kuturbi, did not have particularly remarkable links to decision makers in the ministry or to political elites in government; this was the domain of senior Pertamina staff and directors. Instead, this nationalist network deployed a pro-Pertamina narrative to the media and attempted to shape public discourse on sensitive questions regarding Pertamina's rights and roles. The strategy indicated that the company and its allies believed there was a broad popular preference in favor of Pertamina over both foreign and domestic private ownership and that by launching a public campaign, lawmakers and elected officials would come under increasing pressure to respond to nationalist demands.

The strategy had a discernible impact on state policymakers. For example, after Evita Legowo retired from her position as director general for oil and gas in 2012, she commented that by the end of her tenure, "nationalism" had become the sector's "number one headache" (McBeth 2013). Others in the ministry also complained in interviews about the challenges of managing increasingly widespread nationalist demands for Pertamina to take over foreign blocks while also trying to sustain much needed foreign and private investment. The campaign for Pertamina's first right of refusal gained momentum when particular foreign contracts approached their expiry. The case of the Mahakam block is illustrative because it highlights both the extent of nationalist ambivalence within the bureaucracy and the means via which Pertamina and its advocates could pressure the government by politicizing negotiations over foreign blocks. French oil and gas company Total had been at Mahakam in East Kalimantan either exploring or producing oil and gas since 1968. Japan's Inpex had a 50 percent share in the block; the other half was owned by Total. Mahakam had long been one of Indonesia's most strategic oil and gas blocks, contributing to over 25 percent of the country's entire gas production, while also making up 7 percent of Indonesia's oil supplies (Singgih 2007). Total's production sharing contract was first signed in 1977, and then the Suharto government extended it in 1997. This extension was set to expire in 2017.

Total began negotiations over its contract extension with the Yudhoyono government as early as 2009. But Karen Agustiawan indicated that she wanted Pertamina to take a substantial interest in, or even take over, the block (Detikfinance 2009). Both Total and Pertamina, therefore, had expressed their interest in the block's operatorship. But the strategic and complex nature of the block meant state managers in the ministry were ambivalent about the SOE's capacity to handle the project and maintain production levels. A public campaign in favor of transferring Mahakam to Pertamina began in 2012–13, off the back of the Constitutional Court's decision to dissolve BP Migas (detailed in chapter 3). Emboldened by their victory in the courts, the nationalist coalition that brought down BP Migas turned its attention to Mahakam. Marwan Batubara of IRESS organized this campaign and told the *Jakarta Post* that "the disbandment of BPMigas would ease the group's steps to push the government to meet its demands [on Mahakam]" (Azwar 2012). Representatives from groups affiliated with Pertamina, together with members of Muhammadiyah and NU, plus prominent national economists such as Rizal Ramli and Kwik Gian Kie appeared in the media regularly, held seminars, and organized a petition demanding the government hand the block over to Pertamina and return Indonesia's riches to the state.

The Yudhoyono administration continued to equivocate. Economists, industry experts, and bureaucrats within the ministry spoke increasingly of an impending energy crisis in Indonesia as energy demand continued to rise, while accessible oil reserves were slowly being diminished (Mahfoedz 2014; Platts

2013). President Yudhoyono thus avoided making a decision and instead left the fate of the contentious block in the hands of his successor.

Pertamina continued to lobby for the block during the early years of the Jokowi presidency. Former minister for energy and mineral resources Sudirman Said (2014–16) stated in an interview that Pertamina lobbied hard to be given access to all expiring foreign contracts, but he was skeptical about Pertamina's capacity to manage complex blocks like Mahakam.[8] Amien Sunaryadi, the head of SKK Migas (2014–18), voiced the same concerns and stated that the government needed to prevent Pertamina from capital overreach. Media reports revealed that Pertamina would need to invest over US$2.5 billion annually into the block in order to maintain and extend its production levels (Cahyafitri 2015a). Domestic and international industry experts were also skeptical about Pertamina's capabilities (McBeth 2018). In the words of one local analyst, "While an excess of nationalistic sentiment runs high among policymakers when it comes to the discussion of Mahakam's fate, little attention has been paid to the enormous scale of the operation should Pertamina be left to operate it alone" (Cahyafitri 2015a).

Nevertheless, Jokowi's political advisers supported Pertamina. Luhut Pandjaitan, for example, head of the Presidential Staff Office (Kantor Staf Presiden [KSP]) during Jokowi's first year in office, recommended that Pertamina take over the operating rights for Mahakam, with a share split of 70 percent for Pertamina and 30 percent for Total (*Tempo Magazine* 2015). The minister for state-owned enterprises Rini Soemarno, another of Jokowi's closest allies and key operator during Jokowi's 2014 presidential bid, also advocated strongly for Pertamina's rights to the block (*Tribunnews* 2015). Both Luhut and Rini saw Pertamina's control of Mahakam as an important political legacy for Jokowi that would help him shore up support for a second term in office. After months of intrigue in the media, President Jokowi finally decided in March 2015 not to extend Total's contract, and in June, the government announced it would transfer the operating rights and a 70 percent stake to Pertamina.

The Jokowi administration was consistent in its bullish approach to Pertamina and the state firm's capacity to takeover expiring foreign oil contracts. In 2018, the government rejected Chevron's request to extend its contract for the Rokan block, which at the time produced just over 30 percent of Indonesia's oil (PricewaterhouseCoopers 2017). The decision to hand the block to Pertamina instead was, according to the government, based on the SOE's superior production plan, which would ostensibly save the government billions of dollars in oil imports by channeling crude into Pertamina's refineries for domestic use. The decision attracted criticism from a range of stakeholders, who felt the financial and technological burden of the block would be too much for Pertamina to bear (Bachtiar 2018). But the Jokowi government remained committed to ensuring

Pertamina got control of the block. After ninety years in Indonesia, Rokan was Chevron's last project, having resigned from several other blocks around the archipelago in the years prior. The result was that by 2021, Pertamina was finally and for the first time in the country's history set to become the country's top oil producer.

So despite the regulatory stalemate that marked proposed revisions to the 2001 Oil and Gas Law, the 2000s were marked by a striking incremental transition toward domestic ownership of the country's hydrocarbon resources. Appendix A provides a list of all production sharing contracts with major domestic ownership. Those data demonstrate that during the early and mid-2000s, the trend was for domestic private takeovers of expiring foreign contracts. The data also show that from 2013, Pertamina was allocated the majority of previously foreign-run concessions, including two of the most productive and strategic blocks in the country—Mahakam and Rokan. This shift suggests that although the SOE had failed to change the legal and regulatory domain in its favor, in practice it achieved numerous important victories by squeezing both foreign and domestic capital out of some of the country's most important and most profitable oil and gas concessions. To be sure, foreign capital continued to play an important role in the sector. BP, ConocoPhilips, CNOOC, and Exxon Mobil were still producing large volumes of Indonesia's oil and gas as well (figure 5.1). Many of Pertamina's contracts were also joint operating bodies in which Pertamina partnered with an international or private domestic company to jointly operate the field. Still, as figures 5.1 and 5.2 illustrate, by 2021, the state-owned company had finally become the country's major oil producer, from producing around just one-fifth of the country's oil back in 2012.

To conclude this section, the post-Suharto political economy presented new opportunities for statist nationalist advocates and their localizing agendas. Pertamina had evolved into a more efficient and capable upstream operator, and democratic reform brought new prospects for nationalist actors to access and pressure policymakers in different sections of the bureaucracy. New domestic private actors emerged, too, and their interests and instrumental power prevented the emergence of coherently statist legal framework for investment in the oil and gas sector. At the time of writing in 2022, the Jokowi administration and lawmakers in parliament had still not arrived at an agreement on the terms of a new oil and gas law. In fact, well into Jokowi's second term in office, talk of revising the 2001 Oil and Gas Law had faded into the background. A senior member of Pertamina's communications team and long-term industry analyst described in an interview in 2022 how the momentum to revise the 2001 Oil and Gas Law had changed: "It's not a priority for anyone anymore, not even for Pertamina. . . . So many of the big tenders are done for the moment; in fact,

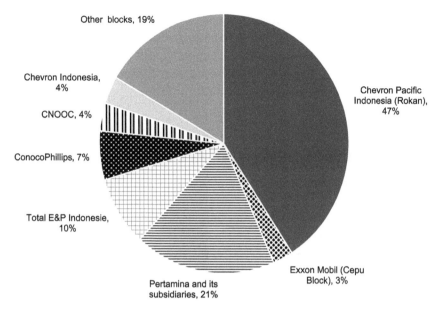

FIGURE 5.1. Major oil producers, 2011

Source: Adapted from PWC (2012)

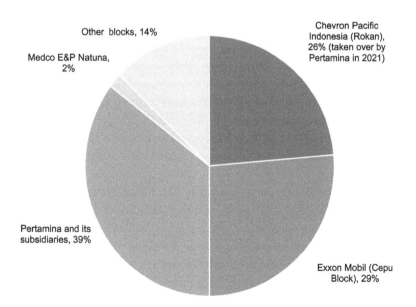

FIGURE 5.2. Major oil producers, 2019

Source: Adapted from PWC (2020)

there have been very few contract tenders in these last years. All the big blocks are now in the company's hands and Pertamina [has to be] more focused on first balancing its massive upstream investments, and actually it can't handle any more big contracts . . . and second its downstream distribution obligations. . . . So at least for now it seems the law is dead."[9]

The Nationalization of Freeport

The most striking trend in Indonesia's mining sector over the course of the post-Suharto period has been, as the previous chapter argued, the rise to prominence of domestic mining firms. At the same time, there were certain limits to the corporate control of resource nationalism in this sector. One particular mine drove government managers and politicians to redesign the state's role in the sector. The Jokowi administration established a new sectoral holding company, with the primary objective to nationalize the Freeport mine in Papua. The Freeport case is arguably the most compelling demonstration of how political imperatives pushed nationalist interventions down a more statist nationalist path—and this push came *after* the boom.

A Politically Salient Mine

The Grasberg mine is the world's largest and most lucrative gold mine and until 2018 had been majority owned and operated by the American mining giant Freeport McMoran since 1967. The company's most recent CoW was set to expire in 2021, but the firm's management sought an early extension deal, arguing that it required contract security before embarking on the next stage of the mine's $18 billion underground expansion. By law, however, the company could only apply for an extension in 2019. In effect, Freeport was asking for an exception. Unlike most other mining contracts, these negotiations attracted intense media and public scrutiny.

This is in part because the company has such a long and troubled history in Indonesia. The Grasberg mine is situated in Papua, one of Indonesia's poorest provinces and a place where a low-level separatist conflict has simmered for decades. Violence has intermittently broken out at the mine between security forces, employees, and Papuans associated with different armed factions of the separatist movement (IPAC 2017). Freeport has been accused of a range of human and labor rights abuses dating back to the Suharto era (Leith 2003). The democratic transition did not bring major change in this regard, and news of strikes, protests, and shootings by security forces and police and intimidation of journalists are a common occurrence (Human Rights Watch 2015). Wide-ranging reports and data compiled by organizations like the Business and Human Rights Resource Centre and the Institute for Policy Analysis of Conflict have documented decades of fraught interactions between the company, the regional government, the local population, and separatist organizations.[10] Many Indonesians in government and others working in the sector and for NGOs felt that Freeport had never approached any of its contract negotiations with the government in good faith. After all, Freeport had avoided fulfilling major parts of its contract—when the company put in a request for an early negotiation of its contract in 2016 with the Jokowi government, the firm had divested only 9.36 percent of its shares despite the contract mandating that 39 percent should have been divested to local parties by this stage. The company's profile in Indonesia was, therefore, unusually public for a mining firm and extremely contentious. Against this backdrop, the negotiations over the 2021 contract extension were framed by both journalists and politicians as a test of Indonesian sovereignty.

The political salience of the Freeport mine intensified during the Jokowi period because the contract negotiations became fraught with public controversy. Luhut Pandjaitan, a government minister and one of President Jokowi's most important political allies and operators, was an avid proponent of the 51 percent divestment regime and was particularly and publicly concerned that Freeport meet its obligation in this regard. He stated that even despite the downturn in commodity prices the new government was grappling with, foreign companies like Freeport were more financially troubled than the state (*Jakarta Post* 2015). And this was true to an extent. The commodities bust and several questionable investment decisions had left Freeport with significant debt, and by 2015, its share price had plunged, and it was in the midst of selling assets and restructuring almost US$20 billion in debt (Sanderson, Hume, and Wilson 2016). However, Luhut's personal ambitions for the mine were revealed to the public just one year into Jokowi's first term in office. In mid-November 2015, Luhut became embroiled in a controversy over Freeport's divestment deal. It was revealed that Setya Novanto, Golkar politician and then parliamentary speaker, together with shady oilman Riza Chalid, had met with Freeport Indonesia informally (Budiartie and Warburton 2015). The pair offered to expedite the company's contract extension in return for private shares in the mine and they named Luhut Pandjaitan as a key facilitator of the deal. The content of the meeting had been recorded by then director of Freeport Indonesia Maroef Sjamsoeddin, which he then handed to the Ministry of Energy and Resources. The full transcript was then leaked to the press.

The story made media headlines for weeks and enflamed tensions within executive government. The scandal laid bare the extent to which senior politicobusiness elites and business actors viewed the foreign firm's divestment obligations as an opportunity for private gain. The public now had incredibly detailed insight into the mechanics of corruption and rent seeking at the highest levels of government and in relation to a mine that was both politically salient and that politicians—including Luhut—routinely described as a national asset that belonged to the Indonesian people.

Negotiating National Control

In response to the media furor surrounding the leaked tape, President Jokowi's position on Freeport began to harden. When he first came to power, Jokowi had no clear agenda for the Freeport contract. In an interview, the minister for energy and mineral resources at the time, Sudirman Said, stated that the president delegated responsibility to him to direct the Freeport negotiations and to find a solution that satisfied "both parties" without articulating a strong personal preference.[11]

But after the tape scandal, it became clear that Jokowi now perceived Freeport's contract as a political liability. In 2016, Jokowi made a point of denying Freeport an early contract extension. Then in January 2017, the Ministry of Energy and Mineral Resources introduced a new set of regulations demanding CoW holders, including Freeport, forfeit their contracts and sign new licensing agreements or they would be denied an export permit. The president's change of tack was a reflection of the importance he now placed on insulating himself from any political attacks on his nationalist credentials when it came to Freeport (Warburton 2018).

This was important to Jokowi because back in 2014, he won the presidential elections by only narrowly defeating Prabowo Subianto, chair of the Gerindra Party (introduced in chapter 4). During that campaign, Prabowo deployed vitriolic nationalist rhetoric as part of his broader populist platform (Aspinall 2015b). At rallies, Prabowo decried the exploitation of Indonesia's land and resources by nameless "foreign forces" and gave impassioned speeches that claimed Indonesia's riches were disappearing while the profits were taken abroad, leaving little for the country's poor masses (Gammon 2014). The narrative was reflective of a wider nationalist mood that Aspinall (2015b, 80) argues emerged in the post–New Order years, whereby "major parties and aspirants to executive office differ very little in policy and programmatic terms, [so] nationalism is a useful legitimating device by which such actors can try to distinguish themselves from rivals and court public support." These conditions prompt nationalist outbidding among elected officials when it comes to sensitive resource projects like Freeport. As one Golkar politician explained in an interview in the months after the presidential elections, members of parliament feel they "need to be seen to be nationalist."[12]A former chairperson of the IMA also commented that during election years, "no one is brave enough to take a policy stance that might appear to favor foreign companies."[13] Against this backdrop and with the 2019 presidential elections looming closer on the horizon, the president treated the Freeport negotiations as a matter of political urgency.

Private sector actors hoped for opportunities to buy into the mine. Beyond the brazen rent-seeking scandal involving Reza and Luhut, there were other politicobusiness elites who had been circling the negotiations. According to media reports, Surya Paloh, chairperson of the National Democratic Party (Nasdem), and Vice President Jusuf Kalla (2014–19) both made serious efforts to pursue shares in the mine via a range of avenues (Cahyafitri and Witular 2015; Lubis 2015). Domestic business groups also expressed serious interest in taking a participating share in the Grasberg mine as part of the government's divestment negotiation. One journalist covering the Freeport negotiations suggested that the usual cast of mining giants, including Edwin Soeryadjaya of Adaro, approached the president to propose a plan for how their firms might acquire Freeport's divested shares.[14] Further, at one point, Medco's acquisition of Newmont's mine in 2016 had been considered by Jokowi as a model for how domestic firms might raise funds to participate in a share deal with Freeport. Many industry experts, and in particular those associated with the foreign expatriate mining community, expressed doubt that the divestment would ever go ahead, but if it did, the capital would likely need to come from the country's private conglomerates.[15] From their perspective, the mine was simply too expensive for any of the SOEs to purchase. But when approached by these sorts of private business interests, the president reportedly told them they would have to wait some time before being given access to Freeport shares—he had resolved that a state-owned company would purchase the entire 51 percent divested shares.

There were two reasons Jokowi took the statist path. First, according to an insider within the Presidential Staff Office, when it came to the case of Newmont, Jokowi backed his ally Arifin Panigoro's pursuit of the mine, but he wanted to keep the country's most strategic mine in state hands.[16] Not only would a state-led takeover sit well with the public, this adviser explained, but Jokowi did not want such an important asset landing in the hands of business elites with questionable political loyalty. With elections due in 2019, the same year the Freeport contract would legally be allowed to request an extension, the president endeavored to present himself as taking a hard line against foreign companies and Freeport in particular, and it was imperative that he was seen to be doing the bidding of the state, not politicobusiness elites or conglomerates. There was also the risk that should Jokowi and his coalition lose the 2019 elections, a different government would divvy up Freeport shares to his or her business network. So Jokowi wanted to show the electorate he could negotiate a historical state acquisition of Freeport Indonesia and control who had access to the company's shares.

The major challenge for Jokowi, however, was that none of the state-owned mining companies had even near the capital to acquire the Freeport mine. Jokowi turned to Rini Soemarno, the minister for state-owned enterprises, who laid out a grand plan to reform and restructure the state-owned sector in which SOEs would be consolidated under new state-run sectoral holding companies. The idea of establishing holding companies had been proposed on and off in the post-Suharto years as a means of consolidating the sector and doing away with some of the smaller and least efficient state companies. Holding companies would also then be in control of more assets, in turn giving them leverage to borrow from banks and rely less on the state for financing. The idea was appealing to Jokowi's developmental sensibilities and his broader economic push to reduce red tape and increase efficiency across the economy and especially in the state sector (Warburton 2018). Under Rini's guidance, Jokowi oversaw significant restructuring of SOEs in key sectors, including mining.

The ministry decided to turn PT Inalum, the 100 percent state-owned aluminum miner, into the sector's holding company. The other three mining sector SOEs, Antam (nickel, bauxite, and gold), Bukit Asam (coal), and Timah (tin), would now sit under Inalum. By pooling the assets of these state companies, the government projected a new holding company would be in control of approximately $6.6 billion in assets (*Nikkei Asian Review* 2017). In turn, according to Rini, the state-owned miners would be able to leverage these massive assets to borrow from banks and "alleviate the government's burden of having to inject capital into these companies when they need to expand" (*Jakarta Globe* 2017). The holding company would become the means via which the state could acquire shares in expensive privately run mines—and the major objective was to purchase the 40.64 percent shares in the Freeport mine that would become available once Freeport and the government could agree on a divestment price and structure.

Establishment of the holding company was finalized in November 2017, and Inalum officially became the state's mining sector holding company (Sugianto 2017). One year later, after drawn-out and difficult negotiations, the Jokowi government arranged for Inalum to raise enough capital to make the $3.85 billion acquisition of a majority stake in the Freeport mine by borrowing from eleven different banks (NS Energy 2018; Reuters 2017). The deal was locked in just months before the 2019 election campaign. The government, thus, pursued a statist approach to ensuring national control of this particular mine. The Freeport case was an exception to a primarily business-oriented form of resource nationalism in this sector. President Jokowi and his advisers turned away the local firms and politico-business elites who sought access to the mine, driven by a strong sense that for this especially lucrative and politically symbolic extractive project, it must be the state that becomes the major shareholder and that controls the revenues of what remains the world's largest and most profitable gold and copper mine.

A Statist Nationalism

This chapter examined the conditions under which a more statist nationalism prevailed in Indonesia's resource sectors during and after the boom. It looked at the ambiguous fate of the 2001 Oil and Gas Law and homed in on the high-profile state acquisition of the Freeport mine. In different ways, both cases are classic examples of how, when a problem, policy, or particular resource contract, has high political salience and state actors believe there is a political risk to siding with private corporate interests, an otherwise strong and influential private business class can be constrained or excluded by the state (Culpepper 2011; Fairfield 2015).

During the boom years, Indonesia's oil and gas sector was marked by policy conflict and confusion, generated by tensions between both a statist and business-centered form of resource nationalism. Throughout the colonial and New Order periods, domestic business had been unable to overcome the high barriers to entry that characterized the upstream oil and gas sector. The post–New Order political economy created new and more favorable conditions for nationalist change. The liberal reforms introduced after Suharto's resignation in 1998 facilitated Pertamina's corporate revival and the company became a much more capable upstream operator than it had been in the past. Moreover, as foreign interest in Indonesia's depleting oil wells began to wane and as foreign contracts approached expiry, more domestic private players were able to move into the upstream market by taking over old foreign-operated wells. The local business interests that entered the sector were generally well-connected tycoons and entrepreneurs, who could leverage their material and political influence to pursue expiring foreign contracts. As a result, Pertamina's efforts to enshrine in law a first right of refusal to these foreign contracts largely failed.

However, more so than in either the mining or plantations sectors, state capital remained a formidable political and economic actor in this sector, and despite legal ambiguity surrounding the sectoral law, there was a slow nationalization of the country's oil wells that took place during the first decades of the twenty-first century, driven by statist advocates in Pertamina, the government, and civil society actors with links to the SOE. This trend stands in distinction to the much more business-driven nationalization that marked the mining sector. I have argued in this chapter that Pertamina's historical influence and structural power, paired with the political traction of pro-Pertamina public campaigns in the democratic era, helped ensure the company secured some of the country's most strategic and profitable oil and gas concessions.

The state's acquisition of the Freeport mine in 2018 and the massive investment in a state-owned holding company also breaks with the dominant pattern of private sector acquisitions in the rest of the mining industry during and following the boom. Although most contract negotiations between mining companies and the government go under the public radar, this particular mine had immense political salience. Freeport's contract expiry date was, in the eyes of the governing coalition and President Jokowi, dangerously close to his bid for reelection. The president decided to turn the mine into a political weapon rather than a political vulnerability. To achieve that goal, the president established a new state holding company that could leverage the massive capital needed to bring the mine under government control. The statist approach was driven by political expediency—the government's objective was to mobilize a perceived public preference for state ownership of the mine and prevent control by one particular business tycoon or group of tycoons in the lead-up to or just following the presidential election.

6

OWNERSHIP, IDENTITY, AND NATIONALIST DEMANDS

So far, this study has traced the trajectory of nationalist policies in Indonesia's major primary commodity sectors, emphasizing the role that different domestic businesses played in determining the direction of nationalist change. Although the government turned to SOEs at key moments, I have argued that the most remarkable feature of Indonesia's experience of resource nationalism in the twenty-first century was the directive role played by an increasingly influential private sector. The last two decades have produced important changes in patterns of ownership, with the mining sector dominated by domestic private interests, the palm oil sector characterized by a mix of major local and international conglomerates, and the oil and gas sector marked by the new entry of domestic firms alongside the massive expansion of Pertamina's assets. The commodity boom and the clientelist features of Indonesia's democratic political economy underpinned the development of a politically influential class of domestic resource giants whose structural and instrumental power reached unprecedented heights in the wider context of the country's history of capitalist development.

Yet, we still lack a clear picture of why corporate actors held such distinct preferences when it came to foreign flows, and what those preferences might tell us about how different sorts of companies perceive and interact with the state and other forms of capital. This chapter grapples with the question of why some business actors become nationalist advocates, while others remained liberal bulwarks. To answer these questions, I bring together qualitative interview material with original survey data to provide a more complete picture of business preferences in each sector and the features of individual companies that are associated with these preferences. Using a survey of business managers, I test the observations I have made so far about the nationalist preferences of major extractive and plantation businesses, and drawing on theoretical expectations generated by scholarship on business-level characteristics and policy preferences, I explore how factors such as the sector, size, and ownership structure of Indonesian companies are associated with differing levels of support for limiting foreign investment. I go one step further than most other business surveys, however, and explore how firm ownership and business owners' identities predict nationalist preferences. I do so because the history of Indonesia's business class is infused with identity-based divisions that remain relevant today. Just a cursory glance at the ethnic composition of the most prominent conglomerates and companies indicates the sustained prominence of ethnically Chinese businesspeople within the country's economy (Forbes 2022), and such patterns of wealth distribution potentially generate particular policy preferences, too.

The survey data confirm, first, that business managers in these sectors have heterogenous preferences when it comes to FDI, and firms in mining and plantations are not coherently nationalist or liberal. In fact, contradicting the expectations of much of the literature on sector-based preferences, mining and plantation companies are on average less nationalist than firms in other parts of the economy. Second, company size matters but in inconsistent ways: the largest agricultural companies are the most open to FDI, in line with the findings of other studies that suggest the larger the firm, the more supportive it will be of cross-border flows of trade and capital. However, in the mining sector, the largest firms are significantly more likely to oppose increasing foreign investment. These findings are, overall, in line with the arguments and observations put forward in this book so far, which have been based on qualitative observations. Importantly, however, even when accounting for a range of other variables, it was businesses with Chinese Indonesian ownership that were significantly less likely to support constraints on FDI. This finding was consistent across all sectors of Indonesia's economy, but the effect was largest in the agricultural sector.

To further understand the relationship between ownership and nationalist preferences, the chapter integrates interview data and information on the profiles of the major producers in each sector. I argue that identity has played a complex but nonetheless important role in determining business preferences for FDI and, in turn, supporting a policy environment that embraces rather than constrains foreign capital in the plantation sector. The sector's evolution over the past two decades has, for a range of reasons described in chapter 4, been marked by a deep integration into regional networks of capital. Yet, I argue, the identity and internationalized nature of some of the country's largest palm oil producers and refiners has not been incidental to this trend of regionalization but rather an enabling condition for such a sectoral shift.

Specifically, in the post-Suharto period, the palm oil sector's many Chinese Indonesian–owned firms and family conglomerates were no longer threatened by or opposed to FDI as they had been in the late 1990s; instead, open ownership structures and the embrace of foreign inflows worked to the advantage of such companies. These sorts of business actors no longer relied as heavily on the state for privilege and protection as they had during the Suharto years. The major pribumi mining firms, on the other hand, on average sought direct ties with the state and demanded protection as a means of business expansion. In fact, where the survey probed corporate managers about their company's lobbying activities and their relations with the state, significant differences along identity lines emerged, and qualitative interviews confirmed a strong preference among Chinese Indonesian businesses for avoiding close and especially public ties with politicians and state actors.

This chapter begins by returning to the literature on business preferences, eliciting a set of expectations about how firm-level characteristics might determine both what business actors want and how they go about pursuing their policy agendas. The second section explains the survey instrument and reveals the results. Section three integrates the survey findings with qualitative reflections on how identity matters for explaining business preferences. I then dig deeper into the identity and internationalization of major domestic firms in each sector and conclude by reflecting on how such business characteristics can help to explain subnational patterns of resource nationalism.

Expectations about Business and Nationalist Preferences

Let us return to extant theories about business preferences and economic policymaking. How should we expect firm-level characteristics to determine the nationalist preferences of Indonesian businesses? Recalling the review presented in chapter 1, a range of scholarship has attempted to explain the source of firms' heterogenous policy preferences. Some research argues that companies' preferences are derived from the sector in which they operate. Firms in the extractives and cash crop sectors, for example, have often been cast as especially protectionist. In these sectors, so the argument goes, firms' products (raw commodities) are fixed, inflexible, and vulnerable to booms and busts, which in turn motivates firms to seek state protection and subsidies (Frieden 1991; Haggard, Maxfield, and Schneider 1997, 39–39; Shafer 1990).

New research on firms and trade policy, on the other hand, emphasize that regardless of sector, companies that are large, productive, and globalized will have distinctly more liberal preferences and will lobby for open trade and investment regulations (Hamilton-Hart 1999; Kim and Osgood 2019; Milner 1988; Yoshimatsu 2000). This is because as a business or group grows large enough and begins expanding interests beyond its home country, it becomes more likely to support the liberal policies that enable international expansion. Natasha Hamilton-Hart (1999, 4) explains that as firms become "internationally-oriented and competitive, they also become more concerned with access to investment sites and markets abroad than with protecting a domestic market." The ownership characteristics of business have also been explored as a potential driver of managers' decisions and preferences for particular sorts of investment regulations, including public versus private, partial state ownership, family-owned businesses, and even the diverse identities of board members (Alon and Kim 2021; Gallo, Tàpies, and Cappuyns 2004; Kesternich and Schnitzer 2010; Nekhili and Gatfaoui 2013). To explore the extent to which these different firm-level characteristics—sector, size, internationalization, and ownership—are associated with different sorts of nationalist preferences among Indonesian businesses, I leverage an original survey of Indonesian business managers.

The Survey

In 2019, as part of a collaborative research program on "Southeast Asia's Rules-Based Order" (SEARBO), Australia's Department of Foreign Affairs and Trade (DFAT) funded a survey of Indonesian business managers. The survey was implemented by the Australian National University's Department of Political and Social Change[1] in partnership with the Indonesia Survey Institute (Lembaga Survei Indonesia [LSI]). As part of the SEARBO team, I contributed to the design and execution of the survey, which was fielded between May and November 2019 using face-to-face interviews with 672 business managers and owners from across all major sectors of the Indonesian economy.[2]

Samples of companies in each sector, except for agriculture, were randomly selected from the list of companies in the government's 2016 economic census. For the agricultural sector, on the other hand, we randomly sampled from the Agriculture Companies Directory 2013, 2016, and 2017, put together by the Indonesia's Central Statistics Agency (Badan Pusat Statistik [BPS]). Of the 700 companies that were originally selected, 500 companies were successfully interviewed. An additional 172 firms were surveyed through repeated random substitution. The nominal nonresponse rate was 4 percent (28 firms) and the minimum response was between 90 and 100 percent per sector. Responses are weighted to be proportional to the population of firms in a given sector according to BPS data.

In terms of the respondents, around 37 percent were business owners, and just over half were directors of firms, with another 6 percent holding the position of executive directors. The survey, thus, successfully recruited senior business managers with a deep understanding of their firm and the sectors in which they operate. Respondents also understood that the survey was designed to elicit their opinions in their capacity as firm owners or managers, and so the questions we asked about policy preferences can be reasonably assumed to represent the interests of their firm, rather than their own personal preferences as ordinary Indonesian citizens. Within the sample, ninety-six came from mining (including oil and gas) and ninety from agriculture.

Such data are rare. Only the World Bank conducts representative opinion surveys of Indonesia's business community as part of its global Enterprise Survey project, but the survey's sectoral reach is limited, and mining and plantation firms are not included in the World Bank's survey. So far, therefore, scholars attempting to systematically assess Indonesian business preferences and lobbying activities have had limited data to work with. This business survey constitutes a first attempt to generate new data with which to explore such topics.

Variables and Descriptive Statistics

What do the firms in this survey look like, and how do extractive and agricultural firms compare? Table 6.1 displays descriptive statistics for all firms that participated in the survey across major sectors of the Indonesian economy, as well as information specifically for mining and agricultural firms. The table includes information on all variables of interest, including support for FDI, company size, ownership, internationalization, and relationships with state actors.

To measure the dependent variable—businesses' FDI preferences—respondents were asked a simple question: "Please indicate whether you agree or disagree with the following statement: Indonesia should be more open to foreign investment," with answers ranging on a Likert scale from strongly agree, agree, between agree and disagree, disagree, or strongly disagree. The results (presented in table 6.1) are remarkable to the extent that differences between average responses among mining and agricultural firms are not so dramatic, though the standard deviations suggest important heterogeneity of preferences within sectors. The survey also shows that although on average mining companies express more opposition to FDI than agricultural companies, both sectors are overall less nationalist than firms in general across all sectors of the economy. The survey thus contradicts sectoral-based theories of firm preferences, which

TABLE 6.1. Descriptive statistics: Full sample and sectoral samples

VARIABLE	FULL SAMPLE			AGRICULTURAL COMPANIES ONLY			MINING COMPANIES ONLY			MIN.	MAX.	CODING	
	OBS.	MEAN	STD. DEV.	OBS.	MEAN	STD. DEV.	OBS.	MEAN	STD. DEV.			VALUES	
Oppose FDI	662	1.49	1.09	90	1.31	1.05	95	1.39	1.1	0	4	Strongly support (0) Strongly oppose (4)	
Size	663	0.74	0.93	90	1.32	1.08	95	1.02	0.93	0	3	Small (0) Very large (3)	
Foreign ownership	428	0.15	0.49	60	0.06	0.36	57	0.19	0.51	0	2	None (0) Some (1)	
Identity of owner	591	0.19	0.39	81	0.27	0.45	86	0.13	0.33	0	1	Majority Chinese Indonesian–owned (1)	
Firm type	660	1.3	0.96	90	2.64	1.08	94	2.3	0.99	0	3	Public (0) Private (1) Private individual (2) Others (3)	
Invests overseas	640	0.04	0.21	87	0.05	0.21	91	0.08	0.28	0	1	Yes (1)	
Diversified	650	0.1	0.31	88	0.15	0.35	91	0.09	0.28	0	1	Yes (1)	
Exports	664	0.13	0.34	89	0.27	0.44	95	0.14	0.34	0	1	Yes (1)	
Lobbying preferences	504	0.51	0.50	77	0.62	0.49	76	0.43	0.5	0	1	Via firm owners (0) Via industry associations (1)	
Good government relations	659	1.97	0.80	90	2.2	0.73	95	2.07	0.85	0	3	Not important at all (0) Very important (3)	

have long argued that resource and agricultural companies prefer protection from foreign capital due to the fixed nature of their assets (Shafer 1990, 1994). Instead, at least on this question of FDI, resource firms appear less nationalist than firms in other parts of the Indonesian economy.

The survey sought representation on firm size across each sector. We used three categories based on number of employees: 5–20 (small), 21–100 (medium), 101–500 (large), more than 500 (very large). When it comes to larger-sized companies—which we are most interested in for the purposes of testing comparative hypotheses and for examining the preferences of structurally and instrumentally powerful firms—both mining and agriculture are home to more "large" and "very large" firms than the rest of the economy. On average, though, agricultural companies are larger than those in the mining industry.

How does ownership structure vary across sectors? First, the level of foreign ownership among the companies represented in the survey is very low, with almost none of the agricultural firms indicating any level of foreign ownership, and for mining, the mean was just 0.19. Also noteworthy is that for both sectors, the N drops down to 60 or below, suggesting that participants were either unsure or did not wish to disclose the extent of foreign ownership or shareholding in their businesses. Respondents were more confident in responding to the question of owner identity. The data show that the proportion of Chinese Indonesian–owned firms in each sector reflects qualitative observations made throughout this book, with many more such firms in the agricultural sector than in mining, or indeed in the rest of the economy more broadly. When it comes to firm ownership type, agricultural and mining firms are not so different to the rest of the sample, with the average respondent coming from a privately owned rather than publicly owned business.

In both sectors of interest, the number of firms with any degree of internationalization is miniscule, reflecting broader trends throughout Indonesia's private sector. For example, the survey asked respondents whether their firm invests overseas. This variable best approximates a measure of internationalization because it provides some indication of a firm's global character. Prior research has demonstrated that in general, Indonesian firms are poorly internationalized (Carney and Dieleman 2011), and the survey data confirm this observation—this indicator returns a mean of just 0.05 and 0.08 for agriculture and mining, respectively. Instead, I rely on whether firms' export as a means of capturing their international orientation; here, more agricultural than mining firms export their products. Still, exports are an indicative but not ideal measure of business internationalization. Later in this chapter I turn to other sources of data to explore how this factor might play a role in determining the sorts of investment policies business wants.

To get a sense of whether preferences for protection are associated with how companies interact with the state, I use two different questions. First, the survey asked respondents how important it is for their company to maintain good relationships with bureaucrats at the national level. Both mining and agricultural firms are more likely to see relations with the state as important compared to the entire sample, suggesting that unsurprisingly, both sectors lean on the state for various licenses and thus share a need to sustain positive connections with the government. Second, however, when asked whether lobbying is more effective when done by individual companies or by industry associations, mining sector respondents were more likely to view individual companies as effecting greater influence over policies and regulations, indicating a preference for more direct, personal relationships with state policymakers. Most agricultural firms, on the other hand, believed lobbying was best done via industry associations, in turn indicating—at least in comparative terms—a degree of distance between national bureaucrats and individual business owners.

A Closer Look at Opposition to FDI

Next, we dig deeper into how different sorts of firms feel about the prospect of increasing FDI. We start with a broad look at the data for businesses across the whole economy, before zooming in on the commodity sectors. Figure 6.1 compares average levels of opposition to FDI for different company types (where the

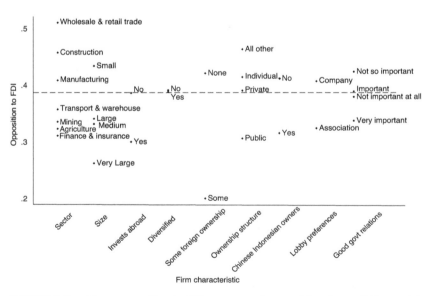

FIGURE 6.1. Mean opposition to FDI across sectors and firm types (full sample)

higher the position on the y-axis, the stronger the opposition to FDI). The horizontal line that runs through the figure indicates mean opposition to FDI for the full sample. The sectoral results confirm that firms in Indonesia's agricultural sector are on average the most welcoming of FDI, followed by mining companies. Across the economy, small businesses are the most nationalist, while the very large ones tend to be more supportive of FDI, which is in line with theoretical expectations about the liberal preferences of large firms (Kim and Osgood 2019). Those who export their products or commodities are also, on average, less opposed to FDI.

Predictably, businesses with some foreign ownership are the least likely to express opposition to increasing foreign investment in the Indonesian economy. Public companies are also less opposed to FDI, again an unsurprising finding given that such companies are also likely to be larger than other sorts of firms. When it comes to the importance that businesses place on sustaining good relations with national bureaucrats, there is no dramatic pattern that emerges, with most respondents clustering around the mean. Importantly, on the question of how owners' identity might shape preferences, we see that majority Chinese Indonesian–owned are more open to increasing foreign investment.

Next, we look specifically at firms in extractives and agriculture. In the agricultural sector, like firms in other parts of the economy, exporters are more open to FDI. On the other hand, there is almost no difference in the preferences of exporters and nonexporters in the mining sector. Size matters in both sectors but in opposite directions. In agriculture (figure 6.2), the very largest firms (500+ employees) are the most supportive of increasing FDI, while the large firms in this sector (with employees between 100 and 500) hold more nationalist preferences. This pattern is in line with one of the main contentions of this book: that it was the middle-tier companies that sought more restrictions on FDI during the boom, while the agribusiness giants—and the smaller firms that often depend on them—prefer a more liberal investment regime. In the mining sector, on the other hand, it is the very large companies that are most nationalist (figure 6.3). The survey data thus confirm the picture painted in chapter 4— that in the extractive sectors, the largest domestic firms are the strongest advocates for a more nationalist policy paradigm because it is these sorts of firms that stand to benefit from divestment and from the slow retreat of foreign companies from operating profitable mines. Finally, firms with majority Chinese Indonesian ownership are on average more liberal toward FDI in both sectors; there is a higher proportion of such firms in the agricultural sector.

There is no major difference in the FDI preferences of agricultural companies that lobby through associations versus those that lobby directly. For mining businesses, however, those that lobby the state directly through company

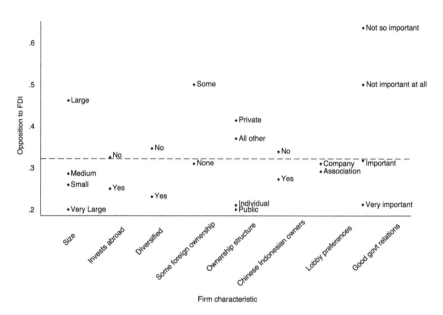

FIGURE 6.2. Mean opposition to FDI across sectors and firm types, agriculture sector only

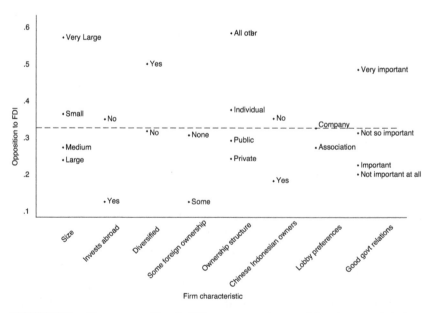

FIGURE 6.3. Mean opposition to FDI across sectors and firm types, mining sector only

owners and managers are on average more nationalist. Equally, mining companies that feel it is very important to sustain positive relationships with national-level bureaucrats are less likely to support an increase in FDI. Such patterns suggest a need for more instrumental types of policy power among those businesses that lobby for protection from foreign investors. Curiously, however, agricultural firms that see good state relations as "very important" are the least likely to oppose FDI. These nuanced relationships are explored further in regression analysis and the qualitative discussion later in this chapter.

Testing Firm Effects on Support for FDI

Motivated by the patterns that emerged from the descriptive statistics, this section probes the effect of particular firm-level characteristics on companies' probability of opposing an increase in FDI. To do so, I turn the outcome of interest, opposition to FDI, into a binary variable such that agreeing or strongly agreeing to the statement "Indonesia should be more open to foreign investment" is coded as 0, and all other responses are coded as 1. Those respondents who sit on the fence when it comes to FDI are, I argue, expressing an ambivalence toward foreign capital that makes them potentially open to supporting specific nationalist interventions. Coding for the remaining variables remains the same. Using simple logistic regression models, I investigate the probability that a particular type of firm will support or oppose FDI, first without any controls. Given that firms with foreign ownership will so obviously be less inclined to oppose foreign investment, I include this variable as a control rather than an independent variable of interest. I also include size as a control for the remaining models, given that size may be associated with factors like public ownership and export status.

The results of the logistic regression are displayed in table 6.2. Among mining firms, the very largest have a remarkably high predicted probability of opposing FDI (0.57, or 0.64 when the controls are included); the rest of the firms in this sector have a probability of between 0.2 and 0.36, suggesting that size constitutes the most important predictor of nationalist support among mining firms, a finding that again confirms the observation that the preferences of major domestic mining interests have been reflected in regulatory changes that pursue nationalization and squeeze out foreign operators. Meanwhile, and as expected, very large agricultural firms have just a 0.2–0.29 predicted probability of opposing FDI when controls are included (though the standard errors are notably high). It is the middle-tier agricultural firms that have the highest predicted probability of opposing FDI in this sector (0.51 with controls). Meanwhile, Chinese Indonesian–owned firms

TABLE 6.2. Predicted probabilities of firm opposition to foreign investment (by firm type)

	MINING		AGRICULTURE	
FIRM TYPE	(1) NO CONTROLS	(2) CONTROLS*	(3) NO CONTROLS	(4) CONTROLS*
Small	0.36 (0.08)	0.24 (0.09)	0.26 (0.08)	0.15 (0.09)
Medium	0.27 (0.08)	0.30 (0.11)	0.29 (0.1)	0.27 (0.12)
Large	0.24 (0.09)	0.23 (0.13)	0.46 (0.1)	0.51 (0.11)
Very large	0.57 (0.19)	0.64 (0.19)	0.2 (0.1)	0.29 (0.17)
Chinese Indonesian–owned	0.18 (0.11)	0.15 (0.14)	0.27 (0.06)	0.21 (0.1)
Non-Chinese Indonesian–owned	0.35 (0.05)	0.37 (0.08)	0.34 (0.09)	0.31 (0.08)
Public ownership	0.29 (0.09)	0.24 (0.16)	0.2 (0.1)	0.17 (0.11)
Private ownership	0.32 (0.09)	0.33 (0.13)	0.35 (0.06)	0.32 (0.07)
Exports	0.3 (0.12)	0.30 (0.19)	0.25 (0.09)	0.16 (0.09)
Does not export	0.33 (.05)	0.26 (0.06)	0.35 (0.06)	0.37 (0.08)
Good relations with state very important	0.48 (0.09)	0.32 (0.11)	0.21 (0.07)	0.09 (0.06)
Good relations with state not important	0.2 (0.18)	0.26 (0.23)	0.5 (0.05)	0.77 (0.14)
Lobbies via association	0.27 (0.08)	0.26 (0.11)	0.29 (0.07)	0.29 (0.08)
Lobbies via company	0.33 (0.07)	0.29 (0.09)	0.31 (0.09)	0.27 (0.11)

Standard errors in parentheses; *Controlling for firm size and some foreign ownership.

have among the lowest predicted probability of opposing FDI, particularly in the mining sector (0.15 with controls). Identity-based differences are less pronounced but still significant in the agricultural sector.

In line with theoretical expectations, companies with public ownership are more open to FDI in both sectors, as are exporters, although this effect is only sustained in the agricultural sector.

The final result of particular note is that mining companies that view good state relations as very important have notably high levels of opposition to FDI; however, in the agricultural sector, company managers who hold this view have the lowest predicted probability of opposing FDI. This finding is especially important because it confirms that those firms in each sector that are the most likely to sustain productive and open channels with state policymakers tend to hold preferences that largely align with the policy framework that prevailed in each sector: more nationalist in the mining sector and more open to investment in the agricultural sector. These results hold even when controlling for firm size and foreign ownership.

Business Ownership, Identity, and Sector

Overall, the survey results paint a revealing picture of how firm-level and sector-level variables predict business support for or opposition to foreign investment. Across both the mining and agricultural sectors, ownership structures mattered, with public ownership and ethnic Chinese ownership associated with a higher probability of openness to FDI. Other sorts of firm characteristics have different effects depending on the sector: the largest firms are more nationalist in the mining sector and more liberal in the agricultural sector; firms that view relationships with national-level policymakers as very important have a higher probability of opposing FDI in the mining sector, but such companies are more likely to support FDI in the agricultural sector. It is also worth noting that the measure of internationalization—exports overseas—does not predict major differences in FDI preferences in the mining sector, but exporters are significantly more supportive of FDI in the agricultural sector.

These results confirm and extend the arguments made so far in this book that have been based primarily on qualitative observations and long-form interviews with stakeholders in each sector. As earlier chapters have demonstrated, foreign divestment is the primary means via which domestic mining giants have built their assets. Throughout the process of first designing and then (especially) implementing the 2009 Mining Law, major local private companies were "waiting in the wings," as one mining executive put it, to benefit from new and more stringent foreign investment rules. Interviews with parliamentarians and senior bureaucrats consistently suggested that divestment was not their priority during the early stages of the bill's deliberation, nor was it necessarily even welcomed by many in the industry. Instead, most believed that foreign investment should be encouraged because such capital can provide opportunities for growth and technological exchange. But the divestment law came to reflect the preferences of the country's dominant private business interests. A decade later and not long after this survey was fielded, the 2020 Mining Law was introduced. The revised law, which one legal academic and anti-corruption lawyer described as having been "written by the Big Five" coal companies,[3] elevated the 51 percent divestment rule to the status of law rather than a ministerial regulation, which ensured these sorts of firms would enjoy future opportunities to strike attractive deals with foreign mining companies. Divestment has long been the primary means of entry and expansion for local firms in this sector, which in turn has generated more support for limiting foreign investment among the largest Indonesian mining companies, rather than the smaller ones.

Why, on the other hand, do the largest agricultural companies, together with the smallest, hold more liberal preferences? The fact that agricultural firms are, on average, more liberal and welcoming toward FDI than firms in any other sector is remarkable not just in the Indonesian context but compared to other middle-income countries with large agricultural sectors. In other such economies, the politics of FDI is very different. Demands from large rural voting populations and domestic companies in agricultural sectors all around the world tend, on average, to compel governments to protect such sectors from foreign inflows. The OECD's index on FDI Restrictiveness illustrates that, on average and all around the world, it is primarily agricultural industries that are targeted for the most restrictive interventions (OECD 2019). In Indonesia, on the other hand, the biggest crude palm oil producers and the smallest enterprises did not participate in nationalist campaigns to stem foreign investment and ownership. The palm oil boom of the 2000s and the international investment that poured into the sector after the end of the Asia financial crisis has in many ways benefited these two types of businesses in particular. For Indonesian firms and especially the largest ones, liberalization provided access to capital and to investment partners, and smallholders, cooperatives, and microenterprises have, in turn, come to depend on the bigger firms for their own prosperity (explained in chapters 2 and 4). One representative from a sectoral business association explained that the biggest local companies in this sector are "very comfortable" with foreign capital: "These big players are also international businesses, they are conglomerates with massive profits and they aren't threatened by foreign investment. And they do foreign investing themselves."[4] In another interview, a corporate communications expert working at a major Indonesian palm oil producer explained that "there's a lot of narrow nationalism in the extractive sectors, from politicians and local business players; in plantations the big companies have a different attitude to foreign capital—if it helps their businesses they welcome it, and don't see it as a threat."[5]

The identities of these big players mattered, too. The data point to differences in the preferences of firms that have Chinese Indonesian ownership, and there are more of these sorts of firms in Indonesia's plantations sector, especially at the top end of the sector. Such firms are less likely to express opposition to FDI. Why might it be that Chinese Indonesian–owned firms are, on average, less opposed to an open foreign invest policy? In interviews, sources within Indonesia's business community offered a range of opinions about how identity matters for businesses' policy preferences in this regard. One Chinese Indonesian business elite with investments across a range of agricultural sectors within Indonesia and in neighboring countries remarked on how, at least anecdotally, Chinese Indonesian businesspeople are generally more internationalized as individuals—they travel abroad from when they are children, receive education in Singapore or North America, and pursue more internationally oriented careers and business trajectories.[6] Pointing to the historical wealth of a slice of the ethnic Chinese community who go on to establish private companies, he and others interviewed for the study felt that there was a cosmopolitanism dimension to this business class that potentially made them less inclined to support economic protectionism.

Other interviewees suggested instead that such firms had a general tendency to shy away from statist interventions for political and historical reasons. One pribumi businessperson with interests in palm oil and who partners with some of the most prominent Chinese Indonesian family conglomerates reflected on how such business actors perceive the state and economic policymakers: "Chinese Indonesian companies are more comfortable using business associations to approach and lobby the state. Many don't want to go directly to or get too close to ministers and members of government. . . . They are worried about things getting political because of history, it is like a habit. . . . And in general they just don't want the state interfering in business. . . . Pribumi businesses don't have to worry and just do their lobbying directly."[7] A representative from APINDO, one of the main national business associations that includes within its members a large number of Chinese Indonesian businesses, explained that from his perspective,

> Chinese Indonesian businesses *are* nationalist, they invest massively in their own country, employ tens of thousands of citizens and do a lot of CSR. . . . So in that sense, we can say they are nationalist. But in terms of FDI, well these are often bigger companies, and they just aren't threatened by FDI—actually, they tend to see foreign investors as partners. Many pribumi businesspeople still see foreign money as something that will compete with them, will take away opportunities—not all of them of course, but it's just a general attitude and comes from the history of business in this country.[8]

That history continues to generate identity-based differences in the preferences that Indonesian businesses hold when it comes to foreign flows of capital. At the end of the 1990s, as the Suharto regime fell apart, Chinese Indonesian tycoons understood they would not be able to rebuild their empires using the old patrimonial template. Prominent Chinese Indonesian business elites instead focused on transforming their firms into more globalized corporate outfits (Borsuk and Chng 2014; Carney and Dieleman 2011; Chua 2008). Writing in the first decade that followed the economic crisis, Christian Chua (2008, 97) emphasized how despite their enormous debts, "Chinese conglomerates were best equipped to start the new era of post-crisis economy from a pole position, with still significant funds at their disposal," and given their capital advantage, most of these Chinese tycoons became "fervent supporters of free markets." Indeed, there was a sense among businesspeople interviewed for this study that Chinese Indonesian businesses preferred, in general, a more distant set of state-business relations and less state intervention in the economy more generally. The picture that emerges, therefore, is one in which both the plantations sector and its largest firms experienced a transformation at the turn of the century that encouraged internationalization and a liberal approach to investment from abroad.

A Closer Look at the Effects of Internationalization

On the question of internationalization, which theorists have identified as a primary predictor of nationalist preferences, the survey data are less clear. Although the comparison of means indicated that firms with investments abroad tend to have more liberal preferences, the number of firms that fit this profile in the survey sample was miniscule and this variable was excluded in the logistic regression analysis. For example, less than 4 percent of agricultural company representatives stated in the survey that their firm invests overseas. At the same time, the data did not suggest major differences between exporters and nonexporters, another measure of a firm's level of internationalization. The survey questions and the sample of respondents have likely not captured how firms' global orientation shapes their investment policy preferences. This section, therefore, takes a closer look at the global footprint of Indonesia's major mining and agribusiness firms.

In general, Indonesian companies across all sectors of the economy have struggled to "go international" at the same rate as firms in other middle-income and developing countries. For example, United Nations Conference on Trade and Development (UNCTAD) data illustrate that Indonesian firms have had far less capacity to conduct cross-border mergers and acquisitions over the past two decades compared to those in other middle-income countries, such as Malaysia, India, Thailand, and to a lesser extent, Brazil and the Philippines (figure 6.4). Indonesia's outward FDI stocks are also far below the average for Southeast Asia and for developing economies globally (figure 6.5). Nor have Indonesian

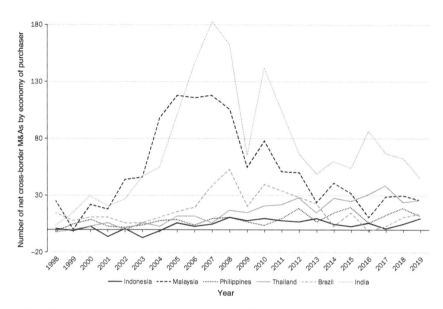

FIGURE 6.4. Number of net cross-border M&As by economy of purchaser, 1998–2019

Source: UNCTAD cross-border M&A database

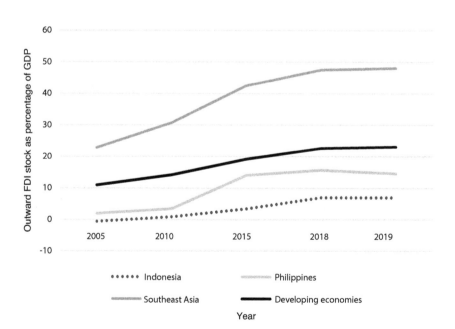

FIGURE 6.5. Total outward FDI stock as percentage of GDP

Source: UNCTAD World Investment Report 2020

companies made UNCTAD's list of 100 nonfinancial multinational enterprises from developing and transition economies. In 2018, Malaysia had five companies in this list, as did India.

Still, some companies have spread their corporate wings beyond Indonesia. Theories reviewed earlier in this chapter suggest that in sectors where the major local firms are internationalized, business demands for nationalist intervention will be weaker, leading to weaker expressions of nationalism in the form of policy change. Conversely, in sectors where the major local business actors are domestically oriented with little internationalization, their demands for government protection and privilege in that sector will be stronger, leading to more assertive manifestations of resource nationalism. To examine these propositions, I bring together information on the global footprint of major domestic firms in each resource sector ("major" is judged in terms of the volume of their exports). Internationalization is measured by identifying where each company is listed and the number of overseas subsidiaries a company has (without counting tax havens) (Carney and Dieleman 2011; Ramaswamy, Kroeck, and Renforth 1996). These details are displayed in table 6.3.

These ownership data suggest internationalization may help to explain the absence of a strong nationalist campaign against FDI in the plantations sector. First, agribusiness companies are far more likely to be listed and headquartered in neighboring Singapore. The top three palm oil producers also tower over their mining counterparts in terms of overseas subsidiaries, although beyond those top three companies, other firms in both industries are in fact comparable, with mining and oil and gas firms on average having more subsidiaries abroad. Strikingly, however, foreign shareholding appears to be both more common and more complex in the palm oil sector, where despite ultimate ownership often being in the hands of an Indonesian citizen, the firms are almost always domiciled and listed in foreign countries.

Indeed, as discussed in chapter 4, distinguishing between foreign or domestic companies in the palm oil industry is not simple. The companies that own the largest plantations are Singapore-listed PT Golden Agri Resources, Indonesia's Salim Group, Singapore-listed Wilmar International, Malaysia-listed Sime Darby (formerly Guthrie), and Jakarta-listed PT Astra Agro Lestari. Golden Agri Resources listed on the Singapore stock exchange in 1999, but it is part of the Sinar Mas Group owned by Eka Tjipta Widjaja, one of Indonesia's wealthiest tycoons. Other prominent Singapore-based companies owned by Indonesian businesspeople include First Resources and Indofood Agri. Indonesia's Fangiono family owns First Resources, but the family has distanced itself from direct ownership through layers of holding companies listed in the British Virgin Islands. Wilmar International is one of the largest listed companies by market

TABLE 6.3. Internationalization of the major mining and palm oil firms owned or established by Indonesian citizens

MINING GROUPS (INCLUDING OIL AND GAS)	LISTED	MAJOR SHAREHOLDERS	FOREIGN SUBSIDIARIES*	AGRIBUSINESS GROUPS	LISTED	MAJOR SHAREHOLDERS	FOREIGN SUBSIDIARIES*
Golden Energy Mines (Sinar Mas)	Indonesia	Owned 37% by GMR Coal Resources (Singapore); 67% Golden Energy and Resources (Singapore), which is controlled by Citibank	38	Wilmar International	Singapore	No shareholders with over 25%; Kuok brothers (Malaysia) own 18%, and rest is owned by mix of Singapore- and U.S.-based companies	1,788
Medco	Indonesia	50.27% owned by Medco Daya Abadi Lestari (Indonesia), which is 100% owned by the Panigoro family (Indonesia)	26	Golden Agri Resources (Sinar Mas)	Singapore	No shareholders with over 25%; owned by mix of foreign companies based in Singapore, United States, Hong Kong, Virgin Islands, and elsewhere	252
Bumi Resources	Indonesia	No shareholders with over 25%; Hong Kong–based Chendong Investment and HSBC Chendong own 22% each	22	Indofood Agri (Salim Group)	Singapore	Owned 71% by Indofood Singapore holdings (Singapore). The ultimate owner of this firm is First Pacific (Bermuda), controlled by Anthony Salim (Indonesia)	119
Indika Energy	Indonesia	Owned 38% by Indika Inti (Indonesia); 30% Teladan Resources (Indonesia)	21	Salim Invomas Pratama (Salim Group)	Indonesia	Owned 72% by Indofood Agri Resources (Singapore); ultimate owner First Pacific (Hong Kong), controlled by Anthony Salim	11
EMP	Indonesia	No shareholders with over 25%; majority are based in Indonesia	11	Musim Mas	Private (Singapore)	Bachtiar Karim (Indonesia)	15**

(continued)

TABLE 6.3. (continued)

MINING GROUPS (INCLUDING OIL AND GAS)	LISTED	MAJOR SHAREHOLDERS	FOREIGN SUBSIDIARIES*	AGRIBUSINESS GROUPS	LISTED	MAJOR SHAREHOLDERS	FOREIGN SUBSIDIARIES*
Pertamina	Indonesia	Indonesian government-owned	10	Eagle High Plantations (Rajawali)	Singapore	Owned 37% by FIC Properties (Malaysia); 37% Rajawali Capital (Indonesia); the rest is owned by mix of foreign shareholders	3
Adaro Energy	Indonesia	Owned 44% by Adaro Strategic (Indonesia); 35% public; approximately 10% individual shareholders based in Indonesia	9	First Resources (Eight Capital)	Singapore	Majority owned by Eight Capital (Virgin Islands) and Eight Capital Trustees (Singapore), which are both owned by Eight Trust (Great Britain)	2
Bayan Resources	Indonesia	Owned 54% Tuck Kwong Low (Indonesia) and the rest Bayan Resources (Indonesia)	9	Sampoerna Agro	Indonesia	Owned 67% Sampoerna Agri Resources (Singapore), which is 100% owned by Xian Investment holdings based in Seychelles, presumably owned by the Sampoerna family (Indonesia)	2
Multi Harapan Utama	Indonesia	Privately owned, reports suggest the major shareholders are Risjad family (Indonesia) and the Pribadi family (Indonesia)	0	DSN (Triputra)	Indonesia	No shareholders with over 25%; 27% Triputra Investindo (Indonesia) 15% Krishna Kapital (Indonesia); remaining shares are held by Indonesia-based companies or individuals	2
Star Energy (Barito Pacific)	Singapore	71% owned by Prajogo Pangestu (Indonesia)	3	Bakrie Sumatera (Bakrie Global)	Indonesia	No shareholders with over 25%; held by a mix of Indonesian and foreign companies and individuals	2

*Excluding subsidiaries in countries listed as tax havens by the European Union (https://eur-lex.europa.eu/legal-content/EN/TXT/PDF/?uri=CELEX:52020XG0227(01)&from=en);
**Private company data sourced from company websites and report.

Source: Orbis database (2020).

capitalization on the Singapore stock exchange and was first established as a joint venture between Indonesian businessperson Martua Sitorus and Malaysian tycoon William Kuok. On the other hand, Jakarta-listed Astra Agro Lestari is a subsidiary of Astra International, which was set up by prominent Suharto-era Chinese Indonesian businessperson William Soeryadjaya and is thus often perceived as an Indonesian company. But since 1999, the Jardine Matheson Group, a Hong Kong–listed company, has owned a controlling stake.

Not only are many of the country's most dominant crude palm oil producers listed overseas, but the largest agri-giants are globalized, international corporations with many investments abroad as well. In 2016, the Boston Consulting Group identified Indonesia's top three palm oil producers—Salim, Sinar Mas, and Wilmar—as the country's "global champions" (BCG 2016). For example, Golden Agri Resources of the Sinar Mas group owns over 250 subsidiaries which are incorporated all around the world (and many more in tax havens), from Singapore, Hong Kong, China, Malaysia, and the Netherlands, and 20 percent of its revenues come from overseas investments in China. Other research has shown that Chinese Indonesian conglomerates in general tend to hold more overseas assets and make more investments abroad than their pribumi business counterparts. Their tendency has been to "set up platforms in Hong Kong or Singapore from which internationalization is pursued" (Carney and Dieleman 2011, 112). A study by Michael Carney and Marleen Dieleman (2011) surveyed the international foreign investments of Indonesia's largest conglomerates and found very few had noteworthy outgoing FDI. The exceptions were Salim and Lippo (the latter's business is mostly focused on property), which the authors describe as the country's "emerging market giants," followed by Sinar Mas (Carney and Dieleman 2011, 115).

There is, quite clearly, an identity-based dimension to these patterns of internationalization as well. As described above, in the aftermath of the New Order's collapse, Chinese Indonesian businesses were no longer compelled to, and thus avoided, tying their economic ventures to individuals within the state. For some of these firms, the move toward greater internationalization was, in part, motivated by the "political risks" of being ethnically Chinese Indonesian entrepreneurs (Chua 2008, 106).

Firm Nationalism

This chapter brought Indonesia's experience of resource nationalism back into conversation with political economy theories about the kinds of firms that seek protection and oppose foreign investment. An original survey of Indonesian firms revealed that within and across sectors, businesses hold heterogeneous preferences when it comes to foreign investment. The survey results provide a rare and representative snapshot of how business characteristics predict support or opposition to FDI in Indonesia. On one level, the data confirm the propositions put forward in the comparative scholarship about the importance of firm size, internationalization, and ownership structures for predicting openness to trade and foreign flows. But this chapter also emphasized the complex relationship between firm- and sector-level variables and pointed to the specific and historically rooted significance of owner identity for explaining distinct preferences for state protection.

So, although mining and agricultural firms are, in general, more liberal than firms in other sectors, different sorts of enterprises had very different sorts of preferences in each sector. Confirming the qualitative observations presented in chapter 6, Indonesia's largest mining firms emerged as the most opposed to FDI, while the largest agrifirms held more liberal preferences. Theorists have further argued that internationalized firms will oppose nationalist trade and investment policy, and a scan of firm profiles revealed that the major palm oil companies are more internationalized than their extractive counterparts.

But there is more to the Indonesian story than firm size and internationalization. The picture that has emerged from both the qualitative analysis and the survey data is one in which firm identity and internationalization are interlinked. Many of Indonesia's local mining giants are domestically oriented pribumi-owned firms. At the turn of the century, the largest and most profitable foreign-operated coal mines were transferred to Indonesian-owned companies. The shift was fortuitously timed just before the global coal boom took off in 2003, and the boom sent profits soaring for Indonesia's new coal miners. Many of these domestic companies, such as Bumi, Adaro, and Indika, are owned by groups of pribumi businesspeople whose business interests were focused primarily within Indonesia. These sorts of local companies expanded their businesses through divestment deals, often leveraging state loans to buy new mines, and eventually demanded more opportunities to take over lucrative and complex foreign mines in the precious minerals sector. Indonesia's upstream oil and gas producers have also made inroads into the industry via acquiring stakes in and taking over foreign wells. These firms are also not highly internationalized—whether privately owned or state-owned. Although Pertamina's leadership had outlined a vision to "go international" like Malaysia's Petronas or Brazil's Petrobras, in reality the company is still focused first and foremost on expanding its domestic oil and gas reserves.

To the extent that Indonesia is home to internationalized corporate giants, they are owned (or mostly owned) by Chinese Indonesian tycoons whose economic preference, since 1998, have become more liberal. Even during the boom years of the mid-2000s and as foreign competitors entered the market, the largest agrifirms remained advocates for an open investment regime and the free flow of capital across international borders. The palm oil sector's liberalization at the end of the 1990s and early 2000s worked in favor of these conglomerates and in turn helped boost the fortunes of smallholders and smaller enterprises, too, dampening the sort of nationalist mobilization that historically has marked this sector and that characterizes the agricultural industries of other middle-income countries. In sum, sectoral transformations and identity-based differences in the firms that dominate each sector are tightly interrelated, and both explain divergent business preferences and nationalist policy trajectories across Indonesia's land and resource industries.

PRIVATE NATIONALISM AND STATE DEVELOPMENTALISM

I have argued throughout this book that a focus on business actors, their owner-ship structures, and their preferences can explain patterns of nationalist interven-tion during and after the boom in Indonesia. In the mid-2000s as commodity prices soared, the Indonesian government introduced a series of nationalist poli-cies in the mining sector, prevaricated when it came to oil and gas, and sustained an open investment regime for the plantations industry. Diving deep into negotia-tions over each sectoral law, this study revealed conflict, ambivalence, and often confusion among senior bureaucrats toward nationalist interventions. The direc-tion of nationalist change could instead be often traced back to major domestic business interests. Domestic mining businesses pushed to secure and enshrine in law stringent divestment requirements for foreign firms; in the oil and gas sector, competition between state and private capital contributed to regulatory stalemate; agribusiness conglomerates, however, were not advocates for capping or con-straining foreign capital, and the plantations sector continue to welcome foreign investment and ownership.

Explaining resource nationalism in Indonesia requires a particular focus on private business because of the nature of the country's political economy and patronage-driven democracy. In the twenty-first century, the global commodities boom and the evolution of Indonesia's expensive electoral system gave economic elites and major domestic business actors new sources of instrumental policy power and influence. The country's political parties and legislatures filled with economic actors whose business portfolios stretched across the infrastructure, land, and resource industries, weaving the worlds of politics and business into an ever-tighter web. As coal and palm oil evolved into the country's top exports and sources of foreign reserve, domestic conglomerates in these industries also enjoyed growing structural power. This book's major contention is, therefore, that Indonesia's agribusiness and extractive companies became increasingly formidable policy actors in the democratic period, more powerful than at any other time in the country's corporate history, such that business preferences came to determine the trajectory of nationalist proposals both during and after the boom.

There were important caveats to my central claim about the superior policy power of domestic private business actors. First, the historical and empirical chapters pointed to the role of prior state policies for nurturing and empowering a domestic business class in agriculture and mining, providing access to land, contracts, and loans, and regulating future divestment opportunities. Local business actors benefited immensely from these prior state actions and were able to capitalize on the boom in mineral, coal, oil, and palm oil prices at the turn of the century. The second caveat concerned the sustained, even enhanced, power of state capital in particular contexts. Despite the regulatory stalemate that characterized the oil and gas sector, Pertamina won a series of strategic contracts and became a top upstream producer for the first time in the country's history. For a range of historical and structural reasons outlined in chapters 2 and 5, state capital sustained enormous political and economic power in this sector, much more so than in either the mining or plantations sectors. The slow nationalization of the country's oil wells was thus driven by a reformed and more efficient Pertamina, by the company's advocates in government, and by civil society. The political salience of the Freeport mine also motivated the Jokowi government to turn to state capital to acquire the American-run project, sensing a strong public preference for state ownership and facing an upcoming reelection campaign.

In this final chapter, I reflect on the implications of these arguments for the country-focused and comparative scholarship. The chapter is organized around the following questions: (a) In what ways do my findings about resource nationalist variation contribute to how we understand the broader nature of state-business relations and economic policymaking in contemporary Indonesia? (b) What are the developmental consequences of domestic ownership and business policy power for Indonesia's resource and land-based industries? (c) Do patterns of ownership matter for environmental protection and social activism? (d) What lessons can be learned from the Indonesian case when it comes to understanding patterns of resource nationalism in other parts of the world?

Contemporary State-Business Relations and Economic Policymaking in Indonesia

Scholarship on post-Suharto Indonesia has produced two influential character-izations of the nature of the state and its relationship with capital. First, a stream of critical political economy work views contemporary Indonesia as dominated by an oligarchic class that is endowed materially and politically and that displays striking continuity with the ruling class of the New Order period (Hadiz and Robison 2013; Robison and Hadiz 2004; Winters 2011). A second pluralist stream emphasizes the highly competitive nature of politics and state-business relations in post–New Order Indonesia (Mietzner 2013a, 2013b) and suggests that fragmented patronage-based networks constitute the organizing logic of Indonesia's politi-cal economy (Aspinall 2013). Pluralists also provide more analytical space for popular forces, arguing that despite the sustained power of an oligarchic elite, civil society and voters themselves should not be rendered powerless in charac-terizations of Indonesia's contemporary democracy (Ford and Pepinsky 2013).

On one level, the political economy of ownership in Indonesia's land and re-source industries presented in this book confirms the picture painted by critical political economists of an unchanged and indelibly fused network of wealthy busi-ness and bureaucratic interests (Hadiz and Robison 2013). In many instances, this book uncovered how influential politicobusiness elites pursued programs for na-tionalizing resource projects that could provide them with opportunities for pri-vate gain. The collection of tycoons that came to dominate these sectors was also familiar—the Salim Group, Sinar Mas, the businesspeople behind Adaro, and the Bakrie Group. The individuals that have managed to accumulate immense mate-rial wealth in these sectors were indeed "incubated" under the New Order. Over a decade ago, Christian Chua's (2008) study of ethnic Chinese business similarly argued that the country's old conglomerates were prospering within the new democratic and more liberal political economy, less tethered to specific patrons in the executive or the military, and less constrained by (though not entirely free of) cultural and political discrimination.

This book has argued that such observations about the sustained dominance of economic elites motivate a set of analytically important questions about varia-tion and change that have been underexamined in the contemporary country literature and largely overlooked by oligarchy theorists themselves. Specifically, why do different sorts of capital seek different rules and regulations? Under what conditions do business preferences change? Do different sorts of economic elites exercise power in different ways? Answering these sorts of questions, I have ar-gued, demands a different political economy approach that treats capitalist actors as heterogenous and changeable, rather than undifferentiated and all powerful (Doner 1991; Frieden 1991; Gourevitch 1977; Hall 1997; Shafer 1990, 1994).

To that end, this book investigated the source of nationalist policy variation by studying the preferences and profiles of business interests in each sector. I showed how the commodities boom helped to lock in a private nationalization of the country's mining sector that was already underway, and the preferences of the major miners for more stringent divestment requirements were reflected in changes to laws and regulations during and following the boom. There was also a general trend toward pribumi ownership in this sector, and the largest companies were mostly, though not entirely, locally oriented and locally listed companies with more protectionist set of preferences when compared to major businesses in the palm oil sector. Such companies also tended to have more overt connections to political office, sometimes with company leaders entering office directly, giving their policy power an especially instrumental character.

Meanwhile, although Indonesia's agricultural sector is subject to a range of state protections and subsidies, the commercial plantation industry sustained a remarkably open investment and ownership policy throughout the course of the post-Suharto period, a policy outcome that, I have argued, must be understood in terms of the role that internationalized domestic actors and foreign flows have played in expanding the sector's contribution to revenues, growth and rural economies. Big local businesses did not seek protection in the palm oil sector, and those preferences can be traced back to the structure and identity of the businesses themselves—the palm oil sector's dominant corporate actors were diversified and often internationalized Chinese Indonesian–owned companies that no longer demanded state protection from foreign flows. Both the qualitative and survey-based data revealed an inclination for open and liberal ownership regimes among Indonesia's ethnically Chinese business owners. Such businesses are over-represented in the agribusiness sector generally and in the top layer of conglomerates that dominate exports and that invest up and down the plantations value chain.

To be sure, businesses and their preferences are shaped to an extent by the features of the sectors in which they invest, and historical state policies and regulations can constrain or nurture domestic investment. For example, the palm oil sector became much more integrated into regional networks of capital at the turn of the century when the IMF compelled the government to remove constraints on foreign capital, and foreign flows helped local firms take advantage of the boom. Corporations owned by Indonesian citizens were often domiciled abroad, a function of how Chinese Indonesian tycoons carved a more internationalized path for their businesses in the wake of the Asian financial crisis. Small plantation enterprises also saw their fate as inextricably tied to foreign capital because the Indonesian government had come to rely on foreign and private investors to expand and develop the sector and to provide rural populations with livelihoods and access to markets.

In many ways, the variation in nationalist outcomes that motivated this book reflect histories of stratified capital accumulation in Indonesia (Robison 1986). The colonial, postindependence, and New Order governments all treated ethnically Chinese Indonesian businesses differently from their pribumi counterparts, and those different histories of state-business relations continue to play out in the contemporary era. Prior research into the corporate success of ethnically Chinese business actors throughout Southeast Asia points to the advantages that cross-border migrant networks, business contacts, and regional capital have bestowed on Chinese entrepreneurs around the region (Mackie 1998a). Importantly, however, scholars have also emphasized that colonial occupation, and later the Suharto regime, shaped ethnically Chinese traders and businesspeople into "comprador capitalists," making such actors both dependent on the state for economic opportunity and privilege and also vulnerable to predation by ruling elites who could "siphon off rents without having to worry that their clients will mobilize [public] support" (Hefner 1998, 22). President Suharto cultivated a politically weak and economically dependent class of Chinese Indonesian business cronies, while at the same time endorsing popular prejudice against the country's wider ethnic Chinese minority community. This history of business-state relations helps to explain why today, Indonesia's large Chinese businesses might seek *less* state protection. Following Suharto's demise and intermittent spikes in public outpouring of anti-Chinese sentiment (Setijadi 2019), Chinese Indonesian business elites have sought to distance themselves from the state and from political figures. Dependence on the state has given way to an embrace of foreign flows and free markets for growth and security (Chua 2008), and on average, these companies hold more liberal policy preferences and tend to pursue internationalization (in some ways and ironically reflecting the negative stereotypes projected onto them in the past). For all of these reasons, the liberalizing influence of major Chinese Indonesian conglomerates derives from their *structural* economic power, as distinct from the direct instrumental form of power exercised by their pribumi counterparts.

The sectoral case studies I have presented in this book also suggest conflict and competition between different networks of private and state capital. State managers and politicians resisted the demands of tycoons in particular instances, pursuing statist outcomes and building state resources, sometimes at the expense of private sector actors. For example, the Jokowi government decided to establish a new holding company for the mining sector so that the state could keep Freeport out of the hands of private business elites. And in the oil and gas sector, conflict between state and private capital led to regulatory stasis and ambiguity, rather than victory for the country's private conglomerates. As chapter 6 demonstrated, Pertamina's rise to prominence as the country's major upstream operator and oil producer provides a compelling illustration of renewed statist power in the democratic era. To be sure, state ownership of strategic mines and oil wells opens the door for politically linked private local firms to capitalize on the many service contracts and subcontracting deals associated with complex resource projects—and there is a long history of such behavior in Indonesia, as described in chapter 2. But Pertamina's rise was never guaranteed, given the push for privatizing this sector at the end of the Suharto period and the entry of a range of new upstream private domestic firms. Rather, the state's support for Pertamina and for a mining holding company must be understood as state managers' efforts to balance the rise of private conglomerates and to exert strategic control over particular projects in the context of growing private policy power throughout much of the twenty-first century. In his study of Indonesia's contemporary political economy, Davidson (2015) found the expansion of state capital in the roads sector was driven by a need to overcome yawning gaps in private investment; in the resource sectors, I argue, the government has also turned to state enterprise to protect specific and politically salient projects from foreign *and* oligarchic control.

So by tracing variation and change in patterns of resource nationalism, this book has attempted to advance the study of Indonesia's contemporary political economy and of the role economic elites play in determining policymaking trajectories in strategic land and resource sectors. The story of resource nationalism suggests that prevailing oligarchic theories should be a starting point, rather than a conclusion, for analyzing Indonesia's contemporary political economy and should motivate a deeper investigation into analytically important differences between business actors, the preferences they pursue, and the kind of policy power they wield.

Nationalization and Developmentalism

Much of this book has been concerned with the causes of nationalist variation, rather than its consequences. In this section, I reflect on the developmental implications of transformed ownership structures in Indonesia's land and resource sectors and the enhanced policy power of the local business actors that dominate production and trade. Resource nationalist efforts in Indonesia, just as in other countries around the world, have often been framed by advocates in the state, political parties, and even by domestic companies as part of a developmentalist project. The literature on developmental states characterizes economic policy as the product of coordinated efforts by state and business to achieve mutual goals of profit, revenue generation, industrial transformation, and growth (Doner, Ritchie, and Slater 2005; Döring, Santos, and Pocher 2017; Evans 1989).

In the resource sectors specifically, scholars have argued that the global commodity boom motivated the return of a developmentalist approach to resource-based growth in many countries around the world and particularly in Latin America (Haslam and Heidrich 2016b, 5; Singh and Massi 2016, 158). This "new developmentalism" is broadly concerned with turning resource sectors into engines of industrial growth, as opposed to export-oriented and foreign-owned enclaves. Such an agenda finds expression in policies that expand the participation of local firms and state enterprises, build corporate champions, and increase the developmental footprint of raw commodity sectors by investing in downstream processing and value adding. In their study of developmentalism in Brazil, for example, Döring, Santos, and Pocher (2017) demonstrate how the Brazilian government intentionally invested in the concentration of ownership by local private companies in mining and steel in order to build domestic corporate champions for national economic goals.

State managers and politicians articulated these sorts of goals in each of Indonesia's primary commodity sectors. I have argued elsewhere that under President Jokowi, Indonesia's resource policy and economic policy more generally took a developmentalist turn, melding heavy state interventionism in some sectors while enabling private capital and the expansion of domestic companies in others (Warburton 2018). One of the government's justifications for enabling the transfer of Indonesia's major mining projects to domestic hands was that local owners would be more willing—or more easily compelled—to invest in downstream industrialization and to expand the industrial footprint of the nickel, bauxite, and copper sectors. This industrializing expression of resource nationalism was regulated in the 2009 Mining Law, which laid out a plan to ban the export of raw mineral ores and to force industrial processing on Indonesian shores, in turn building a more sophisticated minerals industry.

So to what extent has the expansion of domestic ownership in the upstream sector helped to achieve these downstream developmental objectives? On one level, localizing nationalist efforts have indeed enabled progress toward downstream industrialization. Over the course of the decade that followed the introduction of the 2009 Mining Law, the government instituted a ban on nickel ores (first in 2014 and then again in 2020) and prompted a boom in smelting investment in the nickel subsector; however, attempts to ban the export of unprocessed copper and to compel firms to invest in copper smelting facilities was far more difficult. The two foreign multinationals, Freeport and Newmont, which were at that time responsible for 97 percent of Indonesia's copper production, opposed the government's policies and attempted to delay and water down the regulations that would force downstream investments. The two foreign companies communicated regularly about the smelting issue and would often present as a united front in negotiations with the government.[1] Both Freeport and Newmont were operating under contracts of work, and they argued that smelting requirements and export restrictions breached their contracts, and they threatened the government with international arbitration should it execute a full ban on copper exports (Cahyafitri 2014). The government was forced to delay export restrictions on copper, giving the companies more time to invest in smelting facilities.

The domestic acquisitions of Newmont and Freeport were framed by local stakeholders as a step toward realizing the government's industrial goals. When it came to Newmont, for example, both Medco's leadership and government ministers claimed that domestic business and the state could now work together to maximize the mine's developmental benefits in ways that its former American owners had not. In a press interview, the new CEO for AMMAN Minerals (Medco's subsidiary established to acquire the Batu Hijau mine), expressed how the company's culture needed to shift from a "short-term to long-term focus, which hasn't been seen in the past," and that shift included extending the life of the mine and investing in smelting facilities (Wayne 2021). Indeed, not long after the firm's acquisition, Medco committed to investing US$9.2 billion to develop a gold and copper processing facility, and in 2021, the company signed an agreement with a Chinese company to build the smelter. The government's efforts to compel Newmont to make this investment had failed in the years prior. Similarly, the years-long deadlock with Freeport McMoran over a smelting investment came to an end once the state-owned holding company took over the mine. As part of the contract that was signed in 2018 giving the state a majority share, Freeport McMoran also signed an agreement to establish a new smelter within five years of the contract date. The case of downstream industrialization would appear in many ways to confirm the proposition put forward by nationalist advocates, that foreign ownership of major resource projects undermines a long-term and developmental approach to the commercial exploitation of land and resource policy.

However, there are other contexts in which domestic ownership has *not* improved the sector's developmental outcomes. Domestic market obligations (DMOs), where governments compel private companies to direct part of their products onto domestic markets and to sell to local industry or consumers, constitutes another common developmental tool in a government's policy toolbox. The Indonesian government institutes DMOs across a range of sectors in order to ensure supply of products that are critical for domestic industry. In the coal sector, however, the government is perpetually chasing companies for not meeting their DMOs. In December 2021, for example, the government took the extraordinary step of banning coal exports. The state-owned electricity provider PLN was facing a dangerous shortage of coal stocks for its coal-fired power stations, for which both PLN and the government blamed the country's coal companies. Companies have a legal obligation to allocate 25 percent of their production to domestic power plants at a capped price of US$70 per metric ton. But with international coal prices booming at over US$140 per metric ton at the end of 2021, coal miners were neglecting their DMOs and enjoying soaring profits instead (Listiyorini 2022). Media reports suggested that the Ministry of Energy and Mineral Resources had approached companies on numerous occasions in an attempt to compel them to fulfill their commitments to PLN, but at the start of 2022, "the companies only met less than 1 percent, or around 35 metric tons, of the target of 5.1 million metric tons required for domestic needs" (Nirmala and Firdaus 2022). To make up the shortfall and avoid widespread electricity outages, the government stopped all international coal exports. PLN's coal shortages are not purely the fault of private companies; the SOE's inability to sustain long-term contracts and ensure reliable stock is partly a systemic internal problem. But this case illustrates the extent to which the state has been unable to control corporate behavior and enforce state regulations until a crisis looms.

In this sense, the transformation of ownership in the mining sector has not generated the type of state-business relations that underpin an ideal-type developmental state. Resource nationalist efforts in the mining sector I described in chapters 3 and 4 were often characterized by high levels of collusion and particularistic deal making. Competition between different state actors, political elites, and business networks caused much regulatory conflict in the years that followed the 2009 Mining Law. Nationalist regulations were constantly being amended and regulatory regimes were often marked by high levels of institutional uncertainty—for example, there were four different versions of the divestment law from 2010 to 2017. Although some developmental goals, such as building a downstream smelting industry, have been smoothed by high levels of domestic upstream ownership and strong connections between particular upstream firms and state managers, in other instances developmental outcomes that rely on efficient and cooperative state-industry relations, such as adherence to a predictable set of DMO requirements, have been poor. In archetypal developmental states, trade, investment, and industrial policies emerge out of negotiations between well-organized business groups and effective, autonomous bureaucracies (Schneider 2015, 2–4). In post-Suharto Indonesia, attempts to control and compel the country's biggest businesses failed at key moments, and the state struggled to bring corporate behavior in line with developmental objectives that did not suit the immediate profit-driven goals of business groups.

Nationalism and Social Activism

What has been the relationship between resource nationalism and social activism and in particular activism in pursuit of environmental protection? In other country contexts, scholars have demonstrated the ways in which grassroots activists and leftist organizations deploy nationalist narratives in their campaigns against foreign companies and, more generally, against commercial control and exploitation of land and minerals. In her seminal study of Ecuador, for example, Thea Riofrancos (2020) decenters the state from studies of resource nationalism and demonstrates the role of social movement activists in first, pressuring the state to nationalize natural resources and second, opposing extractive regimes and demanding constitutional protection of environmental rights. This kind of bottom-up popular expression of resource nationalism, whereby demands for local control are articulated and mobilized through social movement organizations and community leaders, is most often observed by scholars working in and on Latin America, a region with a long history of leftist, indigenous, and peasant mobilization and organization (Kohl and Farthing 2012; Perreault and Valdivia 2010; see also Bebbington and Humphreys-Bebbington 2011; Yates and Bakker 2013).

Resource nationalism in Indonesia lacked such high-profile popular expression, and as this book has argued, nationalist efforts were largely dominated and directed by corporate and statist elements. During the boom, the fast-paced expansion of plantations and mines across the country motivated a range of campaigns by environmental, anti-corruption, and agrarian social movement organizations at both the national and local levels. However, their efforts never transformed into a cohesive, nationwide movement with significant legislative influence of the sort that scholars describe in countries like Ecuador and Bolivia (Perreault 2013; Riofrancos 2020; Young 2017).

In the mining and oil sectors, the most effective campaigns were often focused on relatively narrow technical issues, including post-mining reclamation activities, licensing processes, and the payment of nontax revenues, rather than on the terms of extraction more broadly. They tended to articulate agendas that set out to improve extraction rather than oppose it. For example, organizations such as Publish What You Pay, the Asia Foundation, Indonesia Corruption Watch (ICW), and the Corruption Eradication Commission (KPK) worked closely with various arms of the Indonesian government in order to reform sectoral mechanisms for ensuring transparency. Their campaigns sought to build the government's capacity to increase the sector's contribution to state revenues, rather than to oppose corporate control of land and resources. There are important exceptions. JATAM (Mining Advocacy Network) and WALHI (Indonesian Forum for the Environment) put forward an ideological argument against neoliberal economic models that enable corporate exploitation of land and natural resources, and adopt narratives that, in many ways, mirror those of counterparts in Latin America. At the same time, such groups have chosen not to couch their campaigns in overtly nationalist terms.

Indeed, civil society activists were deeply ambivalent about resource nationalist policies. In the eyes of many activists, the shift toward domestic ownership in these sectors, and the attendant increase in the structural and instrumental power of local corporate actors, has undermined their efforts to protect the country's land and resources from overexploitation, degradation, and pollution and generated new constraints on their activities and new forms of state repression. In interviews, representatives from JATAM and WALHI would talk of the 2009 Mining Law and related regulations as a kind of "narrow nationalism" or "fake nationalism" that was designed to benefit a small band of big companies and economic elites. These activists were, in many ways, disillusioned with nationalist discourse and the elite-driven form of resource nationalism that was associated with the 2009 Mining Law and especially, years later, the 2020 Mining Law. A member of ICW explained in an interview that their efforts to check and monitor mining companies' royalty payments have targeted local as much as foreign firms, and the evidence they have uncovered of untaxed illegal exports suggests the offenders are primarily local coal and mineral companies: "Many of them [who do not pay export taxes] are local. . . . Some of these companies probably have Korean or Chinese money behind them . . . but the entire sector is to blame, foreign and domestic. And we can't expect politicians in the parliament to have a positive effect [on corruption] because they almost all have personal interests in the industry—in commission VII on natural resources, for example, if they didn't have mining interests before entering the commission, they have them now."[2] To the extent that NGOs leveraged a nationalist argument, they point regularly to Article 33 of the constitution that outlines that land and resources must be used for the benefit of the broader citizenry, which they interpreted as meaning via a fair, clean, and thorough redistribution of the financial benefits accrued through exploitation and extraction.

Meanwhile, in the plantations sector, the most high-profile campaigns oppose the expansion of palm oil into protected forests. Such activism did not take on a nationalist character either, and instead, local NGOs often drew on the international framings of the global climate change movement. NGOs like WALHI, Forest People's Project, and AMAN (Indigenous People's Alliance of the Archipelago), with the backing of transnational environmental organizations like Greenpeace and World Wildlife Forum, have lobbied against the industry's expansion in order to stop the incursion of palm oil into what activists argue is land that should either be protected forest areas or be reserved for other sorts of foods, crops, industries, and livelihoods. Because their activism is linked to, and often funded by, transnational campaigns, Indonesian state and corporate actors have routinely use nationalist arguments *against* these social movement activists, accusing them of representing foreign agents and Western interests whose crusade against palm oil undermines the livelihoods of local farmers, business owners, and the broader national interest (Kabarbisnis 2021).

Throughout the first decade of the post-Suharto period, social activists in a range of sectors pushed legislative agendas that have carved out a space for the rights of smallholders and traditional or indigenous landowners (Dibley and Ford 2019). But anti-corruption and environmental rights groups describe how much more difficult their activities have become in the years following the boom. In an interview, one of the country's most high-profile environmental lawyers and anti-corruption activists, Dr. Laode Syarif, described how each election cycle has produced a parliament with greater numbers of legislators with private sector backgrounds, which he believes has diminished the political will to uphold or improve the country's anti-corruption institutions and regulations.[3] Three laws introduced between 2019 and 2020 powerfully demonstrate the enhanced policy power of business interests over the legislative process: the 2020 Mining Law described earlier, the 2020 Omnibus Law on Job Creation, and the revisions to the 2019 revisions to the KPK Law. The new Mining Law, as described in earlier chapters, not only enshrined the 51 percent divestment rule into law but also reduced limits on concession sizes, and guaranteed contract extensions for CoW holders. The Omnibus Law, meanwhile, shaved away at labor protections and watered down companies' environmental responsibilities by removing obligations to consult with third-party stakeholders, including NGOs, in the environmental approval process (Jong 2019; Mufti and Rasidi 2021). The revised KPK Law eroded the body's investigative tools and enhanced government control over its activities by making KPK employees civil servants, and by establishing an oversight body selected by the executive (A'yun and Mudhoffir 2019). The result is not only reduced legal powers for the KPK but also a shift in the orientation of the organization away from civil society. The new version of the KPK no longer seeks to partner or collaborate with environmental and anti-corruption activists the way that it once did to collect information on predatory state-business arrangements in the land and resource sectors. As Laode explained in an interview, "the influence of business and mining companies in particular is all over these new laws—Mining, Omnibus and KPK."

The new and enhanced policy power of Indonesia's mining and agrifirms has thus deepened the sectors' preexisting environmental problems, made activists' efforts to monitor and enforce environmental regulations more difficult, and produced a less consultative legislative process. In some countries, resource nationalism constitutes an expression of popular imaginaries and seeks to empower communities near sites of extraction and exploitation. In Indonesia, resource nationalist efforts reflect corporate interests, and in many instances nationalist transformations have disempowered activists operating in these sectors.

Beyond Indonesia

What lessons does the study of Indonesia's experience hold for how scholars and policymakers understand and explain patterns of resource nationalism more broadly? Much research on resource nationalism has focused on the state, seeking the source of nationalist change and variation in different sorts of institutional arrangements that enable or incentivize predatory and myopic state actors to squeeze out or expel foreign companies. This book departed from the methodological statism that characterizes much political economy work on the nationalization of land and natural resources, emphasizing the value of asking what drives subnational and sectoral variation. A primary lesson from Indonesia's experience is the analytical value of looking beyond national-level trends and seeking out and interrogating subnational and sectoral variation when it comes to regulating flows of foreign capital. Where much of the cross-national scholarship has historically emphasized the epiphenomenal nature of resource nationalism, Indonesia's experience revealed that even under similar boom conditions, nationalist demands can meet with very different fates within a single country. Comparative studies and journalistic accounts of resource nationalism have tended, understandably, to focus on cases where nationalist advocates prevailed, but examining instances where advocates failed can be analytically revealing. In the Indonesian case, such variation revealed a critical role for private domestic capital in determining distinct nationalist trajectories, in turn providing a window into the evolving nature of state-business relations across sectors and types of firms.

In other middle-income economies with large agricultural and resource industries, we also find uneven patterns of anti-foreign regulation. Brazil, for example, during the commodities boom of the 2000s, enjoyed a huge boost in demand for its agricultural and mineral products, and foreign investment increased in turn (Hopewell 2014, 296). This was especially so in the commercial soybean industry (Barrionuevo 2007). A public campaign against the "foreignization" of farmland emerged (Fairbairn 2015). According to Gustavo Oliveira (2018, 124), it was "large-scale landowners operating primarily with soy production and ranching that supported restrictions to limit foreign competition with their own expansion."[4] On the other hand, we find almost no anti-foreign intervention in Brazil's mining sector during this period. In Brazil, foreign majors such as BHP Billiton, Rio Tinto, Newmont, Xstrata, and Anglo American are all active in Brazil's mining sector, together with smaller foreign operators such as Yamana Gold (Duddu 2014). But even as the boom took off in the mid-2000s, there was little nationalist antagonism expressed by local firms or politicians.

A review of the scholarship on both sectors suggests that like in Indonesia, the structure and ownership of dominant business interests can help to elucidate varied nationalist outcomes. For example, Tomaso Ferrando (2015, 347) suggests a pivotal role for Brazil's soybean producers in the nationalist campaign because these firms saw foreign competition, particularly from China, as a threat to their business.[5] According to Kristen Hopewell (2014, 297), "in the past two decades, there has been a dramatic expansion of Brazilian firms. Of the 40 leading agribusiness companies operating in Brazil, 35 are Brazilian in origin." The industry is very much domestically owned and oriented, and its major firms display only low levels of internationalization. In response to growing nationalist demands from the business community, in September 2010, Brazil's attorney general recommended new limitations on the acquisition of national land by foreigners. President Luiz Inácio Lula da Silva quickly approved the legal opinion and it became binding. In practice, this meant that government agencies now had more responsibility to "monitor" and "authorize" not only foreign companies but also Brazilian companies with majority foreign shareholding that sought to invest in agricultural land.

Unlike the extractive companies in Indonesia's mining sector, in Brazil the mining sector is dominated by one major and highly internationalized domestic firm—Vale. Vale is responsible for 79.8 percent of the country's mineral production (Döring, Santos, and Pocher 2017, 11), it is listed on multiple stock exchanges, and has mining operations all over the world. After purchasing Canadian mining company Inco in 2006, Vale was ranked the world's fifth largest mining company. By 2008, Vale's overseas sales accounted for 84 percent of its revenues (Casanova 2009, 44), and by 2012, the company had operations in thirty different countries. Vale's success as a global mining company relied on an open and liberal mining investment regime in other countries, and its commercial interests were threatened in Guinea, Indonesia, and parts of South America during the boom as a result of nationalist mobilization (Ernst & Young 2014).[6] The ownership and preferences of the largest domestic operators reflects, therefore, the government's approach to FDI in these sectors, much like we saw in Indonesia—though the opposite outcomes prevailed in each sector.

Subnational variation, and a focus on business, also necessitates an approach to resource nationalism that pays specific attention to the different categories of actors that drive and benefit from policy change—state, private, and popular forces. This book has emphasized a need to expand conventional definitions of nationalization beyond state takeovers of private assets and to instead include what are often incremental efforts to chip away at foreign ownership for the benefit of local private actors. Divestment rules in Indonesia's mining sector were largely driven by and benefited big local businesses, and over time new rules pushed out most foreign majors from the coal and upstream minerals sectors and facilitated a slow "private nationalization" of the industry more broadly. Meanwhile, in the oil and gas sector, there was no official policy of nationalization. Instead, the sector was marked by what often appears as an inscrutable degree of regulatory and institutional ambiguity. Regulations were constantly in flux, laws were regularly revised, and often end up containing language that was sufficiently vague to appease nationalist demands while still attempting to maintain an open investment environment. This ambiguity was a function of the constant push and pull between statist and private nationalists.

Identifying distinct state, private, and popular drivers of resource nationalism can help to elucidate differences in the character of resource nationalism from country to country. Beyond Indonesia, in other middle-income countries with large private sectors and patronage-soaked political institutions, the terms of resource nationalism have been similarly marked by tension and conflict between local business and the state, rather than just foreign business and the state. Russia presents an illustrative case. With Vladimir Putin's rise to power in the 2000s, the Russian government shifted toward a more statist approach to ownership in the resource industries. Analysts were especially concerned with the assertive reentry of SOEs into Russia's oil and gas sector (Bremmer 2010), a change widely interpreted as part of Putin's strategy to control and undermine the country's oil barons and oligarchs. Arbatli (2012), however, documents how Putin pursued a strategy of resource nationalism in the oil and gas sector that mixes support for SOEs with selective nurturing of indigenous domestic companies. The president perceived particular local business elites as strategic allies and important patronage resources and thus too politically valuable to exclude from the spoils of resource nationalism. Like in Indonesia, in Russia, resource nationalism is not a statist exercise but rather reflects contentious power struggles between foreign investors, the state, and the country's established economic oligarchs (Arbatli 2012; Domjan and Stone 2010). Asking when and why private business, rather than state enterprises, reap the rewards of resource nationalist policies constitutes an important line of inquiry for scholars and policymakers studying such trends in middle-income economies where patronage resources play a central role in state-business relations.

The state should not, of course, be entirely sidelined when explaining patterns of nationalist agitation. Political economies of state-business relations have long emphasized the ways in which businesses' policy power often evolves out of or is contingent on a supportive set of state institutions and sector-level conditions. Drawing on cases from developmental states in Asia and Latin America, scholars have demonstrated how governments can establish the regulations and institutions to foster private sector expansion, build domestic champions, and then direct investment and business activities in order to achieve specific industrial and developmental goals (Doner 1991; Doner, Ritchie, and Slater 2005; Haggard and Zheng 2013; Hsueh 2012, 2016; Schneider 1997, 2015). Over time, however, corporate giants gain autonomy and are able to mold state policy in line with their preferences. State and business preferences are in many ways mutually constitutive. Indeed, as I demonstrated throughout the historical chapters of this book, the emergence of business-driven forms of resource nationalism in contemporary Indonesia is shaped by historical legacies and the policies of past governments that sought either to sideline or buttress the growth of domestic resource firms.

Although this book does not write the state out of resource nationalism, it has ultimately sought to rebalance the analytical playing field. Academics and policy experts have relied heavily on "the state" to explain varieties of resource nationalism. Myopic bureaucrats, populist politicians, or corrupt state networks are usually framed as the engineers of nationalist constraints on foreign enterprises during the good times of a resource boom. The Indonesian case demonstrated how a surge in commodity prices does not just provide the state with more leverage in its negotiations with foreign resource companies. Instead, booms can boost the structural and instrumental power of domestic firms, in turn transforming business-state relations and patterns of ownership in a country's precious land and natural resource sectors.

Notes

INTRODUCTION

1. Article 33 in the 1945 constitution holds that the economy should be based on familial principles and that strategic sectors, including natural resources, should be controlled by the state.

2. For example, Ernst & Young began producing quarterly updates on resource nationalism from 2012, and Maplecroft developed a new "Resource Nationalism Index" which ranks 190 countries according to the level of risk exposure for nationalist interventions against foreign investors: https://www.maplecroft.com/insights/analysis /resource-nationalism-rises-30-countries/.

3. Interview with journalist at *Asia Times*, September 26, 2013.

4. Boschini, Pettersson, and Roine (2007), for example, argue that point source resources include both plantation crops and minerals, whereas agricultural products such as rice, wheat, and livestock are "diffuse" resources.

5. Orbis is a global database that compiles information on company profiles and ownership structures: https://www.bvdinfo.com/en-gb/our-products/data/international/orbis.

6. This part of the SEARBO project was led by Professor Edward Aspinall (Australian National University) and Professor Paul Kenny (Australian Catholic University).

1. RESOURCE NATIONALISM IN PATRONAGE DEMOCRACIES

1. At the same time, some scholars are careful not to claim that new extractivist models are actually post-neoliberal because of how state-led extractive industries still "deepen dependence on global markets [with] few benefits for (rural) development" (Yates and Bakker 2013, 15).

2. Some scholars of economic nationalism have advocated for a definition less grounded in policy prescriptions. Instead, one school of thought suggests economic nationalism is better understood as a discursive practice and process of legitimation in which an economic policy, whether liberal or protectionist, is cast as benefiting and advancing "the national group" (Abdelal 2001; Helleiner and Pickel 2005; Pickel 2003). Even though the discursive dimensions of both economic and resource nationalism are important, I argue that delineating policy prescriptions is critical for developing precise concepts and precise measures for both phenomena. Indeed, it is impossible to think of a government that does not cast its economic policies as benefiting the nation and its citizenry. If economic nationalism can be associated with protectionist, anti-foreign interventions *and* open trade and foreign investment regimes, the concept becomes blunt and loses much of its analytical purchase.

3. Australia's system for claiming native title is immensely complex, and Aboriginal communities have to prove an unbroken practice of traditions and customs pertaining to a territory since the time of European colonization.

2. HISTORIES OF OWNERSHIP

1. Rice remained the domain of local smallholders, who competed for land with powerful Western sugar cane interests.

2. After discovering oil in Telaga Said in North Sumatra in 1885, Dutch prospectors lobbied the palace to fund their venture. With support from King William III, Royal Dutch was established in 1890 to mine oil in North Sumatra. The company acquired several concessions but expanded primarily by taking over the smaller firms that had emerged in the preceding years (Lindblad 1989, 54).

3. The Royal Dutch Shell Group consisted of three holding companies: Bataafsche Petroleum Maatschappik (BPM), the Asiatic Petroleum Company, and the Anglo-Saxon Petroleum Company. BPM monopolized the production and export of Indonesia's oil. In 1911, the company held forty-four concessions across Sumatra, Java, and Kalimantan (Hunter 1971, 255) and produced 13 million barrels (over 3 percent of the world's oil) (Bee 1982, 3).

4. Article 33 reads:

(1) Perekonomian disusun sebagai usaha bersama berdasar atas asas kekeluargaan.
(2) Cabang-cabang produksi yang penting bagi negara dan yang menguasai hajat hidup orang banyak dikuasai oleh negara.
(3) Bumi dan air dan kekayaan alam yang terkandung di dalamnya dikuasai oleh negara dan dipergunakan untuk sebesar-besar kemakmuran rakyat.
(4) Perekonomian nasional diselenggarakan berdasar atas demokrasi ekonomi dengan prinsip kebersamaan, efisiensi berkeadilan, berkelanjutan, berwawasan lingkungan, kemandirian, serta dengan menjaga keseimbangan kemajuan dan kesatuan ekonomi nasional.
(5) Ketentuan lebih lanjut mengenai pelaksanaan pasal ini diatur dalam undang-undang.

5. See Roosa (2006) for a seminal account of the alleged coup.

6. State-owned gas company Permigan had been dissolved in 1965.

7. Suharto's wife, Siti Hartinah, had family members appointed to strategic positions within Pertamina to ensure easy access to contracts. Suharto's son Bambang Trihatmojo established a shipping company whose success depended almost entirely on personal connections within Pertamina (Borsuk 1998). In 1985, Suharto's other son, Hutomo "Tommy" Mandala Putra, bought Pertamina's subsidiary, Pertamina Oil Marketing (Perta), and established himself as the country's oil broker. The *Asia Times* reported that "Perta was later closed by the government having allegedly milked Pertamina for almost US$1 million per month" (Guerin 2003).

3. THE NEW RESOURCE NATIONALISM

1. Such local demands and the nature of decentralized resource governance was a major topic of concern for political geographers, economists, and anthropologists during the first decade of the post-Suharto area, and such dynamics have been covered in detail in a range of studies (McCarthy 2004; McCarthy and Warren 2009; Resosudarmo 2004, 2005).

2. In 2020, when the law was revised, coal prices were also depressed. The price would spike to new highs in 2021, but the legal revisions took place amid low commodity prices and postboom conditions.

3. As will be explained, district and provincial licensing authority would eventually be rescinded in the revised 2020 Mining Law, and full authority for mining licenses would sit once more with the central government.

4. (1) Setelah 5 (lima) tahun berproduksi, badan usaha pemegang IUP dan IUPK yang sahamnya dimiliki oleh asing wajib melakukan divestasi saham pada pemerintah, pemerintah daerah, badan usaha milik negara, badan usaha milik daerah, atau badan usaha swasta nasional (Government of the Republic of Indonesia 2009).

5. Interview: senior industry consultant and former president director of Rio Tinto Indonesia and Newmont Pacific Nusantara, October 16, 2014.

6. Recall from chapter 4 that by the end of the 1990s, 69 percent of the planted area of oil palm plantation was controlled by eight Indonesian conglomerates (Casson 2000, 14).

7. Interviews: deputy chairman of parliamentary Commission IV, July 14, 2015; plantation industry consultant, September 6, 2014; representative from GAPKI, August 7, 2015; researcher from Center for International Forestry Research, August 14, 2015.

8. Interview: deputy chairman of parliamentary Commission IV, July 14, 2015.

9. Interviews: GAPKI, August 7, 2015; Centre for International Forestry Research (CIFOR) staff, August 24, 2014.

10. At a meeting in early 2017, representatives from Indonesia's major environmental nongovernmental organizations (NGOs) met with the minister for environment and forestry, Siti Nurbaya, to lodge their strong opposition to the bill, arguing it would have a devastating impact on Indonesia's dwindling forests and peat lands and would lead to more land conflicts (Jong 2017).

11. Several interviewees also described how conservative factions within Pertamina lobbied and co-opted members of the ministry and the parliament in order to prevent the draft from becoming law. Interviews: Kuntoro Mangkusubroto, former minister for energy and mineral resources (1998–99), January 12, 2015; Kardaya Warnika, former senior official at the Ministry for Energy and Mineral Resources and former director of BP Migas (2002–5), November 28, 2014.

12. Wahid was head of Nahdlatul Ulama, the country's largest Islamic organization at the time, and was the first reformist president appointed as part of Indonesia's democratic transition.

13. *Energia* is a Pertamina-sponsored publication.

14. Interviews: Kardaya Winarka, former director of BP Migas (2002–5) and former chair of parliamentary Commission VII on energy and natural resources (2014–16), November 28, 2014; Pri Agung, director of industry consulting company Refominer and adviser to parliamentary Commission VII on energy and natural resources, May 6, 2014; Rangga Fadhillah, former journalist for the *Jakarta Post* at the energy desk and industry consultant for Bower Group, May 23, 2014.

15. Interview: Kardaya Winarka, former director of BP Migas (2002–5) and former chair of parliamentary Commission VII on energy and natural resources (2014–16), November 28, 2014.

16. This connection was made routinely by many of the people interviewed for this study, cited in this and later chapters.

17. Interviews: Kardaya Warnika, former director of BP Migas (2002–5) and former chair of parliamentary Commission VII on energy and natural resources (2014–16), November 28, 2014; Satya Yudha, deputy chair of Commission VII (2014–), January 22, 2015; Pri Agung, director of industry consulting company Refominer and adviser to parliamentary Commission VII on energy and natural resources, May 6, 2014.

4. THE RISE OF DOMESTIC BUSINESS

1. Tanoto was incensed at losing his stake in the valuable coal mine and years later launched a case against Deutsche Bank in Singapore, claiming the bank had conspired with Soeryadjaya to sell the shares below market price (Lim 2007).

2. Interviews: former director for business development at the directorate for mineral and coal mining, September 25, 2014; former director general of mineral and coal mining, October 16, 2014.

3. Interviews: Simon Sembiring, former director general of mineral and coal mining (2007–9), April 11, 2014; Sukhyar, former director general for mineral and coal mining (2013–15), October 15, 2014.

4. I base this observation on a thorough examination of *risalah* (recordings of parliamentary deliberations) from parliamentary Commission VII, which manages energy and natural resource policy and negotiated the 2009 Mining Law, and from a thorough search through key industry publications that reported regularly on the law's progress. For example, I reviewed all issues of *Majalah Tambang*, the industry's most prominent publication which covered the negotiations in detail (copies are held at the Australian National Library). There were no articles dealing with the question of divestment from 2005 to 2008.

5. Interview: Mari Elka Pangestu, former trade minister (2009–11), July 13, 2015.

6. Interview: senior bureaucrat at Directorate General Mineral and Coal Mining, September 25, 2014.

7. Interviews: director of Indonesian Mining Association, May 12, 2014; senior industry consultant and former president director of Rio Tinto Indonesia and Newmont Pacific Nusantara, October 16, 2014.

8. Interviews: senior Indonesian industry consultant and former director of a global foreign mining company, Kiroyan and Partners, October 16, 2014.

9. Interviews: senior bureaucrat at directorate for mineral and coal mining, September 25, 2014; senior industry consultant, Kiroyan and Partners, October 16, 2014; representative of the Indonesian Coal Mining Association, May 16, 2014.

10. Interview: government relations consultant for a domestic gold mining company, December 16, 2014.

11. Interview: vice president director of the Indonesian subsidiary of an Australian listed gold mining company, October 17, 2014.

12. Interview: former director for business development at the directorate general for mineral and coal mining, September 25, 2014. The process of renegotiating an existing CoW was fraught. Hatta Rajasa oversaw what became drawn-out and controversial negotiations with foreign CoW holders to change their contracts and compel them to sign up for the new terms outlined in the 2009 Mining Law. Between 2012 and 2014, Hatta was able to compel only 25 out of 112 contract holders to amend their contracts (*Koran Tempo* 2014). Of the twenty-five, nineteen were from the coal sector and were Indonesian owned, which meant negotiations were far easier (domestic companies clearly had no concerns regarding divestment). The other contracts that were successfully renegotiated were mostly in the exploration stage and held by small-to-medium-sized foreign companies. None of the large foreign mining companies, like Freeport, Newmont, or BHP, for example, agreed to the new terms, nor did the many other less high-profile foreign ventures.

13. Interview: Mari Elka Pangestu, former trade minister (2009–11), July 13, 2015.

14. Interview: industry analyst for a foreign embassy in Indonesia, August 11, 2016.

15. Interview: Scott Hannah, corporate communications at Freeport Indonesia, September 2, 2014.

16. Orbis database report, 2020.

17. Orbis database report, 2020.

18. Interview: representative from a national anti-corruption organization and former member of the Corruption Eradication Commission, July 14, 2022.

19. Interview: representative from Bukit Asam, July 13, 2022.

20. Interviews: deputy chairman of parliamentary Commission IV, July 14, 2015; plantation industry consultant, September 6, 2014; representative from GAPKI, August 7, 2015.

21. At other times, however, APKASINDO lobbied to limit the amount of land available to larger private companies, "whether domestic or foreign," and to ensure that farmers' rights to land were properly enforced (Siregar 2013).

22. Interview: executive director of GAPKI, July 7, 2015.

23. Interview: executive director of GAPKI, July 7, 2015.

24. Interview: palm oil industry representative, July 7, 2015.

25. Interview: palm oil industry consultant, January 19, 2015.

26. Interview: Krystof Orbidzinski, CIFOR, September 24, 2014.

27. Interview: deputy chairman of parliamentary Commission IV 2009–14, July 14, 2015.

5. STATE CAPITAL AND CONSTRAINTS ON PRIVATE POWER

1. Initially, production volumes at the block dropped dramatically from 35,000 barrels of oil per day (bpd) in 2008 to just 1,200 bpd in 2013 after technical problems and bad weather delayed the development of new rigs (Detikfinance 2013a; McBeth 2013). But the government kept West Madura in Pertamina's hands, production improved, and in 2016, it stood at 9,300 bpd (Boediwardhana 2016).

2. Company website: http://www.po-and-g.com/oil-a-gas/jambi-merang-block.

3. Confidential interview: representative from Medco Energi, January 10, 2015.

4. Interview: September 29, 2014.

5. Interview: Sudirman Said, minister for energy and mineral resources (2014–16), August 25, 2016.

6. Interview: editor for energy and resources section at *Tempo Magazine*, October 5, 2017; interview representative from Medco Energi, January 10, 2015.

7. Interview: Kuturbi, member of parliament for Nasdem (2014–19), June 26, 2014.

8. Interview: Sudirman Said, minister for energy and mineral resources (2014–16), August 25, 2016.

9. Interview: confidential interview with representative from Bukit Asam, July 13, 2022.

10. See, for example, reports by the Business and Human Rights Resource Center: https://www.business-humanrights.org/en/latest-news/?&language=en&issues=76&companies=757086&operator=1.

11. Interview: Sudirman Said, minister for energy and mineral resources (2014–16), August 25, 2016.

12. Interview: Golkar politician from Commission VII, September 26, 2014.

13. Interview: Syahrir A.B., Chair of the IMA, May 12, 2014.

14. Interview: editor for energy and resources section at *Tempo Magazine*, October 5, 2017.

15. In one confidential discussion, a longtime foreign business analyst based in Jakarta described the divestment negotiations as nothing more than "smoke and mirrors" and suggested the state was really just trying to pressure Freeport to build a smelter and to divvy out small service contract deals to politically connected elites. This assessment turned out to be incorrect. Discussion held under Chatham House Rules at the Australian National University, Canberra, 2017.

16. Confidential interview: member of the Presidential Staff Office, October 5, 2017.

6. OWNERSHIP, IDENTITY, AND NATIONALIST DEMANDS

1. This part of the SEARBO project was led by Professor Edward Aspinall (Australian National University) and Professor Paul Kenny (Australian Catholic University).

2. Some of the results of this survey have been published elsewhere, but these prior papers were concerned primarily with companies' varied experiences of corruption rather than their economic policy preferences (see, e.g., Kenny and Warburton 2020).

3. Interview: representative from a national anti-corruption organization and former member of the Corruption Eradication Commission, July 14, 2022.

4. Interview: representative from APINDO, July 13, 2022.

5. Confidential interview: representative from a Chinese Indonesian conglomerate with major palm oil investments, July 15, 2022.

6. Confidential discussion with group of Indonesian business managers: October 28, 2020, Singapore.

7. Confidential interview: Indonesian businessperson with investments in palm oil and property, April 3, 2018.

8. Interview: representative from APINDO, July 13, 2022.

CONCLUSION

1. Interview, representative from Newmont, January 19, 2015.

2. Interview, Fidraus, Indonesia Corruption Watch, May 6, 2014.

3. Interview, Laode Syarif, July 14, 2022.

4. Oliveira (2018, 124) also argues that support and opposition to localization of the foreign investment regime reflected a subsectoral divide within the agricultural industry: "opposition [to foreign investment restriction] came from landowner associations from regions where the sugar/ethanol industry and the forestry/cellulose industry were expected to lead agribusiness expansion (e.g. the Agricultural Federation of Mato Grosso do Sul—FAMASUL) and the main representatives of those specific agroindustrial sectors (the Union of Sugarcane Planters—ÚNICA, and the Brazilian Association of Planted Forests—ABRAP)."

5. The largest soybean producers were Grupo Bom Futura, an integrated agribusiness company that operates exclusively in Mato Grosso state and has 550,000 ha of soy farmland; Groupo Amaggi, a leading integrated agribusiness company whose interests are focused firmly in Brazil and primarily in Mato Grosso state; and Bom Jesus, a vertically integrated company with 240,000 ha of farmland across the country, concentrated entirely in Mato Grosso state.

6. At the same time, it would be wrong to characterize Vale as a completely independent multinational enterprise in the same category as BHP Billiton or Rio Tinto. Despite being privatized in 1997, analysts refer to Vale as a "quasi-state-controlled company" (Valle and Millard 2017). The government maintained control over the company's strategic decisions and leadership appointments through its "share," and Brazilian state banks and pension funds also had significant interests in the mining giant. This "golden share" provides the government with veto power over important investment decisions, gives it special voting rights, and allows the government to influence leadership appointments within the company. During the presidency of Lula da Silva, analysts pointed to incidents, particularly the ousting of Roger Agnelli in 2011, where government actors exercised influence over company decisions (*Financial Times* 2011).

References

Abdelal, Rawi. 1993. "Entrepreneurship and Protection in the Indonesian Oil Service Industry." In *Southeast Asian Capitalists*, edited by Ruth McVey, 89–101. Ithaca, NY: Cornell University Press.

———. 2001. *National Purpose in the World Economy: Post-Soviet States in Comparative Perspective*. Ithaca, NY: Cornell University Press.

Aditjondro, George Junus. 2006. *Korupsi Kepresidenan: Reproduksi Oligarki Berkaki Tiga: istana, tangsi, dan partai penguasa*. Yogyakarta: PT LKiS Pelangi Aksara.

Adnan, Hanim. 2014. "Indonesia's Oil Palm Dilemma." *The Star Online*, September 27. http://www.thestar.com.my/Business/Business-News/2014/09/27/Indonesias -oil-palm-dilemma-Plans-to-limit-foreign-ownership-still-undecided/.

Alfian. 2010. "Bakrie-Led Venture Picks Up More Shares in Newmont." *Jakarta Post*, March 18. http://www.thejakartapost.com/news/2010/03/18/bakrieled-venture -picks-more-shares-newmont.html.

Alon, Anna, and Oksana Kim. 2022. "Protectionism through Legislative Layering: Implications for Auditors and Investors." *Journal of International Business Policy* 5 (3): 363–83.

Antam. 2013. "Annual Report 2013: Managing Reality, Overcoming Uncertainty." https://cdn.indonesia-investments.com/bedrijfsprofiel/217/aneka-tambang -antam-annual-report-2013-antm-company-profile-indonesia-investments .pdf.

Arbatli, Ekim. 2012. "Oil and (Non)democratic Politics: Explaining Resource Nationalism in Russia and Venezuela" (Order No. 3529453). Available from ProQuest One Academic. (1086353880). Retrieved from https://www.proquest.com/dissertations -theses/oil-non-democratic-politics-explaining-resource/docview/1086353880 /se-2.

———. 2013. "Political Regimes, Investment Risk and Resource Nationalism: An Empirical Analysis." Paper presented at International Academic Conference on Economic and Social Development, Moscow, April 2–5.

Arifin, Bustanul. 2013. "On the Competitiveness and Sustainability of the Indonesian Agricultural Export Commodities." *ASEAN Journal of Economics, Management and Accounting* 1:81–100. https://www.researchgate.net/publication/290483188_On _the_competitiveness_and_sustainability_of_the_Indonesian_agricultural_export _commodities.

Arndt, H. W. 1983. "Oil and the Indonesian Economy." *Southeast Asian Affairs* 10 (January): 136–50. https://search.proquest.com/docview/1308071501/citation/E726162 34C7945C4PQ/1.

Arshad, Arlina, and David Fogarty. 2016. "Palm Oil Companies Ditch Landmark Indonesian 'Zero Deforestation' Pact." *The Straits Times*, July 1.

Ascher, William. 1998. "From Oil to Timber: The Political Economy of Off-Budget Development Financing in Indonesia." *Indonesia* 65 (April): 37–61.

Aspinall, Edward. 2005. *Opposing Suharto: Compromise, Resistance, and Regime Change in Indonesia*. Stanford, CA: Stanford University Press.

——. 2007. "The Construction of Grievance." *Journal of Conflict Resolution* 51 (6): 950–72. https://doi.org/10.1177/0022002707307120.

——. 2013. "A Nation in Fragments: Patronage and Neoliberalism in Contemporary Indonesia." *Critical Asian Studies* 45 (1): 27–54.

——. 2015a. "Oligarchic Populism: Prabowo Subianto's Challenge to Indonesian Democracy." *Indonesia* 99 (April): 1–28.

——. 2015b. "The New Nationalism in Indonesia." *Asia & the Pacific Policy Studies* 3 (1): 72–82. http://onlinelibrary.wiley.com/doi/10.1002/app5.111/abstract.

Aspinall, Edward, and Ward Berenschot. 2019. *Democracy for Sale: Elections, Clientelism and the State in Indonesia.* Ithaca, NY: Cornell University Press.

Aurora, Leony, Jim Schweithelm, Rauf Prasodjo, Paoli Gary, and Blair Palmer. 2015. "Indonesia's Evolving Governance Framework for Palm Oil: Implications for a No Deforestation, No Peat Palm Oil Sector." *Daemeter.* http://daemeter.org/en /publication/detail/44/indonesias-evolving-governance-framework-for-palm-oil -implications-for-a-no-deforestation-no-peat-palm-oil-sector#.Vs6nOsd2NTY.

Auty, Richard. 1994. "Industrial Policy Reform in Six Large Newly Industrializing Countries: The Resource Curse Thesis." *World Development* 22 (1): 11–26.

A'yun, Rafiqa Qurrata, and Abdil Mughis Mudhoffir. 2019. "The End of the KPK—at the Hands of the 'Good' President." *Indonesia at Melbourne Blog,* September 24. https://indonesiaatmelbourne.unimelb.edu.au/the-end-of-the-kpk-at-the-hands -of-the-good-president/.

Azwar, Amahl. 2012. "After BPMigas, the Next Target Is Mahakam." *Jakarta Post,* November 23. http://www.thejakartapost.com/news/2012/11/23/after-bpmigas -next-target-mahakam.html.

Bachtiar, Farahdiba. 2018. "Pertamina Gets Rokan Oil Block from Chevron. What Does This Tell Us?" *The Jakarta Post,* August 30, 2018.

Baihaqi, Bari. 2013. "Petani Minta Lahan Sawit Milik Asing Dibatasi." *Harian Ekonomi Neraca,* January 17. https://www.neraca.co.id/article/23820/petani-minta-lahan -sawit-milik-asing-dibatasi.

Barnes, Philip. 1995. *Indonesia: The Political Economy of Energy.* Oxford: Oxford University Press.

Barr, Christopher. 1998. "Bob Hasan, the Rise of Apkindo, and the Shifting Dynamics of Control of Indonesia's Timber Sector." *Indonesia* 65 (April): 1–36.

Barrionuevo, Alexei. 2007. "China's Appetite for Meat Feeds a Brazilian Soybean Boom." *New York Times,* April 5. https://www.nytimes.com/2007/04/05/business/world business/05iht-soy.4.5164446.html.

Bartlett, Anderson G., Robert Barton, Joe Bartlett, George Fowler, and Charles Hays. 1972. *Pertamina: Indonesian National Oil.* Jakarta: Amerasian.

Basri, M. Chatib, and Hal Hill. 2008. "Indonesia—Trade Policy Review 2007." *World Economy* 31 (11): 1393–1408. https://doi.org/10.1111/j.1467-9701.2008.01134.x.

Bauerle Danzman, Sarah. 2020. *Merging Interests: When Domestic Firms Shape FDI Policy.* Cambridge: Cambridge University Press.

BCG. 2016. "Global Challengers and Champions: The Engines of Emerging Markets." Boston Consulting Group. https://www.bcg.com/publications/2016/growth-global -leaders-challengers-champions.aspx.

Bebbington, Anthony, and Denise Humphreys-Bebbington. 2011. "An Andean Avatar: Post-Neoliberal and Neoliberal Strategies for Securing the Unobtainable." *New Political Economy* 16 (1): 131–45. https://doi.org/10.1080/13563461003789803.

Beckmann, Rick, and Aldi Rakhmatillah. 2014. "Future Still Hazy for Indonesian Plantation Monopolies." *Eco-Business,* October 24. http://www.eco-business.com/opinion /hazy-future-indonesian-plantation-monopolies-continues/.

Bee, Ooi Jin. 1982. *The Petroleum Resources of Indonesia*. Dordrecht, the Netherlands: Springer.

Benda, Harry J. 1956. "The Beginnings of the Japanese Occupation of Java." *Journal of Asian Studies* 15 (4): 541–60. https://doi.org/10.2307/2941923.

———. 1958. *The Crescent and the Rising Sun: Indonesian Islam under the Japanese Occupation, 1942–1945*. The Hague: W. van Hoeve.

Berita Satu. 2013. "Antara Rudi, Wisnu dan Tudingan Suap SKK Migas untuk Konvensi Partai Demokrat." August 17. http://www.indonesiamedia.com/antara-rudi-wisnu -dan-tudingan-suap-skk-migas-untuk-konvensi-partai-demokrat/.

Berrios, Ruben, Andrae Marak, and Scott Morgenstern. 2011. "Explaining Hydrocarbon Nationalization in Latin America: Economics and Political Ideology." *Review of International Political Economy* 18 (5): 673–97.

Bhasin, Balbir. 2000. "Foreign Investment in Gold Mining in Developing Countries: An Analysis of Award and Implementation of the Contract of Work System in Indonesia." PhD diss., University of South Australia. http://search.ror.unisa.edu.au /media/researcharchive/open/9915960078101831/53112378530001831.

Bisnis Indonesia. 2014. "Rizal Ramli: Jangan Takut Hadapi Freeport Dan Newmont!" February 6. http://m.bisnis.com/industri/read/20140206/44/201528/rizal-ramli -jangan-takut-hadapi-freeport-dan-newmont.

Boediwardhana, Wahyoe. 2016. "Pertamina Unit Builds New Oil Rig in East Java." *Jakarta Post*, October 16. https://www.pressreader.com/indonesia/the-jakarta -post/20161015/282016146847845.

Booth, Anne. 1998. *The Indonesian Economy in the Nineteenth and Twentieth Centuries: A History of Missed Opportunities*. New York: St. Martin's.

Borras, Saturnino, Jennifer C. Franco, Sergio Gómez, Cristóbal Kay, and Max Spoor. 2012. "Land Grabbing in Latin America and the Caribbean." *Journal of Peasant Studies* 39 (3–4): 845–72. https://doi.org/10.1080/03066150.2012.679931.

Borsuk, Richard. 1998. "The Suharto Regime Blew Many Chances to Amass Wealth." *Wall Street Journal*, December 30.

Borsuk, Richard, and Nancy Chng. 2014. *Liem Sioe Liong's Salim Group: The Business Pillar of Suharto's Indonesia*. Singapore: ISEAS Publishing.

Boschini, Anne D., Jan Pettersson, and Jesper Roine. 2007. "Resource Curse or Not: A Question of Appropriability." *Scandinavian Journal of Economics* 109 (3): 593–617. http://onlinelibrary.wiley.com/doi/10.1111/j.1467-9442.2007.00509.x/abstract.

Bremmer, Ian. 2010. *The End of the Free Market: Who Wins the War between States and Corporations?* New York: Portfolio.

Bresnan, John. 1993. *Managing Indonesia: The Modern Political Economy*. New York: Columbia University Press.

Brown, David. 1999. "Addicted to Rent: Corporate and Spatial Distribution of Forest Resources in Indonesia: Implications for Forest Sustainability and Government Policy." Report No: PFM/EC/99/06. Jakarta: Indonesia-UK Tropical Forest Management Programme, Provincial Forest Management Program.

———. 2005. *Indonesia: The Great Transition*. Lanham, MD: Rowman & Littlefield.

Budiartie, Gustidha, Ananda Teresia, and Faiz Nasrillah. 2016. "Membidik Saham Batu Hijau." *Tempo Magazine*, April 11. https://majalah.tempo.co/read/ekonomi-dan -bisnis/150491/membidik-saham-batu-hijau.

Budiartie, Gustidha, and Eve Warburton. 2015. "Indonesia's Freeport Saga." *New Mandala* (blog). December 22. http://www.newmandala.org/indonesias-freeport-saga/.

Buehler, Michael. 2012. "'Resource Nationalism' Clouds Indonesia's Economic Prospects." *ASEAN Beat* (blog). September 7. http://thediplomat.com/asean-beat/2012 /09/07/resource-nationalism-clouds-indonesias-economic-prospects/.

Buletin Parlementaria. 2014. "Komisi IV Selasaikan Naskah RUU Tentang Perkebunan." Volume 4 (February). http://www.dpr.go.id/dokpemberitaan/buletin-parlementaria/b-804-2-2014.pdf.

Busch, Matthew. 2017. "Can Indonesia Take on Freeport?" *East Asia Forum* (blog). March 12. http://www.eastasiaforum.org/2017/03/21/can-indonesia-take-on-freeport/.

Busse, Matthias, and Steffen Gröning. 2013. "The Resource Curse Revisited: Governance and Natural Resources." *Public Choice* 154 (1–2): 1–20. https://doi.org/10.1007/s11127-011-9804-0.

Butt, Simon, and Fritz Edward Siregar. 2013. "State Control over Natural Resources in Indonesia: Implications of the Oil and Natural Gas Law Case of 2012." *Journal of Energy & Natural Resources Law* 31 (2): 107–21.

Cahyafitri, Raras. 2015a. "Pertamina's Biggest Gamble: The Mahakam Block." *Jakarta Post*, February 9. http://www.thejakartapost.com/news/2015/02/09/pertamina-s-biggest-gamble-the-mahakam-block.html.

———. 2015b. "Newmont Seeks Support from Investors, Kalla." *Jakarta Post*, February 20. http://www.thejakartapost.com/news/2015/02/20/newmont-seeks-support-investors-kalla.html.

Cahyafitri, Raras, and Rendi A. Witular. 2015. "Deal Shields Govt, Freeport from Legal Row, Corrupt Politicians." *Jakarta Post*, October 16. http://www.thejakartapost.com/news/2015/10/16/deal-shields-govt-freeport-legal-row-corrupt-politicians.html.

Carney, Michael, and Marleen Dieleman. 2011. "Indonesia's Missing Multinationals: Business Groups and Outward Direct Investment." *Bulletin of Indonesian Economic Studies* 47 (1): 105–26. https://doi.org/10.1080/00074918.2011.556058.

Carney, Richard W., and Natasha Hamilton-Hart. 2015. "What Do Changes in Corporate Ownership in Indonesia Tell Us?" *Bulletin of Indonesian Economic Studies* 51 (1): 123–45. https://doi.org/10.1080/00074918.2015.1016570.

Casanova, Lourdes. 2009. *Global Latinas*. London: Palgrave Macmillan. https://doi.org/10.1057/9780230235021_3.

Casson, Anne. 2000. "The Hesitant Boom: Indonesia's Oil Palm Sub-sector in an Era of Economic Crisis and Political Change." Occasional Paper No. 29. Bogor, Indonesia: Center for International Forestry Research (CIFOR). https://www.cifor.org/library/625/the-hesitant-boom-indonesias-oil-palm-sub-sector-in-an-era-of-economic-crisis-and-political-change/.

Casson, Anne, Y. I. K. D. Muliastra, and Krystof Obidzinski. 2015. "Land-Based Investment and Green Development in Indonesia: Lessons from Berau District, East Kalimantan." Working Paper No. 180. Bogor, Indonesia: Center for International Forestry Research (CIFOR). http://www.cifor.org/library/5538/land-based-investment-and-green-development-in-indonesia-lessons-from-berau-district-east-kalimantan/.

Castle, James. 2014. "Indonesia's Fragile Future." *Tempo Magazine*, January 5.

Chalmers, Ian. 1997. Introduction to *The Politics of Economic Development in Indonesia: Contending Perspectives*, edited by Vedi Hadiz and Ian Chalmers, 1–39. London: Routledge.

Childs, John. 2016. "Geography and Resource Nationalism: A Critical Review and Reframing." *Extractive Industries and Society*. 3 (2): 539–46.

Chua, Christian. 2008. *Chinese Big Business in Indonesia*. New York: Routledge.

Click, Reid W., and Robert Weiner. 2010. "Resource Nationalism Meets the Market: Political Risk and the Value of Petroleum Reserves." *Journal of International Business Studies* 41: 783–803. https://doi.org/10.1057/jibs.2009.90.

Clift, Ben, and Cornelia Woll. 2012. "Economic Patriotism: Reinventing Control over Open Markets." *Journal of European Public Policy* 19 (3): 307–23. https://doi.org/10.1080/13501763.2011.638117.

CNN Indonesia. 2015. "Pemerintah Tak Restui Pertamina Kuasai Blok Mahakam?" March 7. http://www.cnnindonesia.com/ekonomi/20150307190711-85-37497/pemerintah-tak-restui-pertamina-kuasai-blok-mahakam/.

Colantone, Italo, and Piero Stanig. 2019. "The Surge of Economic Nationalism in Western Europe." *Journal of Economic Perspectives* 33 (4): 128–51.

Cramb, Rob, and John McCarthy. 2016. *The Oil Palm Complex: Smallholders, Agribusiness and the State in Indonesia and Malaysia.* Singapore: NUS Press.

Cribb, Robert. 1988. "Opium and the Indonesian Revolution." *Modern Asian Studies* 22 (4): 701–22. http://www.jstor.org/stable/312522.

———. 2001. "Genocide in Indonesia, 1965–1966." *Journal of Genocide Research* 3 (2): 219–39.

Cribb, Robert, and Colin Brown. 1995. *Modern Indonesia: A History since 1945.* London: Longman.

Culpepper, Pepper D. 2011. *Quiet Politics and Business Power.* Cambridge: Cambridge University Press.

Damayanti, Doty. 2010. "Gagalnya 'Indonesia Incorporated.'" *Kompas*, December 3. http://bisniskeuangan.kompas.com/read/2010/12/03/08115979/Gagalnya.Indonesia.Incorporated-5.

Dargin, Justin. 2010. "Investor-State Relations in the Chavez Age: The Nature of Resource Nationalism in the 21st Century." Belfer Center Working Paper Series (Spring). Cambridge, MA: Harvard University Kennedy School of Government. https://www.belfercenter.org/publication/investor-state-relations-chavez-age.

Davidson, Jamie S. 2015. *Indonesia's Changing Political Economy: Governing the Roads.* Cambridge: Cambridge University Press.

———. 2021. "Opposition to Privatized Infrastructure in Indonesia." *Review of International Political Economy* 28 (1): 128–51.

D'Costa, Anthony P. 2009. "Economic Nationalism in Motion: Steel, Auto, and Software Industries in India." *Review of International Political Economy* 16 (4): 620–48.

Deacon, Robert, and Ashwin Rode. 2012. "Rent-Seeking and the Resource Curse." Working paper (September 26), Department of Economics, University of California, Santa Barbara. http://econ.ucsb.edu/~deacon/RentSeekingResourceCurse%20Sept%2026.pdf.

Detikfinance. 2008. "Ancora Backdoor Listing Lewat TD Resources." December 9. https://finance.detik.com/bursa-valas/1050493/ancora-backdoor-listing-lewat-td-resources.

———. 2009. "Pertamina Incar Blok Mahakam Dan North Madura." June 16. https://finance.detik.com/berita-ekonomi-bisnis/d-1148765/pertamina-incar-blok-mahakam-dan-north-madura.

———. 2013a. "Produksi Minyak Di Blok Madura Milik Pertamina Jeblok." January 29. https://finance.detik.com/read/2013/01/29/185522/2155653/1034/produksi-minyak-di-blok-madura-milik-pertamina-jeblok-.

———. 2013b. "Petronas Setor Ke Malaysia Rp 190 Triliun, Pertamina Ke RI Cuma Rp 7 Triliun." March 4. https://finance.detik.com/read/2013/03/04/163432/2185238/4/petronas-setor-ke-malaysia-rp-190-triliun-pertamina-ke-ri-cuma-rp-7-triliun.

Devi, B., and D. Proyogo. 2013. "Mining and Development in Indonesia: An Overview of the Regulatory Framework and Policies." Perth: International Mining for Development Centre, University of Western Australia. http://im4dc.org/wp-content/uploads/2013/09/Mining-and-Development-in-Indonesia.pdf.

Dewan Perwakilan Rakyat. 2006. "Daftar Inventarisarsi Masalah (DIM): Rancangan Udang-Udang Tentang Pertambangan Mineral Dan Batubara." Jakarta: Dewan Perwakilan Rakyat.

———. 2014. "Risalah Resmi 2014–2014: Rapat Paripurna DPR RI." Masa Persidangan 1, Rapat 10. Jakarta: Dewan Perwakilan Rakyat.

Dibley, Thushara, and Michele Ford, eds. 2019. *Activists in Transition: Progressive Politics in Democratic Indonesia*. Ithaca, NY: Cornell University Press.

Dick, Howard W. 2002. *The Emergence of a National Economy: An Economic History of Indonesia, 1800–2000*. Sydney: Allen & Unwin.

Dickie, Robert, and Thomas Layman. 1988. *Foreign Investment and Government Policy in the Third World: Forging Common Interests in Indonesia and Beyond*. London: Palgrave Macmillan.

Dieleman, M., and W. Sachs. 2006. "Oscillating between a Relationship-based and a Market-based Model: The Salim Group." *Asia Pacific Journal of Management* 23:521–36. https://doi.org/10.1007/s10490-006-9019-y.

Directorate General for Mineral and Coal Mining. 2019. *Laporan Kinerja Tahun 2019* [Work report for 2019]. https://www.minerba.esdm.go.id/pdf/129-Lakin%202019.

Domjan, Paul, and Matt Stone. 2010. "A Comparative Study of Resource Nationalism in Russia and Kazakhstan 2004–2008." *Europe-Asia Studies* 62 (1): 35–62. https://doi.org/10.1080/09668130903385374.

Doner, Richard F. 1991. *Driving a Bargain: Automobile Industrialization and Japanese Firms in Southeast Asia*. Berkeley: University of California Press.

Doner, Richard F., Bryan Ritchie, and Dan Slater. 2005. "Systemic Vulnerability and the Origins of Developmental States: Northeast and Southeast Asia in Comparative Perspective." *International Organization* 59 (2): 327–61. https://doi.org/10.1017/S0020818305050113.

Doner, Richard F., and Ben Ross Schneider. 2016. "The Middle-Income Trap: More Politics than Economics." *World Politics* 68 (4): 608–44.

Döring, Heike, Rodrigo Salles Pereira dos Santos, and Eva Pocher. 2017. "New Developmentalism in Brazil? The Need for Sectoral Analysis." *Review of International Political Economy* 24 (2): 332–62. https://doi.org/10.1080/09692290.2016.1273841.

Duddu, Praveen. 2014. "The 10 Biggest Foreign-Owned Mines in Brazil." *Mining Technology*, October 26. https://www.mining-technology.com/features/featurethe-10-biggest-foreign-owned-mines-in-brazil-4415407/.

Dunia Energi. 2015. "Blok Migas Habis Kontrak Tak Selalu Diserahkan Pada Pertamina." October 7. http://www.dunia-energi.com/blok-migas-habis-kontrak-tak-selalu-diserahkan-pada-pertamina/.

———. 2019. "Jika Terbuka, Medco Siap Bersaing Perebutkan Blok Corridor." February 19. https://www.dunia-energi.com/jika-terbuka-medco-siap-bersaing-perebutkan-blok-corridor/.

Dwiarto, David. 2014. "Kemenperin: Industry Tambang Wajib Dikuasai Negara." *Asosiasi Tambang Indonesia*, March 25. http://www.ima-api.com/index.php?option=com_content&view=article&id=1744:kemenperin-industri-tambang-wajib-dikuasai-negara&catid=47:media-news&Itemid=98&lang=id.

Eaton, Kent. 2002. *Politicians and Economic Reform in New Democracies: Argentina and the Philippines in the 1990s*. University Park: Pennsylvania State University Press.

The Economist. 1999. "A Survival Guide." January 28. http://www.economist.com/node/184355.

———. 2012a. "Resource Nationalism in Africa: More for My People." February 11. http://www.economist.com/node/21547246.

———. 2012b. "Foreigners Beware." November 24. http://www.economist.com/news/business/21567117-foreign-investors-are-getting-nervous-foreigners-beware.

Embassy of the United States of America, Jakarta. 2000. "Coal Report: Indonesia 2000." Coal Sector Report Indonesia.

Energia. 2014. "Pertamina Sangat Siap Ambil Ahli Kelola Blok Migas Expired." Number 12, March 24. http://www.pertamina.com/media/60d270a3-6512-4a11-aaad -3f3dba849526/energia%2012%20-%2024%20MARET%202014%20ok.pdf.

Erb, Maribeth. 2016. "Mining and the Conflict over Values in Nusa Tenggara Timur Province, Eastern Indonesia." *Extractive Industries and Society* 3 (2): 370–82. https://doi.org/10.1016/j.exis.2016.03.003.

Erman, Erwiza. 2007. "Rethinking Legal and Illegal Economy: A Case Study of Tin Mining in Bangka Island." *Southeast Asia: History and Culture* 37:91–111.

Ernst & Young. 2014. "Resource Nationalism Update." http://www.ey.com/Publication /vwLUAssets/EY-resource-nationalism-in-mining-metals-november-2014 /$FILE/EY-resource-nationalism-in-mining-metals-november-2014.pdf (site discontinued).

Evans, Peter B. 1989. "Predatory, Developmental, and Other Apparatuses: A Comparative Political Economy Perspective on the Third World State." *Sociological Forum* 4 (4): 561–87. https://doi.org/10.1007/BF01115064.

Evans, Peter. 1995. *Embedded Autonomy: States and Industrial Transformation*. Princeton, NJ: Princeton University Press.

Fairbairn, Madeleine. 2015. "Foreignization, Financialization and Land Grab Regulation." *Journal of Agrarian Change* 15 (4): 581–91. https://doi.org/10.1111/joac.12112.

Fairfield, Tasha. 2015. *Private Wealth and Public Revenue in Latin America: Business Power and Tax Politics*. Cambridge: Cambridge University Press.

Fane, George. 1996. "Deregulation in Indonesia: Two Steps Forward, One Step Back." *Agenda* 3 (3): 341–50.

Feith, Herbert. 1962. *The Decline of Constitutional Democracy in Indonesia*. Ithaca, NY: Cornell University Press.

Feridhanusetyawan, Tubagus. 1997. "Survey of Recent Developments." *Bulletin of Indonesian Economic Studies* 33 (2): 3–39. https://doi.org/10.1080/00074919712331 337105.

Ferrando, Tomaso. 2015. "Dr. Brasilia and Mr. Nacala: The Apparent Duality behind the Brazilian State-Capital Nexus." *Revisita de economia politica* 35 (2): 343–59.

Financial Times. 2008. "Indonesia Pulls Out of OPEC." May 29. https://www.ft.com /content/d0e346fe-2c87-11dd-88c6-000077b07658.

——. 2011. "Vale: Signs of Growing Resource Nationalism." April 3. https://www.ft .com/content/a525b29e-5e1c-11e0-b1d8-00144feab49a.

——. 2016. "The Dynasty That Charmed the City." July 18. https://www.ft.com/content /6fe28630-cf30-11e1-bfd9-00144feabdc0.

Forbes. 2007. "A New Chapter." December 14. http://www.forbes.com/global/2007 /1224/044.html.

——. 2022. "Indonesia's 50 Richest." December 7. https://www.forbes.com/lists/indo nesia-billionaires/?sh=2a8d666c2ff7.com.

Ford, Michele, and Thomas B. Pepinsky. 2013. "Beyond Oligarchy? Critical Exchanges on Political Power and Material Inequality in Indonesia." *Indonesia* 96 (1): 1–9. https://doi.org/10.1353/ind.2013.0015.

Frieden, Jeffry A. 1991. *Debt, Development, and Democracy: Modern Political Economy and Latin America, 1965–1985*. Princeton, NJ: Princeton University Press.

Friederich, Mike C., and Theo van Leeuwen. 2017. "A Review of the History of Coal Exploration, Discovery and Production in Indonesia: The Interplay of Legal Framework, Coal Geology and Exploration Strategy." *International Journal of Coal Geology* 178 (June): 56–73. https://doi.org/10.1016/j.coal.2017.04.007.

Fukuoka, Yuki. 2012. "Oligarchy and Democracy in Post-Suharto Indonesia." *Political Studies* 11 (1): 52–64. https://doi.org/10.1111/j.1478-9302.2012.00286.x.

Fuller, Douglas. B. 2016. *Paper Tigers, Hidden Dragons: Firms and the Political Economy of China's Technological Development*. Oxford, UK: Oxford University Press.

Fullerton, Ticky. 2012. "High Stakes: The Politics of Chinese Investment." *ABC News*, October 2. http://www.abc.net.au/news/2012-10-02/fullerton-high-stakes/4289756.

Gallo, Miguel Ángel, Josep Tàpies, and Kristin Cappuyns. 2004. "Comparison of Family and Nonfamily Business: Financial Logic and Personal Preferences." *Family Business Review* 17 (4): 303–18.

Gammon, Liam. 2014. "Prabowo's Dog-Whistling." *New Mandala*, June 12. http://www.newmandala.org/prabowos-dog-whistling/.

GAPKI. 2015. "Perkebunan Sawit tak Abaikan Usaha Kecil Menengah (UKM) lokal/daerah" [Palm oil plantations do not neglect local/regional small and middle-sized firms]. https://GAPKI.id/news/1105/perkebunan-kelapa-sawit-tak-abaikan-usaha-kecil-menengah-ukm-lokaldaerah.

Gardner, David. 2013. "Not All Forms of Resource Nationalism Are Alike." *Financial Times*, August 18. http://www.ft.com/intl/cms/s/0/62be6d98-05df-11e3-ad01-00144feab7de.html?siteedition=intl#axzz2cwGbY9Oa.

Gaskell, Joanne C. 2015. "The Role of Markets, Technology, and Policy in Generating Palm-Oil Demand in Indonesia." *Bulletin of Indonesian Economic Studies* 51 (1): 29–45. https://doi.org/10.1080/00074918.2015.1016566.

Geddes, Barbara. 1996. *Politician's Dilemma: Building State Capacity in Latin America*. Berkeley: University of California Press.

Gellert, Paul. 1998. "A Brief History and Analysis of Indonesia's Forest Fire Crisis." *Indonesia* 65 (65): 63–85. https://doi.org/10.2307/3351404.

———. 2005. "Oligarchy in the Timber Markets of Indonesia: From APKINDO to IBRA to the Future of the Forests." In *The Politics and Economics of Indonesia's Natural Resources*, edited by Budy P. Resosudarmo, 145–61. Singapore: Institute for the Southeast Asian Studies Press.

Gellner, Ernest. 2008. *Nations and Nationalism*. Ithaca, NY: Cornell University Press.

Girvan, Norman. 1975. "Economic Nationalism." *Daedalus* 104 (4): 145–58.

Glassburner, Bruce. 1976. "In the Wake of General Ibnu: Crisis in the Indonesian Oil Industry." *Asian Survey* 16 (12): 1099–112. https://doi.org/10.2307/2643447.

Global Business Guide. 2014. "New Restrictions on Foreign Ownership of Plantations Proposed." August 24. http://www.gbgindonesia.com/en/main/business_updates/2014/upd_new_restrictions_on_foreign_ownership_of_plantations_proposed.php.

Goertz, Gary, and James Mahoney. 2012. *A Tale of Two Cultures: Qualitative and Quantitative Research in the Social Sciences*. Princeton, NJ: Princeton University Press.

Goldstone, Anthony. 1977. "What Was the Pertamina Crisis?" In *Southeast Asian Affairs 1977*, edited by Kim Hanh Huynh, 122–32. Singapore: ISEAS Publishing.

Gomez, Edmund T., and Elsa Lafaye De Micheaux. 2017. "Diversity of Southeast Asian Capitalisms: Evolving State-Business Relations in Malaysia." In *Changing Constellations of Southeast Asia*, edited by Jan Nederveen Pieterse, Abdul Embong, and Siew Yean Tham, 111–36. London: Routledge.

Gourevitch, Peter Alexis. 1986. *Politics in Hard Times: Comparative Responses to International Economic Crises*. Ithaca, NY: Cornell University Press.

Government of the Republic of Indonesia. 2009. Law No. 4 2009 on Mineral and Coal Mining [UU Minerba]. http://prokum.esdm.go.id/uu/2009/UU%204%202009.pdf.

Guerin, Bill. 2003. "Indonesia's First Family of Corruption." *Asia Times Online*, October 31. http://www.atimes.com/atimes/Southeast_Asia/EJ31Ae03.html.

Habir, Ahmad D. 2013. "Resource Nationalism and Constitutional Jihad." *Southeast Asian Affairs* 2013 (1): 121–34. http://muse.jhu.edu/journals/southeast_asian_affairs/v2013/2013.habir.html.

Hacker, Jacob S., and Paul Pierson. 2002. "Business Power and Social Policy: Employers and the Formation of the American Welfare State." *Politics & Society* 30 (2): 277–325.

Hadiz, Vedi R., and Richard Robison. 2013. "The Political Economy of Oligarchy and the Reorganization of Power in Indonesia." *Indonesia* 96 (1): 35–57. https://doi.org/10.1353/ind.2013.0023.

Haggard, Stephan, Sylvia Maxfield, and Ben Ross Schneider. 1997. "Theories of Business and Business-State Relations." In *Business and the State in Developing Countries*, edited by Sylvia Maxfield and Ben Ross Schneider, 36–62. Ithaca, NY: Cornell University Press.

Haggard, Stephan, and Yu Zheng. 2013. "Institutional Innovation and Investment in Taiwan: The Micro-foundations of the Developmental State." *Business and Politics* 15 (4): 435–66. https://doi.org/10.1515/bap-2012-0010.

Hall, Peter. 1997. "The Role of Interests, Institutions and Ideas in the Political Economy of Industrialized Nations." In *Comparative Politics: Rationality, Culture and Structure*, edited by Mark Irving Lichbach and Alan S. Zuckerman, 174–207. Cambridge: Cambridge University Press.

Hamilton-Hart, Natasha. 1999. "Internationalization: What Scholars Make of It?" Working paper 5, Department of International Relations, Australian National University.

———. 2015. "Multilevel (Mis)governance of Palm Oil Production." *Australian Journal of International Affairs* 69 (2): 164–84. https://doi.org/10.1080/10357718.2014.978738.

Hardjono, Joan. 1994. "Resource Utilisation and the Environment." In *Indonesia's New Order: The Dynamics of Socio-Economic Transformation*, edited by Hal Hill, 179–215. Sydney: Allen & Unwin.

Harian Ekonomi Neraca. 2013. "Petani Minta Lahan Sawit Milik Asing Dibatasi." January 14. http://www.neraca.co.id/article/23820/petani-minta-lahan-sawit-milik-asing-dibatasi.

Haslam, Paul A., and Pablo Heidrich. 2016a. "Chapter 13: Towards a Theory of Resource Nationalisms." In *The Political Economy of Natural Resources and Development: From Neoliberalism to Resource Nationalism*, edited by Paul A. Haslam and Pablo Heidrich, 223–35. New York: Routledge.

———. 2016b. "Introduction: From Neoliberalism to Resource Nationalism: States, Firms and Development." In *The Political Economy of Natural Resources and Development: From Neoliberalism to Resource Nationalism*, edited by Paul A. Haslam and Pablo Heidrich, 1–32. New York: Routledge.

Hawkins, Douglas, Yingheng Chen, and Thomas Wigglesworth. 2016. "Indonesian Palm Oil Production Sector: A Wave of Consolidation to Come." Hardman Agribusiness.

Hefner, Robert W. 1998. *Market Cultures: Society and Morality in the New Asian Capitalisms*. Boulder, CO: Westview Press.

Helleiner, Eric, and Andreas Pickel. 2005. *Economic Nationalism in a Globalizing World*. Ithaca, NY: Cornell University Press.

Herberg, Mikkal E. 2011. Introduction to *Asia's Rising Energy and Resource Nationalism: Implications for the United States, China, and the Asia-Pacific Region* by Andrew S. Erickson, Yufan Hao, Weihua Liu, Llewelyn Hughes, Mikkal E. Herberg, Jane Nakano, and Gabe Collins, 6–7. Washington, DC: National Bureau of Asian Research. http://www.nbr.org/publications/issue.aspx?id=236.

Hermansyah, Anton. 2017. "Malaysian Felda Acquires 37 Percent of Rajawali's Eagle High." *Jakarta Post*, April 20. http://www.thejakartapost.com/news/2017/04/20/malaysian-felda-acquires-37-percent-of-rajawalis-eagle-high.html.

Hertzmark, Donald. 2007. "Pertamina: Indonesia's State-Owned Oil Company." In *Baker Institute Policy Report 35 on National Oil Companies*. Houston: James A.

Baker III Institute of Public Policy, Rice University. https://www.bakerinstitute
.org/center-for-energy-studies/role-national-oil-companies-international
-energy-markets/.

Hill, Hal. 1994. "The Economy." In *Indonesia's New Order: The Dynamics of Socio-Economic Transformation*, edited by Hal Hill, 54–122. Sydney: Allen & Unwin.

———. 2000. *The Indonesian Economy.* Cambridge: Cambridge University Press.

———. 2013. "The Political Economy of Policy Reform: Insights from Southeast Asia." *Asian Development Review* 30 (1): 108–30. https://doi.org/10.1162/ADEV_a_00005.

Hill, Hal, and Chatib Basri. 2004. "Ideas, Interests and Oil Prices: The Political Economy of Trade Reform during Suharto's Indonesia." *World Economy* 27 (5): 633–55.

Hill, Hal, and Thee Kian Wie. 2008. "Moh. Sadli (1922–2008), Economist, Minister and Public Intellectual." *Bulletin of Indonesian Economic Studies* 44 (1): 151–56. https://www.tandfonline.com/doi/abs/10.1080/00074910802001553?journalCode=cbie20.

Hopewell, Kristen. 2014. "The Transformation of State-Business Relations in an Emerging Economy: The Case of Brazilian Agribusiness." *Critical Perspectives on International Business* 10 (4): 291–309.

Houben, Vincent. 2002. "Java in the 19th Century: Consolidation of a Territorial State." In *The Emergence of a National Economy: An Economic History of Indonesia, 1800–2000*, edited by Howard W. Dick, 56–81. Honolulu: University of Hawai'i Press.

Houben, Vincent, and Thomas Lindblad. 1999. *Coolie Labour in Colonial Indonesia: A Study of Labour Relations in the Outer Islands, c. 1900–1940.* Wiesbaden: Otto Harrassowitz Verlag.

Hsiao, Hsin-Huang Michael, and Terence E. Gomez, eds. 2013. *Chinese Business in Southeast Asia: Contesting Cultural Explanations, Researching Entrepreneurship.* London: Taylor & Francis.

Hsueh, Roselyn. 2012. "China and India in the Age of Globalization Sectoral Variation in Postliberalization Reregulation." *Comparative Political Studies* 45 (1): 32–61. https://doi.org/10.1177/0010414011421305.

———. 2016. "State Capitalism, Chinese-Style: Strategic Value of Sectors, Sectoral Characteristics, and Globalization." *Governance* 29 (1): 85–102. https://doi.org/10.1111/gove.12139.

Hughes, Jennifer, and Ben Bland. 2014. "Jardines' Influence in Asia Quiet but Widespread." *Financial Times*, March 12. https://www.ft.com/content/4fdea0ac-a90f-11e3-bf0c-00144feab7de.

HukumOnline.com. 2010. "Suara Pengusaha Terpecah Soal Rencana Revisi UU Migas." July 26. http://www.hukumonline.com/berita/baca/lt4c4d6785a5f90/suara-pengu saha-terpecah-soal-rencana-revisi-uu-migas.

———. 2014. "Draft Bill on Plantations." *Indonesian Legal Brief* 2452. http://en.hukumonline .com/pages/lt53e8af992ee13/draft-bill-on-plantations.

———. 2015. "Compang-Camping UU Migas." February 24. http://www.hukumonline .com/berita/baca/lt54ec68c7d2cac/compang-camping-uu-migas.

Human Rights Watch. 2015. "Something to Hide? Indonesia's Restrictions on Media Freedom and Rights Monitoring in Papua." November 10. https://www.hrw.org /report/2015/11/10/something-hide-indonesias-restrictions-media-freedom-and -rights-monitoring-papua.

Humphreys, David. 2013. "New Mercantilism: A Perspective on How Politics Is Shaping World Metal Supply." *Resources Policy* 38 (3): 341–49. http://www.sciencedirect .com/science/article/pii/S0301420713000391.

Hunter, Alex. 1968. "Minerals in Indonesia." *Bulletin of Indonesian Economic Studies* 4 (11): 73–89. https://doi.org/10.1080/00074916812331331282.

———. 1971. "Oil Developments." *Bulletin of Indonesian Economic Studies* 7 (1): 96–113.

Hutchcroft, Paul D. 1991. "Oligarchs and Cronies in the Philippine State: The Politics of Patrimonial Plunder." *World Politics* 43 (3): 414–50.

ICIS News. 1999. "Corruption Cost Pertamina $6.1bn in 2 Yrs." July 12. http://www.icis .com/resources/news/1999/07/12/83568/corruption-cost-pertamina-6-1bn-in-2 -yrs/.

Indonesia Investments. 2018. "Coal." https://www.indonesia-investments.com/business /commodities/coal/item236.

Indonesia Statistics Agency. 2017. "Directory of Palm Oil Companies in Indonesia—2017." https://www.bps.go.id/publication/2018/11/13/740d97a49dcc8038a6f43cb2 /direktori-perusahaan-perkebunan-kelapa-sawit-indonesia-2017.html.

Indonesian Mining Association. 2002. "Indonesian Mining Industry in the Period of Transition, between 1997–2001."

Info Sawit. 2014. "Revisi UU No. 18 Tahun 2004 Disahkan, Asing Boleh Kuasai Kebun Nasional." http://www.infosawit.com/mobile/index.php/artikel/baca/revisi-uu -no--18-tahun-2004-disahkan--asing-boleh-kuasai-kebun-nasional.

Institute for Policy Analysis of Conflict (IPAC). 2017. "Policy Miscalculation on Papua." No. 40. October 21.

Investor Daily. 2007. "Dampak RUU Minerba, Perusahan Tambang Asing Terbebas Kewajiban Divestasi." October 24. https://kaltimprimacoal.wordpress.com/ruu -minerba/.

Isham, Jonathan, Michael Woolcock, Lant Pritchett, and Gwen Busby. 2005. "The Varieties of Resource Experience: Natural Resource Export Structures and the Political Economy of Economic Growth." *World Bank Economic Review* 19 (2): 141–74. http://wber.oxfordjournals.org/content/19/2/141.

Jaffrelot, Christophe, Atul Kohli, and Kanta Murali, eds. 2019. *Business and Politics in India*. Oxford: Oxford University Press.

Jakarta Globe. 2017. "Indonesia's New Mining Holding Company to Control 6.6b in Assets." November 22. https://jakartaglobe.id/context/indonesias-new-mining-holding -company-to-control-6-6b-in-assets/.

Jakarta Post. 2000. "Reforming Pertamina." March 1.

———. 2008. "Ancora Has Big Investment Plans for Mining Sector." December 10. http:// www.thejakartapost.com/news/2008/12/10/ancora-has-big-investment-plans -mining-sector.html.

———. 2012. "Editorial: Twist in Newmont Divestment." August 1. http://www.thejakar tapost.com/news/2012/08/01/editorial-twist-newmont-divestment.html.

———. 2014. "Notable Achievements during Karen Agustiawan's Six Years at PT Pertamina." August 19. https://www.pressreader.com/indonesia/the-jakarta-post/2014 0819/282286728430076.

———. 2015. "Discourse: President Knows Well Those Orchestrating the Event: Luhut." November 20. http://www.thejakartapost.com/news/2015/11/20/discourse-president -knows-well-those-orchestrating-event-luhut.html.

———. 2020 "Explainer: New Rules in Revised Mining Law." May 14. https://www .thejakartapost.com/news/2020/05/14/explainer-new-rules-in-revised-mining -law.html.

Jiwan, Norman. 2013. "The Political Ecology of the Indonesian Palm Oil Industry: A Critical Analysis." In *The Palm Oil Controversy in Southeast Asia: A Transnational Perspective*, edited by Jayati Bhattacharya and Oliver Prye, 48–75. Singapore: ISEAS Publishing.

Johnson, Harry G. 1965. "A Theoretical Model of Economic Nationalism in New and Developing States." *Political Science Quarterly* 80 (2): 169–85. https://doi.org/10.2307 /2147738.

Jong, Hans Nicholas. 2017. "Mounting Outcry over Indonesian Palm Oil Bill as Legislators Press On." *Mongabay*, July 21.

———. 2020. "Indonesia's Omnibus Law a 'Major Problem' for Environmental Protection." November 4. https://news.mongabay.com/2020/11/indonesia-omnibus-law-global-investor-letter/.

———. 2021. "Deforestation in Indonesia Hits Record Low, but Experts Fear a Rebound." *Mongabay*, March 9.

Jonker, Joost, and Jan Luiten van Zanden. 2007. *A History of Royal Dutch Shell: From Challenger to Joint Industry Leader, 1890–1939.* Oxford: Oxford University Press.

Julianto, Pramdia Arhando. 2016. "DPR: RUU Perkelapasawitan Akan Akomodasi Semua Pihak." Kompas.com, December 14. https://money.kompas.com/read/2016/12/14/161800326/dpr.ruu.perkelapasawitan.akan.akomodasi.semua.pihak.

Junita, Fifi. 2015. "The Foreign Mining Investment Regime in Indonesia: Regulatory Risk under Resource Nationalism Policy and How International Investment Treaties Provide Protection." *Journal of Energy & Natural Resources Law* 33 (3): 241–65. https://doi.org/10.1080/02646811.2015.1057028.

Kabarbisnis. 2021. "Didanai Asing, DPR Minta NGO Lingkungan Transparent." August 13. https://www.kabarbisnis.com/read/28108499/didanai-asing-dpr-minta-ngo-lingkungan-transparan.

Kahin, George McTurnan. 1952. *Nationalism and Revolution in Indonesia.* Ithaca, NY: Cornell University Press.

Kano, Hiroyoshi. 2008. *Indonesian Exports, Peasant Agriculture and the World Economy, 1850–2000: Economic Structures in a Southeast Asian State.* Singapore: NUS Press.

Karl, Terry. 1997. *The Paradox of Plenty: Oil Booms and Petro-States.* Berkeley: University of California Press.

Kaup, Brent, and Paul Gellert. 2017. "Cycles of Resource Nationalism: Hegemonic Struggle and the Incorporation of Bolivia and Indonesia" *International Journal of Comparative Sociology* 58 (4): 275–303. https://doi.org/10.1177/0020715217714298.

Kenny, Paul, and Eve Warburton. 2020. "A Firm-Centered Analysis of Corruption and Reform: Evidence from Indonesia." ASPA Preprints. https://preprints.apsanet.org/engage/apsa/article-details/5f434ae5b8a1230019967b7f.

Kesternich, Iris, and Monika Schnitzer. 2010. "Who Is Afraid of Political Risk? Multinational Firms and Their Choice of Capital Structure." *Journal of International Economics* 82 (2): 208–18.

Khaliq, Abdul, and Ilan Noy. 2007. "Foreign Direct Investment and Economic Growth: Empirical Evidence from Sectoral Data in Indonesia," No. 200726, Working Papers, University of Hawaii at Manoa, Department of Economics. https://EconPapers.repec.org/RePEc:hai:wpaper:200726.

Kim, Kyunghoon. 2018. "Matchmaking: Establishment of State-Owned Holding Companies in Indonesia." *Asia & the Pacific Policy Studies* 5 (2): 313–30.

Kim, In Song, and Iain Osgood. 2019. "Firms in Trade and Trade Politics." *Annual Review of Political Science* 22: 399–417. https://doi.org/10.1146/annurev-polisci-050317-063728.

Koch, Natalie, and Tom Perreault. 2018. "Resource Nationalism." *Progress in Human Geography* 43 (4): 611–31. https://doi.org/10.1177/0309132518781497.

Kohl, Benjamin, and Linda Farthing. 2012. "Material Constraints to Popular Imaginaries: The Extractive Economy and Resource Nationalism in Bolivia." *Political Geography* 31 (4): 225–35.

Kolstad, Ivar, and Tina Søreide. 2009. "Corruption in Natural Resource Management: Implications for Policy Makers." *Resources Policy* 34 (4): 214–26.

Kontan. 2013. "Petani Sulit Beli Saham Perusahaan Sawit." November 7. http://industri.kontan.co.id/news/petani-sulit-beli-saham-perusahaan-sawit.

Kooroshy, Jaakko, Felix Preston, and Sian Bradley. 2014. "Cartels and Competition in Minerals Markets: Challenges for Global Governance." Chatham House the Royal Institute of International Affairs. https://www.chathamhouse.org/sites/default/files/field/field_document/20141219CartelsCompetitionMineralsMarketsKooroshyPreston BradleyFinal.pdf.

Koran Tempo. 2014. "Baru 25 Perusahaan Tambang Teken Renegosiasi." March 7. https://koran.tempo.co/read/ekonomi-dan-bisnis/336642/baru-25-perusahaan-tambang-teken-renegosiasi.

Kurniawan, Roffie. 2015. "Energi Mega Secures Approval for Bentu Block Plan of Development." *Rambu Energy,* October 13. https://www.rambuenergy.com/2015/10/energi-mega-secures-approval-for-bentu-block-plan-of-development/.

Kurtz, John, and James Van Zorge. 2013. "The Myth of Indonesia's Resource Nationalism." *Wall Street Journal,* October 1. http://online.wsj.com/article/SB1000142405 27023043731045791086220702635 60.html?mod=wsj_streaming_stream.

Lagaligo, Abraham. 2008. "Nilai Tambah: Jangan Sekedar Bisa Mimpi." *Majalah Tambang,* May.

Latul, Janeman. 2011. "Debt for Indonesia's Bakrie Group Is Business as Usual." Reuters, November 13. https://www.reuters.com/article/us-bakrie-rothschild-debt/debt-for-indonesias-bakrie-group-is-business-as-usual-idUSTRE7AC00E20111113.

Lee, Janice, Jaboury Ghazoul, Krystof Obidzinski, and Lian Koh. 2014. "Oil Palm Smallholder Yields and Incomes Constrained by Harvesting Practices and Type of Smallholder Management in Indonesia." *Agronomy for Sustainable Development* 34 (2): 501–13.

Leith, Denise. 2002. "Freeport and the Suharto Regime, 1965–1998." *Contemporary Pacific* 14 (1): 69–100. https://doi.org/10.1353/cp.2002.0023.

——. 2003. *The Politics of Power: Freeport in Suharto's Indonesia.* Honolulu: University of Hawaii Press.

Lim, Guanie, Edmund Terence Gomez, and Chan-Yuan Wong. 2021. "Evolving State-Business Relations in an Age of Globalisation: An Introduction." *Journal of Contemporary Asia* 51 (5): 697–712. https://doi.org/10.1080/00472336.2021.19 34720.

Lim, Kevin. 2007. "Court Rules No Conspiracy by Deutsche in Adaro Case." *Reuters.* September 21. https://www.reuters.com/article/idUSSIN1552020070921.

Lindblad, J. Thomas. 1989. "The Petroleum Industry in Indonesia before the Second World War." *Bulletin of Indonesian Economic Studies* 25 (2): 53–77. https://doi.org/10.1080/00074918812331335569.

——. 1997. "Survey of Recent Developments." *Bulletin of Indonesian Economic Studies* 33 (3): 3–33. https://doi.org/10.1080/00074919712331337165.

——. 2008. *Bridges to New Business: The Economic Decolonization of Indonesia.* Singapore: NUS Press.

——. 2015. "Foreign Direct Investment in Indonesia: Fifty Years of Discourse." *Bulletin of Indonesian Economic Studies* 51 (2): 217–37. https://doi.org/10.1080/00074918 .2015.1061913.

Lindblom, Charles Edward. 1977. *Politics and Markets: The World's Political Economic Systems.* New York: Basic Books.

Listiyorini, Eko. 2022. "Indonesia Lifts Ban on Coal Exports on Improving Local Supply." February 1. https://www.bloomberg.com/news/articles/2022-02-01/indonesia-lifts-ban-on-coal-exports-on-improving-local-supply.

Lubis, Uni. 2015. "Luhut, Golkar Dan Jokowi Di Pusaran #Papamintasaham Freeport." *Rappler* (blog). http://www.rappler.com/indonesia/116079-luhut,-golkar-dan-jokowi-di-pusaran-papamintasaham-freeport.

Lucarelli, Bart. 2010. "The History and Future of Indonesia's Coal Industry: Impact of Politics and Regulatory Framework on Industry Structure and Performance." Working paper 93, Program on Energy and Sustainable Development, Stanford University.

———. 2015. "Government as Creator and Destroyer." In *The Global Coal Market: Supplying the Major Fuel for Emerging Economies*, edited by Mark Thurber and Richard Morse, 294–374. Cambridge: Cambridge University Press.

Luong, Pauline Jones, and Erika Weinthal. 2010. *Oil Is Not a Curse: Ownership Structure and Institutions in Soviet Successor States*. Cambridge: Cambridge University Press.

MacIntyre, Andrew. 1991. *Business and Politics in Indonesia*. Sydney: Allen & Unwin.

Mackie, Jamie. 1961. "Indonesia's Government Estates and Their Masters." *Pacific Affairs* 34 (4): 337–60. https://doi.org/10.2307/2752627.

———. 1991. "Towkays and Tycoons: The Chinese in Indonesian Economic Life in the 1920s and 1980s." *Indonesia*: 83–96. https://doi.org/10.2307/3351256.

———. 1998a. "Business Success among Southeast Asian Chinese: The Role of Culture, Values, and Social Structures." In *Market Cultures: Society and Values in the New Asian Capitalisms*, edited by Robert W. Hefner. Singapore: ISEAS Publishing.

———. 1998b. "Indonesia: Economic Growth and Depoliticisation." In *Driven by Growth: Political Change in the Asia-Pacific Region*, edited by James William Morley, 123–41. Armonk, NY: M. E. Sharpe.

———. 2003. "Pre-1997 Sino-Indonesian Conglomerates, Compared with Those of Other ASEAN Countries." In *Ethnic Business: Chinese Capitalism in Southeast Asia*, edited by Brian C. Folk and K. S. Jomo, 105–28. New York: Routledge.

Mahdavi, Paasha. 2020. *Power Grab: Political Survival through Extractive Resource Nationalization*. Cambridge: Cambridge University Press.

Mahfoedz, Lukman. 2014. "Energy Crisis: Needs Urgent Action Now." *Jakarta Post*, September 18. http://www.thejakartapost.com/news/2014/09/18/energy-crisis-needs-urgent-action-now.html.

Majalah Tambang. 2007. "Indonesia Audit Wants Freeport Gold Royalty Tripled." August.

Maplecroft. 2019. "Resource Nationalism Rises in 30 Countries." March 21. https://www.maplecroft.com/insights/analysis/resource-nationalism-rises-30-countries/.

Marston, Andrea J. 2016. "Alloyed Waterscapes: Mining and Water at the Nexus of Corporate Social Responsibility, Resource Nationalism, and Small-Scale Mining." *WIRES Water* 4 (1): e1175. https://doi.org/10.1002/wat2.1175.

Mattangkilang, Tunggadewa. 2012. "Churchill Mining Update: East Kutai Chief Not Worried about Pending $2 Billion Suit." *Jakarta Globe*, July 13.

Matthews-Green, Shameen. 2018. "DRC Mining Code Changes: Where to Now?" *Mining Review Africa*, Edition 4. https://www.miningreview.com/magazine-article/drc-mining-code-changes-where-to-mining-companies/.

McBeth, John. 2013. "Nationalism Undermining Indonesia's Oil, Gas Sector." *Straits Times*, January 9.

———. 2014a. "How to Kill an Industry in Indonesia." *Asia Times*, February 10.

———. 2014b. "Indonesia's Plantation Bill May Undermine the Sector." *Straits Times*, September 23.

———. 2018. "Widodo's Smoke and Mirrors Hide Hard Truths." *Asia Times*, January 23.

McCarthy, John. 2004. "Changing to Gray: Decentralization and the Emergence of Volatile Socio-legal Configurations in Central Kalimantan, Indonesia." *World Development*, 32 (7): 1199–223.

———. 2010. "Processes of Inclusion and Adverse Incorporation: Oil Palm and Agrarian Change in Sumatra, Indonesia." *Journal of Peasant Studies* 37 (4): 821–50. https://doi.org/10.1080/03066150.2010.512460.

———. 2012. "Certifying in Contested Spaces: Private Regulation in Indonesian Forestry and Palm Oil." *Third World Quarterly* 33 (10): 1871–88. http://www.tandfonline.com/doi/abs/10.1080/01436597.2012.729721.

McCarthy, John, and R. A. Cramb. 2009. "Policy Narratives, Landholder Engagement, and Oil Palm Expansion on the Malaysian and Indonesian Frontiers." *Geographical Journal* 175 (2): 112–23. http://www.jstor.org/stable/40205283.

McCarthy, John, and Rob Cramb. 2016. "Conclusion." In *The Oil Palm Complex: Smallholders, Agribusiness and the State in Indonesia and Malaysia*, edited by Rob Cramb and John McCarthy, 442–64. Singapore: NUS Press.

McCarthy, John, and Carol Warren, 2009. *Communities, Environments and Local Governance in Indonesia: Locating the Commonweal*. London: Routledge.

Medco Energi. 2016. "MedcoEnergi Leads 'Indonesia, Inc.' to Bring Back Indonesia's Strategic Assets from Newmont." June 30. http://www.medcoenergi.com/en/subpagelist/view/12/2389.

———. 2021. "Medco Energi Production Report." July 15, 2022. https://www.medcoenergi.com/en/production?csrf_test_name=a5c8ba822a302ff4b765800bf1468083&group_id=0&period=yearly&from_year=2008&to_year=2021&block=0&go=Go.

Mehlum, Halvor, Karl Moene, and Ragnar Torvik. 2006. "Cursed by Resources or Institutions?" *World Economy* 29 (8): 1117–31. https://doi.org/10.1111/j.1467-9701.2006.00808.x.

Mietzner, Marcus. 2013a. *Money, Power and Ideology: Political Parties in Post-authoritarian Indonesia*. Singapore: NUS Press.

———. 2015. "Dysfunction by Design: Political Finance and Corruption in Indonesia." *Critical Asian Studies* 47 (4): 587–610.

Migdal, Joel Samuel. 1994. "The State in Society: An Approach to Struggles for Domination." In *State Power and Social Forces: Domination and Transformation in the Third World*, edited by Atul Kohli, Vivienne Shue, and Joel Samuel Migdal, 7–30. Cambridge: Cambridge University Press.

Milner, Helen V. 1988. *Resisting Protectionism: Global Industries and the Politics of International Trade*. Princeton, NJ: Princeton University Press.

Ministry for Agriculture. 2009. "Rancangan Rencana Strategis Kementrian Pertanian Tahun 2010–2014." https://ppid.pertanian.go.id/doc/1/Renstra%20Kementerian%20Pertanian%202010-2014.pdf.

Ministry of Energy and Mineral Resources. 2011a. "List of Mining Licenses: Southeast Sulawesi." Jakarta: Government of the Republic of Indonesia.

———. 2011b. "Indonesia Mineral and Coal Mining: Company Profiles 2011." Directorate General of Mineral and Coal, Supervision Program. Jakarta: Government of the Republic of Indonesia.

Monaldi, Francisco. 2015. "Latin America's Oil and Gas: After the Boom, a New." *Revista Harvard Review of Latin America* 15 (1): 2–7. http://hdl.handle.net/10469/8262.

———. 2020. "The Cyclical Phenomenon of Resource Nationalism in Latin America." *Oxford Research Encyclopedias*. https://oxfordre.com/politics/view/10.1093/acrefore/9780190228637.001.0001/acrefore-9780190228637-e-1523.

Mongabay. 2016. "Indonesia Palm Oil Giant Joins No-Deforestation Pledge Amid Criticism from Politicians." Mongabya, February 18. https://news.mongabay.com/2016/02/indonesian-palm-oil-giant-joins-no-deforestation-pledge-amid-criticism-from-politicians/.

Mufti, Lailuddin, and Pradipa Rasidi. 2021. "Selling the Omnibus Law on Job Creation." Edition 146: October–December. https://www.insideindonesia.org/selling-the-omnibus-law-on-job-creation.

Muhtadi, Burhanuddin. 2019. *Vote Buying in Indonesia: The Mechanics of Electoral Bribery*. Singapore: Springer Nature.

Neilson, Jeffrey, Angga Dwiartama, Niels Fold, and Dikdik Permadi. 2020. "Resource-Based Industrial Policy in an Era of Global Production Networks: Strategic Coupling in the Indonesian Cocoa Sector." *World Development* 135 (November): 105045. https://doi.org/10.1016/j.worlddev.2020.105045.x.

Nekhili, Mehdi, and Hayette Gatfaoui. 2013. "Are Demographic Attributes and Firm Characteristics Drivers of Gender Diversity? Investigating Women's Positions on French Boards of Directors." *Journal of Business Ethics* 118 (2): 227–49.

Nikkei Asian Review. 2014a. "Uncertainty Hangs over Indonesia's Foreign Plantations." August 19. https://asia.nikkei.com/Business/Uncertainty-hangs-over-Indonesia-s-foreign-plantations.

———. 2014b. "Cargill Warns on Indonesian Palm Oil Curbs." September 5. https://asia.nikkei.com/Politics-Economy/Economy/Cargill-warns-on-Indonesian-palm-oil-curbs.

———. 2017. "Indonesia Pressing Ahead with SOE Mergers." January 12. http://asia.nikkei.com/Business/AC/Jakarta-accelerates-merger-of-state-owned-energy-mining-companies.

Nirmala, Ronna, and Ari Fidraus. 2022. "Indonesian Coal Industry Protests January Export Ban, Pledges to Ease Domestic Shortfall." January 3. https://www.benarnews.org/english/news/indonesian/indonesian-coal-firms-protest-january-ban-01032022150138.html.

NS Energy. 2018. "Inalum Concludes $3.85bn Deal to Acquire Majority Stake in Grasberg Mine." December 24. https://www.nsenergybusiness.com/news/inalum-concludes-3-85bn-deal-to-acquire-majority-stake-in-grasberg-mine/.

Nusantara Resources. 2020. "Annual Report 2020." https://www.asx.com.au/asxpdf/20210429/pdf/44vzw3gtltgmrd.pdf.

OECD FDI Regulatory Restrictiveness Index. 2019. https://stats.oecd.org/viewhtml.aspx?datasetcode=FDIINDEX&lang=en#. Accessed July 15, 2020.

Offshore Energy Today. 2010. "Indonesia: Husky Receives Madura Strait Production Sharing Contract Extension." October 29. http://www.offshoreenergytoday.com/indonesia-husky-receives-madura-strait-production-sharing-contract-extension/.

Oil and Gas Financial Journal. 2007. "Transforming Pertamina into a Competitive Powerhouse: An Interview with Ari Soemarno." January 12. https://www.ogj.com/home/article/17293297/transforming-pertamina-into-a-competitive-powerhouse.

Oliveira, Gustavo de L. T. 2013. "Land Regularization in Brazil and the Global Land Grab." *Development and Change* 44 (2): 261–83. https://doi:10.1111/dech.12009.

———. 2018. "Chinese Land Grabs in Brazil? Sinophobia and Foreign Investments in Brazilian Soybean Agribusiness." *Globalizations* 15 (1): 114–33.

Orji, Anthonia. 2020. "Indonesia Economy Sees Weakest Growth in Almost Two Decades." *Channel News Asia*, May 5.

Osgood, Ian, Dustin Tingley, Thomas Bernauer, In Song Kim, Helen V. Milner, and Gabriele Spilker. 2017. "The Charmed Life of Superstar Exporters: Survey Evidence on Firms and Trade Policy." *Journal of Politics* 79 (1): 133–52.

Patunru, Arianto, and Sjamsu Rahardja. 2015. "Trade Protectionism in Indonesia: Bad Times and Bad Policy." Lowy Institute for International Affairs, July 30. http://www.lowyinstitute.org/publications/trade-protectionism-indonesia-bad-times-and-bad-policy.

Pepinsky, Thomas B. 2008. "Capital Mobility and Coalitional Politics: Authoritarian Regimes and Economic Adjustment in Southeast Asia." *World Politics* 60 (3): 438–74. https://doi.org/10.1017/S0043887100009059.

————. 2009. *Economic Crises and the Breakdown of Authoritarian Regimes: Indonesia and Malaysia in Comparative Perspective.* New York: Cambridge University Press.

Perreault, Tom. 2013. "Nature and Nation: Hydrocarbons, Governance, and the Territorial Logics of 'Resource Nationalism' in Bolivia." In *Subterranean Struggles: New Dynamics of Mining, Oil, and Gas in Latin America,* edited by Anthony Bebbington and Jeffrey Bury, 67–90. New York: University of Texas Press.

————. 2021 "Materializing Space, Constructing Belonging: Toward a Critical-Geographical Understanding of Resource Nationalism." In *The Routledge Handbook of Critical Resource Geography,* edited by Gabriela Valdiva, Matthew Himley, and Elizabeth Havice, 126–39. London: Routledge.

Perreault, Tom, and Gabriela Valdivia. 2010. "Hydrocarbons, Popular Protest and National Imaginaries: Ecuador and Bolivia in Comparative Context." *Geoforum* 41:689–99.

Perrone, Nicolas Marcelo. 2013. "Restrictions to Foreign Acquisitions of Agricultural Land in Argentina and Brazil." *Globalizations* 10 (1): 205–9. https://doi.org/10.1080/14747731.2013.760946.

Pertamina. 2016. "Embracing Change, Leveraging Challenges." Pertamina Annual Report 2016.

Pham, Van Thuy. 2014. "Beyond Political Skin: Convergent Paths to an Independent National Economy in Indonesia and Vietnam." PhD diss., Leiden University. https://openaccess.leidenuniv.nl/bitstream/handle/1887/25770/Dissertation._V.T.Pham.pdf?sequence=17.

Pickel, Andreas. 2003. "Explaining, and Explaining with, Economic Nationalism." *Nations and Nationalism* 9 (1): 105–27. https://doi.org/10.1111/1469-8219.00077.

Plouffe, Michael. 2015. "Heterogeneous Firms and Policy Preferences." In *The Oxford Handbook of the Political Economy of International Trade,* edited by Lisa L. Martin, 196–212. New York: Oxford University Press.

Poczter, Sharon, and Thomas Pepinsky. 2016. "Authoritarian Legacies in Post–New Order Indonesia: Evidence from a New Dataset." *Bulletin of Indonesian Economic Studies* 52 (1): 77–100. http://dx.doi.org/10.1080/00074918.2015.1129051.

Post, P. 1996. "The Formation of the Pribumi Business Elite in Indonesia, 1930s–1940s." *Bijdragen Tot de Taal-, Land- En Volkenkunde* 152 (4): 609–32. https://research.vu.nl/en/publications/the-formation-of-the-pribumi-business-elite-in-indonesia-1930s-19.

Power, Thomas. 2016. "Cashing In." *New Mandala* (blog), August 8. http://www.newmandala.org/cashing-in/.

Power, Thomas, and Eve Warburton, eds. 2020. *Democracy in Indonesia: From Stagnation to Regression?* Singapore: ISEAS Publishing.

Prakasa and Oxfam. 2016. "Mapping Policies and Stakeholders of Foreign Direct Investments in Indonesian Agriculture Sector." https://repository.theprakarsa.org/media/publications/293904-mapping-of-policies-and-stakeholders-in-d0d32b1c.pdf.

Pramudya, Eusebius Pantja, Otto Hospes, and C. J. A. M. Termeer. 2017. "Governing the Palm-Oil Sector through Finance: The Changing Roles of the Indonesian State." *Bulletin of Indonesian Economic Studies* 53 (1): 57–82. https://doi.org/10.1080/00074918.2016.1228829.

PricewaterhouseCoopers. 2016. "Oil and Gas in Indonesia: Investment and Taxation Guide." 7th ed. https://www.pwc.com/id/en/energy-utilities-mining/assets/May%202016/PwC%20Indonesia-oil-and-gas-guide-2016.pdf.

————. 2017. "Oil and Gas in Indonesia: Investment and Taxation Guide." 8th ed. https://www.pwc.com/id/en/energy-utilities-mining/assets/oil%20and%20gas/oil-and-gas-guide-2017.pdf.

Puente, Ignacio, and Ben Ross Schneider. 2020. "Business and Development: How Organization, Ownership and Networks Matter." *Review of International Political Economy* 27 (6): 1354–77. https://doi.org/10.1080/09692290.2020.1727548.

PWYP. Unpublished. "Confidential Unpublished Report: Natural Resource Control and Authoritarianism: Politically Exposed Persons in the Ownership of Structures of Indonesia's Largest Forestry and Coal Business Groups." Jakarta: Publish What You Pay.

Rajah, Roland, and Stephen Grenville. 2020. "Keeping Indonesia's Economy Afloat through the COVID-19 Pandemic." Lowy Institute Policy Brief, July 3. https://www.lowyinstitute.org/publications/keeping-indonesia-s-economy-afloat-through-covid-19-pandemic.

Ramaswamy, Kannan, K. Galen Kroeck, and William Renforth. 1996. "Measuring the Degree of Internationalization of a Firm: A Comment." *Journal of International Business Studies* 27 (1): 167–77. http://www.jstor.org/stable/155377.

Republika. 2013. "Sepertiga Lahan Sawit Dikuasai Asing." http://www.republika.co.id/berita/koran/ekonomi-koran/14/11/14/nf0os929-sepertiga-lahan-sawit-dikuasai-asing.

Resosudarmo, Budy, ed. 2005. *The Politics and Economics of Indonesia's Natural Resources*. Singapore: Institute of Southeast Asian Studies.

Resosudarmo, Budy P., Ani A. Nawir, Ida Aju P. Resosudarmo, and Nina Subiman. 2012. "Forest Land Use Dynamics in Indonesia." In *Land, Livelihood, the Economy and the Environment in Indonesia: Essays in Honour of Joan Hardjono*, edited by Anne Booth, Chris Manning, and Thee Kian Wie, 20–50. Jakarta: Yayasan Pustaka Obor Indonesia.

Resosudarmo, Budy P., Julius A. Mollet, Umbu R. Raya, and Hans Kaiwai. 2014. "Development in Papua after Special Autonomy." In *Regional Dynamics in a Decentralized Indonesia*, edited by Hal Hill, 443–59. Singapore: Institute of Southeast Asian Studies.

Resosudarmo, Budy, and Arief Yusuf. 2006. "Is the Log Export Ban an Efficient Instrument for Economic Development and Environmental Protection? The Case of Indonesia." *Asian Economic Papers* 5 (2): 75–104.

Reuters Staff. 2014. "Indonesia Lawmakers Draft Bill to Slash Foreign Ownership of Plantations." August 15. https://www.reuters.com/article/indonesia-plantations-law-idUSL4N0QL1X620140815.

——. 2015. "Indonesia Energy Minister Reminds Berau to Lower Foreign Ownership." Reuters, May 7. https://www.reuters.com/article/berau-energy-asia-resource/indonesia-energy-minister-reminds-berau-to-lower-foreign-ownership-idUKJ9N0VC01N20150507.

——. 2017. "Indonesia's Inalum Given Control of State Miners ahead of Larger Freeport Stake." Reuters, November 28. https://www.reuters.com/article/us-indonesia-freeport-inalum/indonesias-inalum-given-control-of-state-miners-ahead-of-larger-freeport-stake-idUSKBN1DS0DM.

Rickard, Stephanie J. 2021. "Open Economy Politics Revisited." In *The Oxford Handbook of International Political Economy*, edited by Jon C. W. Pevehouse and Leonard Seabrooke. Oxford: Oxford University Press.

Ricklefs, M. C. 2008. *A History of Modern Indonesia since c. 1200*. New York: Palgrave Macmillan.

Rigzone. 2015. "Pertamina's January–July 2015 Oil, Gas Production Up 9.8% to 571,000 Boepd." September 4. https://www.rigzone.com/news/oil_gas/a/140454/pertaminas_januaryjuly_2015_oil_gas_production_up_98_to_571000_boepd/.

Riofrancos, Thea N. 2020. *Resource Radicals: From Petro-Nationalism to Post-extractivism in Ecuador*. Durham, NC: Duke University Press.

RMOL.Co. 2011. "Kementerian ESDM Larang Pertamina Monopoli Migas." November 10. https://ekbis.rmol.id/read/2011/11/10/45200/kementerian-esdm-larang-pertamina-monopoli-migas.

Robison, Richard. 1986. *Indonesia: The Rise of Capital*. Sydney: Allen & Unwin.

Robison, Richard, and Vedi R. Hadiz. 2004. *Reorganising Power in Indonesia: The Politics of Oligarchy in an Age of Markets*. New York: Routledge.

Robison, Richard, and Amdrew Rosser. 1998. "Contesting Reform: Indonesia's New Order and the IMF. *World Development*, 26 (8): 1593–609.

Roosa, John. 2006. *Pretext for Mass Murder: The September 30th Movement and Suharto's Coup d'État in Indonesia*. Madison: Wisconsin University Press.

———. 2020. *Buried Histories: The Anticommunist Massacres of 1965–1966 in Indonesia*. Critical Human Rights.

Ross, Michael L. 2001. *Timber Booms and Institutional Breakdown in Southeast Asia*. Cambridge: Cambridge University Press.

———. 2015. "What Have We Learned about the Resource Curse?" *Annual Review of Political Science* 18:239–59.

Rosser, Andrew. 2001. *The Politics of Economic Liberalization in Indonesia: State, Market and Power*. Richmond, UK: Curzon.

S&P Global. 2013. "Total Sees Indonesia Mahakam Block's Gas Reserves Falling to 1.3 Tcf in 2018." June 6. https://www.spglobal.com/commodityinsights/en/market-insights/latest-news/natural-gas/060613-total-sees-indonesia-mahakam-blocks-gas-reserves-falling-to-13-tcf-in-2018.

Sanderson, Henry, Neil Hume, and James Wilson. 2016. "Freeport-McMoRan Chief Vows to Complete Debt Reduction Plan." *Financial Times*, November 13. https://www.ft.com/content/8dfcca58-a1f5-11e6-aa83-bcb58d1d2193.

Schneider, Ben Ross. 1997. "Big Business and the Politics of Economic Reform: Confidence and Concertation in Brazil and Mexico." In *Business and the State in Developing Countries*, edited by Sylvia Maxfield and Ben Ross Schneider, 191–215 Ithaca, NY: Cornell University Press.

———. 1998. "Elusive Synergy: Business-Government Relations and Development." *Comparative Politics* 31 (1): 101–22. https://doi.org/10.2307/422108.

———. 2014. "Studying Political Economy in Latin America: Gaps and Methods." *Latin American Politics and Society* 56 (1): 20–22.

———. 2015. *Designing Industrial Policy in Latin America: Business-State Relations and the New Developmentalism*. New York: Palgrave Macmillan.

Sender, Henny. 2011. "Adaro Executives Enjoy Rise in Coal Demand." *Financial Times*, July 5.

Sentana, I. Made. 2005. "Indonesia's Adaro Coal Mine in Tug-of-War." *Wall Street Journal*, April 1. http://www.wsj.com/articles/SB111229920048894579.

Setijadi, Charlotte. 2019. "Anti-Chinese Sentiment and the 'Return' of the Pribumi Discourse." In *Contentious Belonging: The Place of Minorities in Contemporary Indonesia*, edited by Greg Fealy and Ronit Ricci, 194–213. Singapore: ISEAS Publishing.

Shafer, D. Michael. 1990. "Sectors, States, and Social Forces: Korea and Zambia Confront Economic Restructuring." *Comparative Politics* 22 (2): 127–50. https://doi.org/10.2307/422310.

———. 1994. *Winners and Losers: How Sectors Shape the Developmental Prospects of States*. Ithaca, NY: Cornell University Press.

Singgih, Vincent. 2007. "Energy Firms Losing Appetite as RI Remains Aloof." *Jakarta Post*, May 15. https://www.pressreader.com/indonesia/the-jakarta-post/20170515/281956017709517.

Singh, Jewellord T. Nem, and Eliza Massi. 2016. "Resource Nationalism and Brazil's Post-neoliberal Strategy." In *The Political Economy of Natural Resources and Development: From Neoliberalism to Resource Nationalism*, edited by Paul A. Haslam and Pablo Heidrich, 158–73. London: Routledge.

Sippel, Sarah Ruth, and Timothy Weldon. 2020. "Redefining Land's Investability: Towards a Neo-nationalization of Resources in Australia?" *Territory, Politics, Governance* 9 (2): 306–23. https://doi.org/10.1080/21622671.2019.1703797.

Siregar, Zulhidayat. 2013. "Kasih Masukan Ke DPD, Apkasindo Berharap Revisi UU Perkebunan Berpihak Kepada Petani." RMOL.Co, May 21.

Solomon, Michael. 2012. "The Rise of Resource Nationalism: A Resurgence of State Control in an Era of Free Markets or the Legitimate Search for a New Equilibrium?" Southern African Institute of Mining and Metallurgy. http://www.polity.org.za /article/the-rise-of-resource-nationalism-a-resurgence-of-state-control-in-an-era -of-free-markets-or-the-legitimate-search-for-a-new-equilibrium-july-2012-2012 -07-17.

Spiegel, Samuel J. 2012. "Governance Institutions, Resource Rights Regimes, and the Informal Mining Sector: Regulatory Complexities in Indonesia." *World Development* 40 (1): 189–205. https://doi.org/10.1016/j.worlddev.2011.05.015.

Stevens, Paul. 2008. "National Oil Companies and International Oil Companies in the Middle East: Under the Shadow of Governments and the Resource Nationalism Cycle." *Journal of World Energy Law and Business* 1 (1): 5–30. https://doi.org/10 .1093/jwelb/jwn004.

Stratfor. 2018. "What Explains the Ups and Downs of Resource Nationalism?" August 1. https://worldview.stratfor.com/article/what-explains-ups-and-downs-resource -nationalism.

Sugianto, Danang. 2017. "Holding BUMN Tambang Terbentuk, Saaynya Caplok Freeport." *Detikfinance.* November 30. https://finance.detik.com/bursa-dan-valas /d-3749272/holding-bumn-tambang-terbentuk-saatnya-caplok-freeport.

Sukirno. 2013. "Inilah 16 Perusahaan Milik Luhut Panjaitan." *Bisnis Indonesia*, November 3.

Sulaiman, Stefanno Reinard. 2019. "Recent Energy Deals Signal Postelection Pragmatism Play." *Jakarta Post*, July 24.

Suryadinata, Leo. 2012. *Southeast Asian Personalities of Chinese Descent: A Biographical Dictionary, Volume I & II*. Singapore: ISEAS Publishing.

Susanto, Ichwan. 2018. "Baleg Tidak Akan Paksakan RUU Perkelapasawitan." *Kompas*, March 29. https://kompas.id/baca/utama/2018/03/29/baleg-tidak-akan-paksakan -ruu-perkelapasawitan/.

Sutton, Peter. 2003. *Native Title in Australia: An Ethnographic Perspectives*. Cambridge: Cambridge University Press.

Syahrul, Yura. 2015. "Rizal Ramli Sebut Panigoro Akan Caplok 76 Persen Saham Newmont." *Katadata*, November 25. http://katadata.co.id/berita/2015/11/25/rizal-ramli -sebut-panigoro-akan-caplok-76-xpersen-saham-newmont.

Szakonyi, David. 2020. *Politics for Profit: Business, Elections and Policymaking in Russia*. Cambridge: Cambridge University Press.

Tabor, Steven R. 2015. "Constraints to Indonesia's Economic Growth." Working paper no. 10, ADB Papers on Indonesia, Asian Development Bank. https://www.adb .org/sites/default/files/publication/178041/ino-paper-10-2015.pdf.

Taylor, Michael, and Yayat Supriatna. 2014. "Indonesia Lawmakers Draft Bill to Slash Foreign Ownership of Plantations." Reuters, August 15. https://www.reuters .com/article/indonesia-plantations-law-idUSL4N0QL1X620140815.

Teguh Hidayat & Partners. 2012. "J Resources, Backdoor Listing with a Little Magic." March 26. http://www.teguhhidayat.com/2012/03/j-resources-backdoor-listing-with .html.

Tempo. 2014. "Hatta Rajasa: We Were Convinced of Winning." February 18. http://en .tempo.co/read/news/2014/02/18/241555412/Hatta-Rajasa-We-were-Convinced -of-Winning.

———. 2015. "Aturan Pengelolaan Wilayah Kerja Migas Rugikan Pertamina | Bisnis | Tempo.Co." May 27. https://m.tempo.co/read/news/2015/05/27/090669970/aturan -pengelolaan-wilayah-kerja-migas-rugikan-pertamina.

Tempo Bisnis. 2012. "Surya Paloh Dan Edwin Rebutan Gunung Emas." October 22. http://bisnis.tempo.co/read/news/2012/10/22/090437013/surya-paloh-dan -edwin-rebutan-gunung-emas.

Tempo Interactive. 2012. "The Sudwikatmono Clan in Indonesia's Coal Industry." August 16. http://en.tempo.co/read/news/2012/08/16/055424016/The-Sudwikatmono -Clan-in-Indonesias-Coal-Industry.

Tempo Magazine. 2002. "Berebut Batu Bara Kalimantan" June 16. https://webcache .googleusercontent.com/search?q=cache:Gqip8dNZxo0J:https://majalah.tempo .co/read/investigasi/120085/berebut-batu-bara-kalimantan+&cd=16&hl=en&ct =clnk&gl=sg.

———. 2006. "Cerdik Menggapai Puncak." May 8. https://majalah.tempo.co/read/ekonomi -dan-bisnis/119256/cerdik-menggapai-puncak.

———. 2012. "Losing the Upstream Battle." November 25.

———. 2015. "Gas Vegas." April 7. https://magz.tempo.co/konten/2015/04/07/LU/29843 /Gas-Vegas/33/15.

Tempo.co. 2017. "Menteri Luhut: Dibahas Proses BUMN Akuisisi Freeport | Bisnis | Tempo.Co." February 27. https://m.tempo.co/read/news/2017/02/27/090850607 /menteri-luhut-dibahas-proses-bumn-akuisisi-freeport.

Teoh, Cheng Hai. 2013. "Malaysian Corporations as Strategic Players in Southeast Asia's Palm Oil Industry." In *The Palm Oil Controversy in Southeast Asia: A Transnational Perspective*, edited by O. Pye and J. Bhattacharya, 19–47. Singapore: ISEAS Publishing.

Tharakan, Pradeep. 2015. "Summary of Indonesia's Energy Sector Assessment." Working paper no. 9, ADB Papers on Indonesia, Asian Development Bank.

Thee, Kian Wie. 2010. "Understanding Indonesia: The Role of Economic Nationalism." *Journal of Indonesian Social Sciences and Humanities* 3:55–79. http://dspace.li brary.uu.nl/handle/1874/203612.

Tribunnews. 2015. "Menteri Rini Yakin Pertamina Mampu Danai Blok Mahakam." June 21. http://www.tribunnews.com/bisnis/2015/06/21/menteri-rini-yakin-pertamina -mampu-danai-blok-mahakam.

Tse, Pui-Kwan. 2001. "The Minerals Industry of Indonesia." *Minerals Yearbook 2001*. United States Geological Survey. https://d9-wret.s3.us-west-2.amazonaws.com /assets/palladium/production/mineral-pubs/country/2001/idmyb01.pdf.

Tufte, Edward R. 1980. *Political Control of the Economy*. Princeton, NJ: Princeton University Press.

USAID. 2013. "Economic Effects of Indonesia's Mineral-Processing Requirements for Export." United States Agency for International Development. http://pdf.usaid .gov/pdf_docs/pbaaa139.pdf.

Valle, Sabrina, and Peter Millard. 2017. "Vale Chief Executive Ousted as Brazil Seeks New Blood." *Sydney Morning Herald*, February 26. http://www.smh.com.au/business /mining-and-resources/vale-chief-executive-ousted-as-brazil-seeks-new-blood -20170226-gulndc.html.

van der Eng, Pierre. 1998. "Exploring Exploitation: The Netherlands and Colonial Indonesia 1870–1940." *Revista de historia economica—Journal of Iberian and Latin American Economic History* 16 (1): 291–321. https://doi.org/10.1017/S021261090 0007138.

——. 2014. "Mining and Indonesia's Economy: Institutions and Value Adding, 1870–2010." Primced Discussion Paper Series no. 57, Hitotsubashi University. http://www.ier.hit-u.ac.jp/primced/documents/No57_dp_up_Pdf_2014.pdf.

van der Pas, Hilde, and Riza Damanik. 2014. "The Case of Newmont Mining." Transnational Institute. Policy Briefing (November). https://www.tni.org/my/node/1591.

van Leeuwen, Theo M. 1994. "25 Years of Mineral Exploration and Discovery in Indonesia." *Journal of Geochemical Exploration* 50 (1): 13–90. https://doi.org/10.1016/0375-6742(94)90021-3.

van Zanden, Jan Luiten, and Daan Marks. 2013. *An Economic History of Indonesia: 1800–2010.* London: Routledge.

Varkkey, Helena. 2012. "Patronage Politics as a Driver of Economic Regionalisation: The Indonesian Oil Palm Sector and Transboundary Haze." *Asia Pacific Viewpoint* 53 (3): 314–29. https://doi.org/10.1111/j.1467-8373.2012.01493.x.

Vatikiotis, Michael. 1989. "Oil in Troubled Waters: Foreigners Find Risks in Indonesia's Private Sector." *Far Eastern Economic Review* 145 (35): 44.

Veltmeyer, Henry. 2013. "The Political Economy of Natural Resource Extraction: A New Model or Extractive Imperialism?" *Canadian Journal of Development Studies/Revue canadienne d'études du développement* 34 (1): 79–95. https://doi.org/10.1080/02255189.2013.764850.

Vernon, Raymond. 1971. *Sovereignty at Bay: The Multinational Spread of US Enterprises.* New York: Basic Books.

Viva. 2010. "Asing Kuasai 50% Perkebunan Sawit Nasional." December 18.

Vivoda, Vlado. 2009. "Resource Nationalism, Bargaining and International Oil Companies: Challenges and Change in the New Millennium." *New Political Economy* 14 (4): 517–34. https://doi.org/10.1080/13563460903287322.

Vogel, David. 1987. "The New Political Science of Corporate Power." *Public Interest* 87 (Spring): 63–80. https://www.proquest.com/docview/1298115506?pq-origsite=g scholar&fromopenview=true&imgSeq=1.

Warburton, Eve. 2014. "The Business of Politics in Indonesia." *Inside Indonesia*, July 2. https://www.insideindonesia.org/the-business-of-politics-in-indonesia.

——. 2017a. "Resource Nationalism in Indonesia: Ownership Structures and Sectoral Variation in Mining and Palm Oil." *Journal of East Asian Studies* 17 (3): 285–312. https://doi.org/10.1017/jea.2017.13.

——. 2017b. "Resource Nationalism in Post-Boom Indonesia: The New Normal?" Lowy Institute for International Policy, April 27. https://www.lowyinstitute.org/publica tions/resource-nationalism-post-boom-indonesia-new-normal.

——. 2018. "Nationalism, Developmentalism and Politics in Indonesia's Mining Sector." In *Indonesia in the New World: Globalisation, Nationalism and Sovereignty*, edited by Mari Elka Pangestu, Chatib Basri, and Arianto Patunru, 90–108. Singapore: ISEAS Publishing.

Warburton, Eve, and Edward Aspinall. 2019. "Explaining Indonesia's Democratic Regression: Structure, Agency and Popular Opinion." *Contemporary Southeast Asia* 41 (2): 255–85.

Warburton, Eve, Burhanuddin Muhtadi, Edward Aspinall, and Diego Fossati. 2021. "When Does Class Matter? Unequal Representation in Indonesian Legislatures." *Third World Quarterly* 32 (6): 1252–75. DOI: 10.1080/01436597.2021.1882297.

Warta Ekonomi. 2021. "Energy Selesaikan Akuisisi Nusantara Resources Limited." October 6. https://wartaekonomi.co.id/read365741/indika-energy-selesaikan -akuisisi-nusantara-resources-limited.

Wayne, Michael. 2021. "Gold Standard: Rachmat Makkasau." *CEO Magazine*, July 1. https://www.theceomagazine.com/executive-interviews/mining-metals/rachmat -makkasau/.

Wilson, Alana, Fred McMahon, and Miguel Cervantes. 2013. "Annual Survey of Mining Companies: 2012–2013." Fraser Institute. http://bit.ly/1P2V4US?__unam =b07cbf6-15db5101f7b-29d014ca-2&_ga=GA1.2.454296826.1442194644.

Wilson, Jeffrey. 2011. "Resource Nationalism or Resource Liberalism? Explaining Australia's Approach to Chinese Investment in Its Minerals Sector." *Australian Journal of International Affairs* 65 (3): 283–304. https://doi.org/10.1080/10357718.2011.563779.

———. 2015. "Understanding Resource Nationalism: Economic Dynamics and Political Institutions." *Contemporary Politics* 21 (4): 1–18. https://doi.org/10.1080/13569775 .2015.1013293.

Wing, Thye Woo, Bruce Glassburner, and Anwar Nasution. 1994. "Macroeconomic Policies, Crises, and Long-Term Growth in Indonesia, 1965–90." World Bank Macroeconomic Studies Series. Washington DC: World Bank. http://documents .worldbank.org/curated/en/1994/06/698280/macroeconomic-policies-crises -long-term-growth-indonesia-1965-90.

Winters, Jeffrey A. 2011. *Oligarchy*. New York: Cambridge University Press.

Wolf, Christian O. H. 2009. "Overview of the Political and Economic Arguments in Favor of and against the Establishment of a NOC." SSRN Scholarly Paper ID 1514623. https://papers.ssrn.com/abstract=1514623.

World Bank. 2000. "Indonesia: Oil and Gas Sector Study." Washington, DC: World Bank. https://openknowledge.worldbank.org/handle/10986/15255.

———. 2015. "High Expectations." Indonesia Economic Quarterly Update. http://www .worldbank.org/content/dam/Worldbank/document/EAP/Indonesia/IEQ-MAR -2015-EN.pdf.

Yadav, Vineeta, and Bumba Mukherjee. 2016. *The Politics of Corruption in Dictatorships*. Cambridge: Cambridge University Press.

Yasuyuki, Hikita. 1996. "Japanese Companies Inroads into Indonesia under Japanese Military Domination." *Bijdragen Tot de Taal-, Land- En Volkenkunde* 152 (4): 656–98.

Yates, Julian S., and Karen Bakker. 2013. "Debating the 'Post-neoliberal Turn' in Latin America." *Progress in Human Geography* 38 (1): 62–90. https://doi.org/10.1177/0309 132513500372.

Yeung, Henry W. 2006. "Change and Continuity in Southeast Asian Ethnic Chinese Business." *Asia Pacific Journal of Management* 23 (3): 229–54.

Yoshimatsu, H. 2000. *Internationalisation, Corporate Preferences and Commercial Policy in Japan*. New York: Springer.

Young, Kevin A. 2017. *Blood of the Earth: Resource Nationalism, Revolution, and Empire in Bolivia*. Austin: University of Texas Press.

Zadek, Simon, Maya Forstater, Han Cheng, Jason Potts, and Gabriel A. Huppe. 2014. "Meeting China's Global Resource Needs: Managing Sustainability Impacts to Ensure Security of Supply." Institute for Sustainable Development. https://www .iisd.org/sites/default/files/publications/china_supply_synthesis_report.pdf.

Zen, Zahari, Colin Barlow, Ria Gondowarsito, and John McCarthy. 2016. "Oil Palm and Socio-economic Improvement in Indonesia." In *The Oil Palm Complex: Smallholders, Agribusiness and the State in Indonesia and Malaysia*, edited by Rob Cramb and John McCarthy, 78–108. Singapore: NUS Press.

Index

Page references in *italics* refer to illustrative materials.